PHILIP
A STRANGE CHILD

THE LIFE OF AN
EIGHT-YEAR OLD BOY
IN CARE

Philip J. Howard

i

Printed by: Octoprint The Old Foundry, Foundry Lane,
Chippenham, Wiltshire. SN15 1JB

Published by: Dalkeith Publishing
P.O. Box 4 Bournmouth BH1 1YL

First Printed June 2007

ISBN 978 0 9555878 0 1

This book is dedicated to the lasting memory of Sister Pearl, who put her boys on the right path to adulthood during her many years of service with The National Children's Home.

Also to the other current and past members of staff at the NCH who have helped in researching my childhood, by searching their files and allowing this book to be completed, and finally to John who remains at Highfield for eternity.

INTRODUCTION

Some of those who were in care will have happy memories; others regard their time in care as being unhappy, or will have repressed the memories of their childhood. For me, many of my memories in care were of unhappiness, but if I had not been taken into care, my life may well have been unhappier.

This book originally was not going to be a book of my entire childhood, but merely a record of what was in my NCH file, however without the history of my early years, it could be difficult to understand why I might have had problems during my stay in care.

For most, the files that were kept on them during care have remained private. Some will have been given a copy of their file if they have shown interest in their childhood, but for the majority their files remain on a shelf slowly gathering dust. The subjects will never see their content, as many do not realise that their files have been saved.

My file is the most important possession of my past. It gives my life from various points of view, some of which I might want to question, but it was these views that went into my file that were going to govern the matters of my care.

There might be the argument, that the staff who wrote the items did not intend them to be read by the child, the parent or even the public, but if they were telling the truth, there would not be any reason why such matters should remain hidden. With the approval of the NCH, it would be possible to look at any of the other 65,000 files of children who were in their care. These files could be extremely useful to researchers of childcare.

My file is at the end section of the book; this originally came as a pile of photocopied pages. The end section is now in chronological order. Handwritten notes that appeared in odd documents have been added to the main documents to make it easier to follow, together with other items that relate to my childhood and make it easier to understand how the adults were trying to tackle my problems. As to the title of my book? It is a comment the Houseparent made about me to the Child Care Officer.

THE NATIONAL CHILDREN'S HOME

The Children's Home was founded in 1869 by the Reverend Thomas Bowman Stephenson, Francis Horner and Alfred Mager, all committed Methodists who wished to provide education, training, and most importantly, a good home for orphans and destitute children.

The Children's Home established itself in London and quickly expanded into other areas of Britain, becoming known as the National Children's Home in 1907, and opening many Children's Homes and Junior Approved Schools over the next 60 years. In the 1960s there were 30 NCH branches in operation, ranging from small branches of 15 children to the larger branches with 200 children.

1869. NCH founded by Rev Thomas B. Stephenson, a young Methodist Minister, who converted a disused stable into a home for orphans and abandoned children in Lambeth, London.

1871. The Lambeth home is given approval by the Wesleyan Methodist Conference and moves to Bonner Road.

1872. A second home is opened in Edgworth, Lancashire - a rural location.

1900. Rev T. B. Stephenson retires and Arthur E. Gregory takes his place as principal of the Children's Home.

1912. A. E. Gregory dies suddenly and is replaced as principal by Rev William Hodson Smith. Rev T.B. Stephenson dies after a long illness.

1913. A new branch opens at Harpenden (Highfield). It was possible to transfer the whole community of 350 children from London to this new branch.

1933. Rev Hodson Smith retires and is replaced by Rev John H. Litten as principal.

1943 Anne Pearl starts her training period at Danesford Branch (NCH Junior Boy's Approved School). 1944 Ordination into the Sisterhood, then as Sister Pearl at Harpenden 1948-1966.

1950. Rev John Litten retires and is replaced by Rev John W. Waterhouse as principal.

1969. NCH celebrates its centenary. Rev J. Waterhouse is replaced as principal by Rev Gordon E. Barritt.

A DIFFERENT LIFE

Most children born in the 1950s would have had a predictable life to look forward to. The average family of mother and father living at home with two or three children was the norm. For some reason I was going to be different.

My mother had decided not to marry my father, even after his proposal of marriage, but to bring me up on her own. This was a major obstacle. The other was that my father came from Ceylon, resulting in me having a lightly tanned appearance. In 1957 such matters were frowned about by most.

For the first five years of my life, all these matters were of little importance to me. It was only after I started school at the age of six, did I find that I was not the same as all the other boys of my age.

From the age of six, my mother moved around the country with me, resulting in many changes of school. Around the age of eight, various adults thought that due to certain family circumstances, it might be best if I was put in a Home.

The National Children's Home did its best to give children a good start in life. Without their intervention, my life would never have been as varied and as interesting as things have turned out. Had I lived in the London flat from the age of eight, with little opportunity for my mother to supervise me, there would have been a very good chance that with my ability to get into mischief, some more serious events would soon have occurred.

Most of the other children that were in the flat I was placed in had been there for most of their lives. I could not fit in. Having seven years of freedom, I found it difficult to conform to all the rules and the way our lives were regulated. The adults could not understand why I always appeared to be causing problems both in the Home and at school.

After three years in their care, it was thought best by the NCH that I was returned to my mother. When it came to leaving school at the age of 16, I had managed to attend twelve schools in a period of ten years.

MY LIFE BEFORE GOING INTO CARE

The start to my life came in 1957. For my early years, there are few of my own memories, but with what I have been told, I can build a picture of what life at this early stage was like. My mother had been born and brought up during her younger years in London, the second eldest in a family of five children with slightly over 20 years age gap between the youngest and eldest. My mother was 35 when I was born, my father apparently slightly younger.

My mother needed to support me financially; from early morning to mid

Life in London aged 3

afternoon, she continued in restaurant work. In these early days, it was my grandmother who saw to my daily needs. Having only recently finished bringing up her youngest son who was nearing 20 and who still lived with them, a new arrival to look after was not that much of a difficulty; with more or less 40 years' experience of child care, I was not going to be that much of a problem.

In my early years my appearance had a slightly tanned look. I had rosy cheeks, a thin build and fast movements. I could have passed for one of many origins; with no father around, if no serious questions were asked, there was no reason to reveal my true details.

Our flat was the top floor of a detached house in Cricklewood, London NW2. Originally, when it was built, the entire house would have been occupied by one family. Now divided into two, with our family living upstairs and another family downstairs, more use was made of the building.

The house and the complete area had been built between the 1880s to 1890s. The road in which our house was situated had been one of the first parts of the development, and as the other roads were built up, the odd extra house was squeezed into each road – so those houses gradually became smaller and had less ornate finishes to them. If they had a slight advantage, it was that their ceilings were lower and it took less to heat them.

There was one disadvantage to the building's layout, this was having only a single main entrance. The communal hall divided the lower flat in two, although our upper flat, once you were up the wide open staircase, was relatively private; the lower flat, having rooms that led onto the main hall, was not. In a similar fashion a passage that led to a side door equally invaded the privacy of the lower flat. It was down to both families being good neighbours that little conflict took place.

This slightly unusual layout may have been fine for adults, but for a young growing child it was a disadvantage. In my first two years other than noise I might make when crying, or slightly later when I find that any object that can be picked up and banged would make a noise, I caused only a slight nuisance.

From the time that I became a toddler my presence was more of an issue. In today's terms I might have been labelled hyperactive at that point – I was very active and on the move all the time, with slightly out-of-control movements. The floor and I had regular contact. A first-floor flat was not the best location to be brought up in, when this coincides with a building that has only a garden and outdoor area for the lower flat. With the need to keep me away from the main staircase, restrictions to my movements had to be made.

If I had any annoying qualities it was down to my energetic ways, that started from the moment I got up to the time I went to bed; a bad temper and vocal opinion also gave me a slightly unlovable personality. Whilst I was around, there was neither quiet nor stillness. The only point when I was quiet for any length of time was when I caught the measles, but I was soon over the worst and back to my slightly demanding self.

My life was not totally confined to the indoors; during the morning I would on most days be taken shopping by my grandmother. Often two separate journeys were needed to carry the various groceries the family needed, and with only a cool larder to store food in, shopping was almost a daily task. Early on in life I had the luxury of being taken out in my pushchair for most journeys, but when it became apparent that I was capable of walking quite long distances, although I might start out in a pushchair, the return trip often had the shopping travelling in comfort and me walking alongside. My active movements demanded total control of me: a stout pair of leather reins were always required to keep me from darting along the pavement to view some interesting object in the far distance or across the busy roads.

By far the most interesting shop was the fishmonger's. This was a very traditional affair, set up from a small shop quite a distance from the edge of the pavement and built outwards with counters and tables covered in ice. It was my grandmother's habit to visit this shop first. Early on in the morning the fish were fresh and nice; by late morning to early afternoon, the best choices had gone and the aroma was starting to get a little strong.

From early on in my life I had found that there were two attractions in this shop, and often made requests to visit the fish shop when we went out, even if my grandmother did not have fish on the day's menu. The ice sprinkled around the fish was not something a small boy was allowed anywhere near. Additional ice was stored at the rear in fine broken chunks, and as ice from the display melted it was replaced from this pile. This pile was also out of bounds to a boy of around three. It was in an area near a small grating for water to run away and a small amount of waste ice, that became the interesting plaything.

There were a few times during the shopping trip when my reins could be released without any fear of me running away. When the shopping was finished they were required to prize me away from the ice. The coldness of the ice never seemed to cause me any discomfort and without any instructions I had invented small ice balls rather than snowballs. An added bonus, extra ice could be trodden down into the grate to make a hard surface to build on. Had I been wearing shoes this last activity would have been forbidden. When going out with my grandmother if there was the chance that we might go near to the fishmonger, I always wore my wellingtons.

Eventually my grandmother would have completed the purchase of the fish and I would be now encouraged to come along. I was a little foolish to try and hide a small amount of ice to take home in the gap between my leg and the inside of my wellingtons – within minutes it had all melted away. When out with my grandmother it was necessary to obey any instruction given: if ignored, the rest of the trip could be very miserable indeed.

If I'd been good then the second attraction at the fishmonger's was allowed. A deep metal container with live eels might revolt most people but I was fascinated by them. Between 20 and 30 long black eels would be swimming around, so tight that it was often impossible to see where one eel ended and the next started. I'd been told never to touch them, as they would bite me. Apparently I was sensible enough to look and wonder at the wriggling mass. If one of the staff was not busy I might be handed one of the long wooden sticks that they used for separating the eels and allowed to prod them gently. Eels were one item my grandmother never seemed to buy. I knew they were for eating, but I never actually discovered how you took one home. The grocer's also provided a learning experience, with everything from watching bacon being sliced to large lumps of cheese getting cut down to more manageable lumps that would fit on the tea table.

The one drawback of having to go shopping for food was the number of clothes and shoe shops that were in between our flat and the shops we had to visit. Most of the journey seemed to be spent with my grandmother looking in the windows. A sale on, and even more time was spent trying on the various bargains that appeared but it was seldom that anything was ever actually purchased. For the rest of the trip I would be told that the items were the wrong colour, it was the wrong season, or a host of other reasons for not buying the item. I found no real way of persuading my grandmother to speed up the search for these elusive bargains. With my mother the threat of, or an actual temper tantrum was enough to move us on; behaviour in this way was certainly not tolerated by my grandmother.

The only thing that was slightly worse than gazing pointlessly into clothes shops, was being taken out when it was necessary to buy clothes for me. There was slight rivalry between my mother and grandmother, it was over the clothes I should wear. My mother's choice was more for cardigans or jumpers with design embellishments; my grandmother was more for something plain. Often I might wear my grandmother's choice in the morning and if taken out later in the day by my mother then redressed in her choice of clothes.

By mid-morning, we would return to the flat. If I had been good, a glass of squash or milk and the odd biscuit now came my way; whilst my grandmother would put the kettle on to get a pot of tea ready. If she decided she fancied something other than tea then a solitary bottle of Guinness would be brought out. The glass was just too small to take the entire bottle of this black liquid with its interesting creamy head that formed as if by magic. If I had been good then a special miniature drinking glass would be taken from the cupboard and the last part of the bottle would be poured in for me. Not the average drink for a young child, but to me it was interesting and its quantity did no harm.

The rest of the morning I was free to amuse myself. The front window gave a good view of local events, although by this time of the day there were few people about. Eventually lunch was ready, and once that was finished I was encouraged to go for a little nap. If I managed to get to sleep, I would be woken in time to listen to the children's story on the radio. Once over, the programmes reverted to more adult themes and I was left once more to my own devices.

Occasionally, if it was a nice, I would be taken to the park by my mother. The park was quite a distance away, and on the days I walked there most of my energy had been used up by the time we arrived. There was little inclination to do much running about until the moment it was decided it was time to go home.

The most interesting part of the park was to be allowed to run up the grassy sides of the communal air-raid shelters that were still standing from the last war. The speed at which I could run down depended on how confident I felt. Occasional trips and falls did no real damage, but it appeared I had little ability to put my hands out in front of me when I was about to fall so I acquired a good assortment of bruises and many nose-bleeds.

The other attraction in the park was the swings. My requests to be pushed higher each time were ignored; my size dictated from quite an early age that the safety child swings with bars across to hold the child in place were of little use, as my feet touched the ground. I was allowed on the ordinary swings with orders to keep a good hold.

Eventually it would be time to return home for tea. If things progressed without further problems I was then allowed to watch the television, the signal for me going to bed being the start of the News. From this point on the adults wanted peace and quiet. There was little protest on my part. Having used up all my energy, all I could do was hope I had been good enough to have a story read to me in bed. With me asleep, the family had a few hours of peace and quiet. The following morning I would be up as early as possible and ready for another day of learning about what things were, and generally getting under everyone's feet who were not sensible enough to have left the house at the earliest opportunity.

If there were things missing in my life – like a father and other children – I didn't really notice. I was quite content with my daily life. On a Saturday I would be taken out for the entire day by my mother. Bus rides, exploring the London Underground, playing in the park, watching the events on the River Thames, visiting museums and interesting trips to the larger shops allowed a good basic education of life around me to evolve. On the days I was taken out for the day, those still in the flat breathed a sigh of relief at the peace and quiet that had descended.

Sunday, also gave my mother the opportunity to take me out again. Often our day's events would involve the park and a picnic if it was fine. The whole day could be spent together, though if there was enough open space I'd be allowed to run about without any restriction. When I eventually ran out of steam it was judged time to eat and when all the food had been eaten and I'd run about some more, the slow return journey would then take place. If the weather was dull or raining I would still be taken out. Long bus rides and looking at famous buildings were far better than having to stay indoors.

I was active for almost every minute of the day. If my mother decided to go in one direction and I had decided that the other direction looked more interesting for whatever reason, a battle of wills would then ensue. I was an expert at throwing a tantrum. In an open park, there were few others to hear my demands; in a crowded street or bus then I had an audience, and knew on most occasions I would be able to wear her down and get my own way. On odd occasions however I came off worse – a quick swipe across my rear soon had me falling into line.

My school education should have started at the age of about four. I was quite a handful, and although my grandmother could quite easily cope with me, it was felt that if I could go to nursery school I would be able to mix with those of my own age rather than be surrounded by adults as I was now. There was an ideal nursery school a five-minute walk away. However, there were no available places, no matter how deserving the child was. Had my name been put down a couple of years earlier there might have been room: by applying now I would get to the top of the list in about a year and a half, just at the point when I would be going to infant school. So my life during my fourth year was very similar to my third. I devised more ways of getting adult attention – my quick ability to move and my short temper did not really change.

Sweets came as a reward for good behaviour or after a punishment. I was soon able to work out the amount of time I needed to be perfect to get a reward. Once the sweets were mine and finished, I was able to return to my true self. My grandfather was also the source of the occasional sweet. A small child might have rejected his selection, but I soon developed a liking for his limited choice: Victory V lozenges, Bronchial Cough Sweets and on occasions Winter Mixture boiled sweets.

Left to my own devices I could quite happily amuse myself for short periods. It was wise of my grandmother to make occasional visits to see what I was up to; I could use my imagination. At an early age, a large strong box could become an inexpensive plaything; the only problem would be at the end of its life getting

rid of the thing. Around the ages of three and four whilst out shopping with my grandmother, spotting a large unwanted box was an excuse to plead to be allowed to take it home.

On some occasions on our return journey, if the box was thought to be clean and manageable, it was allowed. If it fitted on the pushchair with the shopping inside, then it was quite an easy matter to take it home. If it was too large, it had to be fairly close to home to stand any chance of becoming mine. Other general safe playthings could range from discarded rolls of bus tickets to a host of items that to an adult were simply rubbish, but to a child with imagination they were wonderful possessions.

The wireless or television could amuse me for a short time each day. The early afternoon would bring the afternoon story for children; late in the afternoon there would be a short period of television before my tea and eventual bed. One series that I did find interesting was a regular short story series featuring horses. 'Tum' in later life had a lot to answer for. If I wanted to listen to the wireless, there were two choices — stay with my grandmother and accept her mostly dull talking matters on the Home Service, or go into my uncle's room. This was slowly turning into my playroom, as it had a nice smooth linoleum surface where I could play with my cars, and turn on his wireless. I was too young to be able to tune into many of the stations that could be found on his set. However the station it would first lock onto that gave clear sound was Hilversum. As it was mainly music, I was quite happy with that.

On a few occasions, my grandmother forgot to check on the progress of my playing, it always ended in trouble. Having watched a children's television programme about hair-cutting at a barber's, I decided that perhaps I could amuse myself on that theme. Keeping scissors and sharp instruments out of my hands was a regular matter. Unlike most children at the age of about four, cutting my hair or scalping some object that resembled hair did not immediately spring to mind.

The fashion for men in the early 1960s was to have neat hair held in place with modern white hair cream. My uncle had decided on economy in purchasing his supply: it came in a quite large dispenser with a pump handle. When the adults found my play activity they had little idea of what had gone through my mind. I had neatly squeezed the white rather greasy cream onto the tops of chairs, doubling for the imaginary people that could have been sitting there. Once the top of the chair backs had been covered I set about using any other surface for

the rest of the cream. If the white dollops had been joined together, it would have stretched a couple of feet or so. Spread over several items of furniture, the coverage was far more. Apart from wasting a large tub of hair cream, cleaning up the mess was the main problem. On the areas that were solid wood and the like there was no real problem; on the tops of chairs that were covered with cloth and on parts of the walls, the large greasy stains were immovable. Confined to my bedroom in tears was the general result after such forms of play.

The other major mess I managed to cause was with paint. Usually any painting I attempted was on the kitchen table, providing there was no laundry or clothing around that would suffer the odd spillage. If the table was not free, my bed with its blankets and sheets removed made a flat surface; the mattress was protected with a rubber sheet, so little damage could be caused by any mess I might make. With a small container of water and a selection of paints I could be left alone on my own without the ability to cause much of a nuisance, and with no need to clean everything up until it was time for bed I could have several short sessions at painting to prevent boredom.

One afternoon I decided that I wanted to be like some other children in the park and have coloured wellingtons rather than the standard black pair that had been purchased for me. I was bright enough to realise that if I painted my boots with the paints I normally used, the first puddle I went through would wash the colour off. I headed for the confines of my uncle's bedroom. He was a keen model-maker and I knew he kept a supply of model paints that didn't wash off. There was a disappointment in the colours he possessed, due to his need for accuracy in colouring the trains and buses he constructed. Instead of a nice bright red, I would have had to settle for maroon, but an attractive shade of blue compensated for the lack of red. While most of his pots of paint were very small, a few were slightly larger, and the blue shade was one of these.

Knowing that if I returned to my room with the paint I might get into trouble, I hid under his bed after finding a small paintbrush and something to take the top off the tin of paint. Actually painting my wellingtons took more time than I imagined; the small modeller's brush only allowed tiny amounts of paint to be applied. I speeded up the process by pouring part of the paint onto the sides of the boots and then using the brush to make the painted area larger. I soon found that modelling enamel is a very sticky paint and managed to get some on my hands and a small amount on the floor. I was disappointed in my efforts as I had been unable to cover my two boots entirely. I carefully put the top back on the tin and placed it on the shelf with the other tins, and left my boots under the bed to dry. Not wanting to get any paint on my clothes, I went off to wash my hands.

I found that unlike the paint I normally used, washing my hands with water did not work. Eventually after several attempts to remove the paint from my hands I went in search of my grandmother. The amount of paint was nothing major but it took her a little while to bring my hands back to their normal state. Being quite wise to my forms of play she now asked where I had found the paint. Eventually I led her back to my uncle's room and showed her the paint tin. Looking around the room there was little sign of me spilling paint or actually painting anything. My bedroom and the other areas I might have taken the paint to were also checked, as there were no signs of any problems, my grandmother just took it that I was playing with one of the tins where a top had not been put fully back. I was told off for touching the paint and was given to understand that in future it would be best to stick to my own paints.

Later in the afternoon when my mother returned I was keen to show her my painting results. My wellingtons had not entirely dried off and although the paint was no longer in its runny state it was still a little tacky. A second cleaning session was now called for. My grandmother now found out that my activity having been out of sight was the reason for not being found out. Getting a second telling-off was not fair; it was not as if I had been naughty again. I was sent off to bed in tears. My wellingtons were past saving and were consigned to the dustbin. The small area of blue paint under my uncle's bed dried off and was on the linoleum forever. The following day, I appeared to be of good enough behaviour to be taken by my grandmother for a replacement pair of wellingtons. I might have asked for a red pair but I had not been good enough to have any choice. An ordinary pair of black wellingtons were purchased for me with a warning not to paint them.

The other area of trouble I regularly became involved in was trying to find out how things worked. To the adults it was being destructive with my possessions; to me it was merely an attempt to take an item apart to find out how it worked and then put it back together again. It was this last activity that normally ended in failure. A kaleidoscope with its small plastic coloured inserts makes interesting shapes when viewed. All I wanted to do was find out how the plastic pieces went together. With a small accordion, it was how the air moved the small reeds that was of interest; with a small metal xylophone, the two metal bars that made each note made no sound when taken apart. How they worked was interesting.

Most of these experiments ended with the plaything confiscated and thrown away, as it appeared to be useless after I had taken it apart. If I only had been allowed to keep it, I might have been able to find out more on how it worked. Once an item had been attacked, replacement articles were seldom purchased. I just moved onto the next item that caught my eye. Play sessions like these often ended with me being sent to bed in tears to mull over my actions. Around this time I was warned by my mother that there were schools that took bad boys and if I did not stop my bad behaviour, I would be going to one.

HOLIDAYS

At the age of four, during the summer I was taken to the seaside for two weeks. Our location was a chalet on stilts at a small resort near Clacton. The holiday appeared to start out in dull weather. On arrival, the sun came out and remained for almost every moment of my waking day. My mother had the knack of managing the best two weeks of sunshine for the entire year.

I was fascinated with the basic living conditions; water came from a communal standpipe in the dirt road. There was no mains drainage; water from the washing-up was simply chucked on the garden. What fascinated me more was the lavatory. Each dwelling had its own shed at the bottom of the garden; inside was what appeared to be a small oil drum with a wooden lavatory seat on top. To get the bucket collected you needed to display a letter C on the front of your chalet. Early in the morning, a group of men came round with a vehicle that resembled a large dustcart and dealt with the bucket. It was possibly at that moment I decided on a line of work when I grew up. An engine driver was not for me; this early morning work was going to be my choice.

A small local shop was available to buy all the groceries we needed. Most mornings I was treated to bacon and egg, fried almost in the open air compared with the dusty air of London. The breakfasts were wonderful. The other favourite treat was to have a small mousse that came as a small frozen block. There were instructions to let it thaw for a period before eating. I never managed to let it completely thaw before eating it.

I had inherited the skill of being able to stay out in the sun without getting sunburnt. My skin never turned red, it went from my slightly tanned look to almost dark brown in a matter of days. To keep the sun off the back of my neck, I was equipped with a desert-type cap with long white flowing tail and a clear green see-through visor. It worked for most of the time, however my active play meant it was often off.

Eventually the holiday ended and we returned to London. It was another year before we returned for a second two weeks' holiday, and again for most days my mother had managed to pick fine weather.

One problem with holidays and longer journeys with my mother was coach travel. With a limited budget, travel by coach was often the only solution. Knowing my difficulties lasting on a coach journey of three hours or more without visiting the lavatory, my mother had solved the problem until I was five by insisting that I wear waterproof pants under my trousers. After a protest from me, I was soon told it was either obey her or not go on holiday. I followed the orders but they never were needed.

Travel sickness always affected me. Even if I had apparently not eaten for many hours, my ability to produce an amount of sick that gave the impression I had recently had a massive meal was always a mystery. Often our journey would end at that point, sometimes miles from anywhere. Following such an incident our travel was often by local bus. I was completely fine from that point on.

HOW TO PASS THE TIME

In the flat in London if my grandmother was busy I was quite content to look out of the front window to see what was going on outside. If we had been on a main road, there would have been plenty to see, but as our road was quiet I had to pick certain times of the day to look outside. The rag and bone man was possibly the most interesting; as we were almost at the end of a road he often used to stop to see if there was any other trade around before turning into the next road. None of the adults had been able to explain why he was still called a rag and bone man. Although he might accept old clothing and rags, there were

no bones on his horse-drawn cart. On occasions when I had been out shopping, I had been allowed to pat the head of his horse. The call that he yelled out as he went along the road was simply not something I could understand, until on one of the occasions that I was patting his horse he explained that the call was for the goods he was after. Some people used to leave things on the kerb for him to collect. Almost opposite there was an old lavatory cistern that had been left out, I was waiting to see him pick it up. A man walking along the pavement glanced down at the cistern, possibly wondering what such a thing was doing in the middle of the pavement, and did not notice the lamp post that he now walked into.

My earliest experimentation with electricity must have been at the age of around five. I was fascinated by the shapes of light that were made in the electric fire. Part of the fire had a plastic type of cover that was meant to represent coal. To give the effect of the coal burning, a couple of bulbs were inside that gave a reddish glow. At some point, I had managed to remove the coal-effect part, followed by one of the two bulbs.

The fire had not been on for very long so it was only warm to the touch. Soon the bulb was in my hand. Looking at the end I saw that it had three small lugs on the end, rather than the normal two I had noticed on other light bulbs. For curiosity, I now put my finger into the area where the bulb had been removed from. At this young age all I could describe was the feeling of a person grabbing you and immediately jolting you. For a short while, I was rather stunned. There was no real pain, just an odd shaking sensation; I replaced the bulb, followed by the cover. There was no feeling that I wanted to cry, it was just a stunned sensation. Keeping quiet saved me from getting into any trouble. None of the adults found out about my latest bit of inquisitiveness. The 240 volts that went into me for that short moment could have done real harm, but at that age, I simply put it down to curiosity.

During the week, my grandmother was the main person that I saw. If I was a nuisance, I had to answer to her. My grandmother did not waste any time telling my mother if I was ever badly behaved; I was punished well before her return from work. By the time I saw my mother I was on my best behaviour. If I was out shopping with my grandmother and causing a minor nuisance – normally through boredom, there was often a telling off. If I took the hint and did not cause any further disruption for the rest of our time out, once we arrived home, no more was said about the matter.

A second warning whilst we were out and I knew I had to be absolutely perfect until we arrived home. That might get me off the punishment, but normally it was too late. If I had made a fuss at the point of the second telling off I was really in trouble. For the occasional disobedience when we had been out, as soon as I entered the kitchen after we arrived home, my grandmother would sit down on a chair and beckon me to come forward and lie across her knee. A light but not painful spanking of three or four hits with her hand would now be administered. I would then be sent to my room. Once I had made up my mind to be good I could return; it was up to me to decide when the punishment was over.

If when we arrived home after having been naughty and my grandmother started to put the shopping away, then either put the kettle on or poured herself a glass of Guinness, I knew I was past the minor stage of disobedience. Other than taking my coat off I was not allowed to leave the kitchen. Even using the excuse that I needed to visit the lavatory would not work; my grandmother didn't want me hiding in there to avoid the punishment that was about to befall me. Even if I had decided to lock it from the inside, it was easy to open from the outside with a small screwdriver.

There was some fear, as I knew exactly what was coming next; it would just be a wait of about five minutes whilst she relaxed with her drink before attending to me. This delay was a good idea, when she did punish me, she was much calmer. From the age of four I had found out that this punishment hurt. I could start crying now or when the smacks started; my grandmother was not going to take any notice of my feelings.

 The punishment when it came was harder slaps with her hand on my bottom; they were not done in a way that would cause me any physical harm, just enough to bring tears to my eyes. By the time I was five I knew exactly how much it was going to hurt. Once over I would be escorted to the bathroom for a wash, and then taken to my bedroom to quieten down. When I decided I could be good, it was possible to go back to my playing. After a spanking, a treat was normally given to me on my return to the kitchen if I promised to be good. A few squares of chocolate or sweets allowed me to forget all about earlier events.

My worst ever punishment had been shortly before my sixth birthday. To my grandmother the age of six was the point by which I should have learnt to behave. I had deserved to be punished that day as I really was causing a nuisance, and was badly behaved. Instead of the normal hand, my grandmother had used a small cane; this was kept in the kitchen for closing the top window. Originally it had been a parasol, but now only the thin cane remained. Instead of being put across her lap I was told to face the wall. Unlike the three or four hits with her hand, I was only given two hits on my bottom with this cane. It was far more painful but soon over.

I was sent to my room to contemplate my actions; from that point on I knew how to behave. I did get my reward on my return to the kitchen, but it was not any different from the reward following an ordinary spanking, which I thought was slightly unfair as this time it had hurt more.

At the age of five, I should have started infant school. Our flat was located on the very border of the borough; the nearest infant school that might have space was a good half-hour walk. My mother had already gone off to work at that time so she could not have taken me, whilst my grandmother was still looking after her son in the flat, just at the time I would need escorting to school, and with it being uphill for most of the journey to school, there was some reluctance over the idea that I should start school.

My mother had the idea that the pair of us would move in the spring to a new location, so it was not really worth starting school in these winter months. Spring came but no firm plans for moving emerged. Spring became summer and still no real plans were made. It did not seem worth starting me in the middle of term; it might be best to start with the next school year in September.

The school year started but I did not. It was not a case of not getting an education; my grandmother had many years' experience of bringing up children and did not let me stay idle. Time was spent drawing, writing my name and learning to read. There was encouragement in this field with her starting a story and making me get really interested, then we would work through the final part, word by word with me doing the reading.

I was quite happy with this life. Having been led past a school on days we had been out for our walk, and looking at those noisy children behind the big iron railings, it did not really give me any thoughts to demand to take part.

By the end of the year my mother's plans were made; around mid December we left London and headed to the West Country to a small seaside town. Travelling in the holiday season was not easy, and coupled with very bad winter weather, a shortage of fuel for the trains, a train dispute and a totally unreliable timetable, and you have the makings of a rather irritable child surrounded by a larger number of cross, overcrowded passengers.

SCHOOL

December 1962, it was cold, very cold. The coldest part of the year was not the best time for our move. Eventually after a final bus ride, we arrived at the small seaside town where we were going to live. Not knowing the area it took some time before we found our new home. A power failure with the local street lighting did not help matters.

My mother had taken a job as a housekeeper-matron and to help with anything else that needed doing at a small private school. This was attended by children aged between four and eight years, mostly in preparation for them to join private preparatory schools later in life. Part of my mother's wages would include my place at this school rather than to a local council school in the locality. The building was a large semi-detached house with an additional bungalow at the rear. Originally the school had taken in several boarders, but it was now almost entirely restricted to day pupils. I was not going to be on my own; there was one boarder, slightly younger than I was.

We arrived during the holidays. Christmas that year was a little unusual: I had been used to having the rest of the family around; now it was a rather strict lady, my mother and a boy plus a Siamese cat and a Dachshund – both animals disliking the company of children. The weather was the worst for many years. It snowed and snowed, fun at first for children, but when you return indoors to a cold, sparsely heated building, it is not that nice.

Before we set out on our journey, my mother had received a very nice little booklet on the school and the facilities it offered. In reality everything was economised to the bare minimum. Food was very basic and meagre in portions, every possible expense to keep the building running was spared. A small bungalow in the grounds was even let out to lodgers to bring in some extra income. During the very cold winter, the bungalow became flooded after a pipe burst. As the lodgers were away over the holidays, the heating had been turned off with disastrous results. Christmas had my mother dragging a soaked carpet out of the bungalow, and trying to get the building dry. I tried to help, but an indoor paddling pool to a small boy is only fun.

Actual school terms contained the least number of possible school days; ideal for children, but at this point having just reached six I was eager to start school. The school had a uniform that was required to be worn by all. To save some money, most of my uniform comprised of clothing left by former pupils or items that had not been claimed from the lost property box. With my ability to grow quite fast the saving was welcome.

I now needed to mix with other children. Until this point I had made no contact with children of my own age. At past Christmas times I had met my cousins, but given the limited space in the flat, no real play had ever been achieved. Very occasionally in the park, my grandmother might have allowed me to play a catching game with a ball if a child were on their own with a parent, but no real group play had ever been achieved.

The other major difference was that I had to share the attention of an adult. Until this moment providing an adult was not actually busy, any question or problem I wanted to ask about normally received immediate attention. Having to share with a group of other children was new for me. Before starting school I had read all the small books on going to school. Life now slightly resembled the books, but the nice activities that were shown in the books did not seem to happen. If I had started school a year earlier, I might have been more settled, everyone around me had over a year of school behind them: for me everything was so new.

Unless we were alone, I was not to address my mother as Mummy, Mum or Mother. I had to address her by our surname, as I would address any other adult. This was to make me equal to every other child in the school who might need to address my mother. My mother had some help with her work. When we first arrived, the cook was from Spain. Straight away we made friends, as both of us were dark haired and had slightly tanned skin. Many at first thought that I was her child. Later on, she left and a lady from Holland took her place. The headmistress liked to take on workers from other countries; as they were partly here to study, they were more willing to work longer hours for minimal pay. I soon settled in quite happily with this new lady whilst my mother was busy and learned a few words of Dutch. Apparently I picked these up quite easily; my many hours as a young child spent on my own listening to Dutch radio broadcasts seemed to have ingrained a few words into my vocabulary already.

My mother's job was originally to be housekeeper and to lend a hand in the school if necessary. When the headmistress learnt that my mother had looked after children as part of her work previously, a little more involvement in the school was organised. After school, I had my tea with the other boy in the sitting room with the headmistress. We each had a small chair and a table to put our tea on. Tea took place during the early evening news; it was thought that we both might learn a little about what was happening in the world that day. If we had been good, we were allowed to stay for the following programme. If either of us had been in trouble, both of us would be going to bed early. I always thought this unfair; had we both been naughty then I could quite understand the punishment. I had been quite used to a telling-off and occasional physical punishment from my mother or the adults in our flat. On arrival here, the headmistress explained to my mother that she was against a child ever being hit for any reason. The odd light slap from my mother ended. However, the punishments that I now had to endure were far worse.

A telling-off seemed to go on for so long. Once it was over there was often further punishment of not being allowed to go outside or taken down to the beach. When it came to tea, if either of us had not been good, then cake would not be given to us, but would be left on the main table during tea.

The worst punishment I ever experienced at the school was when the parents of the boy who was boarding came to take him out for a day out. They had previously arranged that I'd go with them. Everything that morning seemed to have been fine. But at some point I must have done some minor thing wrong in front of the headmistress. We were both ready to go out and in our best clothes. Suddenly I was told to go to my room. It was at that point his parents arrived to take us both out. The headmistress informed them that I had been naughty and did not deserve such a treat. With my mother expecting me to be out all day, she had already left the house so did not know I had been sent to my room. I spent the entire day in my best clothes stuck in my room.

At night once we had gone to bed, we were both expected to stay in our rooms until morning. I was quite used to getting up in the night or early morning and visiting the lavatory if needed. Now I was told that I had to go back to using a pot under the bed. Before we went to bed, each of us was made to go and sit on the lavatory, to make sure that if there was a need to go during the night we would only use the pot to pee in. He knew that if he ever had an accident in the night, he was not to cause a fuss. If he was uncomfortable, he was to take off his soaked pyjama trousers and put a second dry pair on. He was then allowed to get into the spare bed that was always made up ready. My arrival had changed these rules; I now occupied the spare bed.

Any night problem and he was upset. Making any noise during the night inevitably led to trouble. Our room was next to that of the headmistress; crying out in the night or making a noise, even if we were only talking, soon brought her in. A quick telling-off at that point was a minor event; the punishment for the following day was always something we had time to think over.

It was suggested by the headmistress that if either of us had an accident during the night, it was fine once a dry pair of pyjamas had been put on to share the other bed. Our beds were quite big enough for two of us to share without any discomfort. In a way, both of us were quite happy with this rule; if we were sharing a bed, we could talk as much as we liked without being caught by her.

The event of getting out of bed and trying to take aim at the pot was something we both hated. It was always dark; we were not allowed to switch on the light. The following morning there was a telling-off if our aim had not been perfect. A cold night and every reason could be thought of over not having to leave one's bed. In the morning, there was never any telling-off or a punishment if there had been a wet bed. As long as he had not made a fuss in the middle of the night everything was fine.

My first report after four months did give some hope.
Spring Term Report of 1963.
Division – Transition.
Age 6 years 4 months.
Scripture, History & Geography: Philip takes an interest in these stories and answers well.
Arithmetic & English: *Philip tries hard with his written work, but should learn to concentrate on his tables; he does not listen.*
Reading: Has made a good start and is progressing slowly but steadily.
Drawing: *Fair.*
Percussion Band: *Will do better when attentive.*
Singing: *Fair.*
Elocution: *Many sounds need much care, but he tries hard.*
Conduct: *Fairly good.*
General Remarks: *Philip is gradually learning to be a co-operative member of the group; he tries hard with his work but is considerably behind others of his age.*

I made slow if erratic progress, but in time, it was hoped I would settle in with the others. With no actual cash coming from my mother, a few economies were made on my education. I was a fidget and tall for my age; this became apparent when my school desk fell apart. Their construction was never intended for everlasting use and constantly having to stand on a supporting wooden beam on the desk to get up, caused the desk to fall apart. For any other child a replacement desk would have been found; I was treated now to two apple crates turned on their sides. If I were special in some way, it was now down to having the only desk with a coloured picture of fruit on the top.

There were other areas where I did not really fit in. My diction was not that clear. I might have been early at just before the age of six for losing all my front teeth, and this had the result that almost everything I now uttered was with rather a splutter. I also had an accent which did not help matters; it was not a true Cockney accent, but compared with the local dialect it was different.

Another difference for me was in my looks; in my mind I had never experienced any problems over my slightly tanned skin and red cheeks. The summer dark tan from my holiday had vanished; I was my normal light tanned complexion. My mother was slightly upset when one of the girls at going home time asked my mother if her older sister from another school could come and see 'the brown boy'; apparently I was a new attraction. Within two terms, it was decided that an alternative school might be of more use to me. My mother made enquires at the local infants' school in town to see if there was a vacancy for me.

The move to my second infant school was quite a happy one. A benefit to my mother was that her wages were increased by a very small amount, simply because a token amount of her wages was no longer taken to pay the term fees of the private school. The new school was in the town. Like any ordinary child I now had to become used to walking to school and waiting at the end of the day to be collected. In an effort to help me, I was by put back by a year; this would allow me to make up the missing year.

The morning outing to school was enjoyable; if the tide was out it was a quick walk along the beach, if it was in and our way impassable it was a slightly longer uninteresting walk to school using the local roads. In the afternoon if our beach route was manageable, I was allowed to use up any excess energy; a little sand getting on my clothes could be dealt with quite easily once we arrived back.

The new school was totally different from my introduction to school life. Here we all sat in little groups; that we were allowed to talk during the lesson as long as the teacher was not talking was ideal. I was soon able to make several friends. Most lessons were more interesting as things were attempted in small groups, all of us helping each other rather than sat in neat rows.

The only lesson that I was having difficulty with was English. Before I had started at my first school I had a basic reading skill and knew the alphabet of 26 letters in full and was quite able to read the early stage text books without any help. At this school the alphabet was different; there were extra letters and this was confusing to me. The Initial Teaching Alphabet I was now taught had 44. The reading books were all in this new style of writing and I found it almost impossible during my first few weeks to make any sense of any storybook.

My writing also had to change. At my original school I had become used to the first stages of a script type lettering. Although our written letters were not actually joined up, each letter was formed in this style. Our workbooks had extra fine printed lines to show where the tails to letters should reach and any top parts of the letters like t, k and l should touch. At this new school, letters had to be printed in an upright style and fit between two lines in our workbooks.

Other lessons were far more fun. Sand play, cooking and other interesting events took place on most days. But one event in the early afternoon did not suit me: having to lie on the floor on soft mats shortly after lunch and listen to a story was not to my liking. If I could have sat at a desk and listened it would have been fine, but lying down was difficult for me. I was not the only one; a girl in our class also found this story session rather hard to concentrate on.

If only one of us had caused minor disruptions with our fidgeting the lesson might have been all right: two of us was too much. Both of us were now sent outside for an extra playtime and apart from any other children while the quiet lesson continued. In time the teacher regretted allowing us out for these extra periods alone as it seemed to allow us extra time to plan mischief for later in the day – nothing very major, just jokes and games we could play on our friends. The girl did not act like the other girls I had met, if she had been upset in any way; a boy soon received a thump – her speed and strength was far more than I could ever manage, I had someone who liked to stick up for me and who simply liked acting like a boy rather than a girl.

When it emerged that we both lived in the same road and by taking different routes had not had much contact with each other, our life became much more fun. Within a short time, my mother would collect the girl from her house in the morning and we would walk or run to school along the beach. Most afternoons her mother would collect her as she had an older brother in a nearby junior school.

If we decided to annoy our teacher, it was to see which of us dared to come into school wearing our wellingtons. In dry weather, we were the only two to arrive in wellingtons owing to our walk along the beach and were often missed. It was fun to be picked on by our teacher then being able to complain that she had not complained about the other. At first we were sent out of the room to change but it was soon realised we were doing minor thing like this on purpose. Unless our antics started to disrupt the lesson we were generally ignored.

Having a friend to protect me was wonderful; it was not that I really needed any protection. Having been placed one year back, I was a slight oddity. At the age of almost seven I was a whole year older than the rest of the class, and if you added my height I could easily pass as an eight – or even a nine-year-old. I was teased a little by smaller children who knew I would not be able to fight back. Help came to me from the girl who could settle a few odd matters for me without any chance of either of us getting into trouble. If it did have one advantage, I was the one picked to do little errands or help with things and if I needed any help, there was a willing girl that was easy to pick as my partner.

Art was the best way of spending time at school: an easel with paint and paper and I was happy. My main subject was railway engines. As we had to share the range of coloured paints, I simply wanted to possess the jar of black paint. We were meant to have three different colours and swap over during the lesson. I just took the one jar and only used the other colours when encouraged by the teacher. All railway engines were black, weren't they?

The small seaside town gave me more freedom than staying in London. There was the opportunity to get out of the house and explore more of the area. For my mother, living at the seaside meant that if there was any free time that is where we should be. Originally, my mother might not have intended to take a second child out along with me. However, the boy who boarded at the school would have felt quite miserable if I were taken out for a walk and other treats, and he was left indoors. Most of the times that I was taken out, the boy a year younger than myself now came with us. I was a little jealous of having someone else to share my mother's attention, but I allowed such things to continue without too much protest.

If my playmate had been my own age there would have been more fun, but he was not at the age where my mother could really allow him to go very far. On the beach he tended to stay quite close to my mother when I went and ran off into the distance. There was little harm I could come to; the sea was always either up to the edge of the beach with a nice shallow area to paddle or totally out and somewhere in the far distance. One matter that stopped me from running off in the direction of the sea to find out exactly where it had gone to, was patches of dark oozing mud that you could not only get stuck in, but was difficult to remove from clothes.

Several miles of desolate beach near to where we lived meant I could be allowed freedom without causing annoyance to anyone. A few seagulls might have been disturbed by my running and shouting but they could easily find more quiet areas away from where I wanted to play.

Vast sand dunes provided hours of entertainment. Unlike the sand by the seashore that could be used for building things, even after heavy rain the dunes seemed to remain dry. My mother could find a nice sheltered spot and sit down for a rest; the pair of us could then play happily for a short while. My boredom normally ended such a sit down, and a different location further up the beach and a second rest could be made. My mother was quite capable of long walks along the sand; I could have easily managed such distances as well, but having the younger boy with us meant that our walks often needed to end earlier than both of us would have liked.

Nearer the town, the beach tended to get more crowded. The reason for going to this part of the town was to get sweets or visit the local café for a snack; things that were totally lacking at our remote area of the beach. The best treat for me was a small bar of chocolate and a bottle of ginger beer. I was often encouraged to share the chocolate. Ginger beer was not a taste that the other boy enjoyed, so to keep him happy my mother normally purchased a carton of orange squash or a small bottle of pop. I was quite happy; the bottle of ginger beer was bigger than either of the drinks he was ever given. To most boys of six, ginger beer might not normally have been their first choice, but to me this drink had some flavour.

A second treat was to be each allowed a donkey ride and I soon advanced to riding one of the two ponies that the man possessed, but still firmly under his control. On a trip out to our remote part of the beach, we came across a group of young girls with their ponies. They had set up in slight unofficial competition to the man with the donkeys, but they were at a far enough distance not to be noticed or to have any real impact on his trade as few people came to this end of the beach. As the area was more deserted, the girls were more willing to walk and run with the ponies during the ride, and for longer distances. At some point a decision would be made to make the turn and return to the starting point. The return trip was always at a run and if it was seen that you were capable of staying on, then quite a speed was possible.

On the days that we did go out, whilst a donkey ride was often given to the younger boy, I normally refused a pony ride at this point. Later on under duress I managed to get my mother to our end of the beach where the girls might be with their ponies. My mother was never asked how old I was. In time I soon progressed from one of the smaller ponies to the largest of the group. It was possible to get a fast pace in both directions; the ride might have ended sooner, but often I was allowed a second lap to give the ride good value in time and distance. On the final trip back I was often allowed full control of the pony.

Once it was made sure that I had the reins gathered up, the lead rein would be unclipped and the pony released to head back to the main group in the far distance. To the girls my height, signs of my second teeth might have given them the impression I was about eight. If they had realised I was only six I bet the rides would have been at a far more leisurely and controlled pace. Although I never actually managed to fall off, my light weight meant that I needed to cling on tightly to avoid being thrown off at the fast speed.

The afternoons my mother were given off from work were often spent at the beach. If the boy was taken out by his parents when they visited him, it was possible to go further along the beach. I still had to be watched; the further you went the more interesting the finds: dead sheep that had been washed up amongst the dunes, and plenty of areas where barbed wire that remained from the war was still located amongst the more remote dunes. Lumps of wood and other debris could make marvellous items to play with; having been in the sea for long periods of time they were perfectly clean. If I found treasure like this it allowed my mother to take longer rests. Eventually it was necessary to return to the school and its rather strict order of life.

If I played up or needed occupying in some way, there were always plenty of tasks I could help out with. Some were quite interesting: setting out the upper classroom with things for the following day's lessons, often meant that odd extra pieces of drawing paper could be had and the more interesting shades of pencils obtained. Chores on the days when I had not been on my best behaviour could be anything from wiping down the play coats belonging to the other children to putting a shine on their spare shoes or cleaning their boots in readiness for group activities on the beach.

The stay at the seaside did not last very long; my mother was getting a little restless owing to the rather poor irregular pay that she and another member of the staff received. General ideas of leaving had been mooted between them for a little while. Whilst my mother and I lived on the premises and our food was supplied, the other member of the staff had to pay rent for a small local flat and also purchase her own food. With their wages dependent on payment from two lodgers in the small flat that adjoined the school, at the end of some weeks there were no wages until several days later. The decision was eventually reached that they were both going to leave together otherwise the one who remained would have the extra work.

My mother was aiming to get another job as a housekeeper; the other lady was going to return to Holland from where she originated, having come to this country to improve her English. Her family had a large farmhouse; my mother was invited to come and bring me. We could have an extended holiday and other work might be possible. Irrational moves like this would have been something my mother could have easily accepted. It was only for the simple reason that neither of us had a passport that the offer was not taken up. If there had been further time to get a passport for both of us, then our trip could easily have happened. My mother was tired of this location and wanted a new start as soon as possible.

Soon our cases were packed; a few extra clothes came my way – several garments from other boys that had been abandoned, usually because the boy had left the school or outgrown the item, became mine. These items of clothing were normally used by other boys when their own clothing had been mislaid or forgotten; at odd times even items belonging to the boarder or myself had to be lent to the day pupils when necessary.

Clothing that would last me for the next year was carefully packed into my case. Some of my outgrown clothing was left in its place; my mother thought that was only fair, the amount exchanged being about equal.

The day we all left brought total disruption for the plans for the cooking and general upkeep of the school and lodgers. Although both staff had given reasonable notice of leaving, no replacement staff had been arranged; it was thought that my mother might have changed her mind and stayed on, but her plans were made and there was no going back. We were off on a new journey. I was told that we were moving to another seaside rather than back to London.

AUTUMN 1963

Our new location was in a small village near the coast. Again, we arrived in almost darkness, so our new home looked rather dark and slightly frightening. My mother was now a housekeeper at an isolated house. This was set in five acres of land. I was allowed to visit some of the garden area when there were no guests, but generally, I was confined to our small garden at the side of the house where our flat was. My mother normally looked after just a lady and gentleman during the week; however at the weekends their grown-up children attended; the time spent with me at these periods decreased.

Having been used to other houses surrounding us, this isolated house took a little getting used to. The house was at the end of a long tree-lined drive; there were no local street lights anywhere near, so at night there was only moonlight. The house had formerly been used as a convalescent home. Next to our flat was a small summerhouse, which had a more macabre use in years past as a mortuary.

The wages my mother received for housekeeping were not a large amount. Three pounds a week had to pay for our food, heating etc. In the normal way, a housekeeper would have expected to receive these items as part of her wages, but in this job, she was expected to pay for her own supplies. As a bonus, we were allowed some vegetables from the garden. Food, clothing and heating were perhaps the main expenses of the week. With careful planning, my mother seemed to make ends meet. A few savings could occasionally be made; the farm next door supplied us with misshapen eggs at a reduced price. During the week, my main meals were in the form of school lunches. At two shillings and sixpence for the week, it ensured I was well fed.

If I was going to play near to the house I had to remain clean and tidy; there were few real playthings to amuse me – all I had was a few model cars; there was a limit to the number of times you can push them around. There were two swings in the side field, made totally out of metal. Neglect over the years had made them difficult to use and rather fragile, so only light use could be attempted.

A small bicycle was given to me by the owners of the house; this had lain unused for many years. I was forbidden to take it out of the grounds; if I had gone out onto our lane, the steep hill would have made the bicycle uncontrollable.

The gravel path made it quite difficult to cycle; any indentations in the gravel path that I made had to be put right by the use of the rake before I came indoors. The lightness of the gravel meant that if I attempted to wear shoes or plimsolls they soon became very uncomfortable when a single piece of stone would become lodged inside. On most days I wore my long leather riding boots which the owners of the house had also given me.

I could easily manage to put the boots on, but I needed the help from my mother in removing them. On returning indoors, I had to wait until my mother returned to our part of the house to help me take them off. Providing they were clean I was allowed to wear them indoors but any mud on the floor normally confined me indoors for the rest of the day.

My mother decided that as I was older I should now have slightly different punishments if I was naughty. The main worry for her when she did punish me, by stopping my treats or confining me to the flat if I had been naughty, was that I might do something more disagreeable in retaliation for a long drawn out punishment. If this were something that affected her employers, then she might lose both job and home.

During the previous year, I had become used to the very boring regime of missing treats or being sent to bed very early. At this new location there was no headmistress living here to dissuade my mother from smacking me. My mother explained what she had in mind. In an odd way, I was happier to go back to the punishments that had been given to me before I had gone to that school. Once a punishment had been given, that was the end of the matter. Not having any sweets or treats and being sent to bed early seemed to last for ever.

My temper was normally the main reason for getting into trouble. As we lived in the house of my mother's employer, I would have to be restricted in both where I went and the amount of noise I made.

When my mother found out that my bedroom here was relatively sound-proofed through having a strong kitchen wall and storage room surrounding it, sending me to my bedroom where I could cry and make a noise after a quick punishment solved the problem of me annoying her employers.

We came to an agreement that for any minor matter I did wrong, I would go back to having a slap on my legs or bottom with her hand. This to me was something I was quite happy to return to. Knowing that there were a selection of sweets in my mother's room at the school, and not being allowed to have any had been one of the worst punishments. My mother now explained that as I was a year older I could expect a little harsher punishment for things that were naughty.

I thought my mother meant a caning, as my grandmother had done, but it appeared that her idea of the next stage in punishment was that instead of her hand, my school plimsoll would be used. I could only ask if there would be anything worse than the plimsoll. It appeared that restricting me to my room for the entire day and confiscating my sweets would be the ultimate punishment. Having already experienced almost a year of such punishment, I made the decision that I did not want to return to that form of reprimand.

I was told never to tell any of my friends, or anyone else, that I received the plimsoll from her. If they told their parents I misbehaved and was punished, I might find they were told not to play with me.

With my active forms of play and annoyance, I soon experienced the odd slap across my legs over minor matters, and took it as part of my play activities. Fun was trying to dodge my mother's hand as it was approaching my legs. She did not have the time to pursue me throughout the flat; in most cases if I reached the safety of my room, I was not in any position to cause any more problems and was left alone. When I thought it was safe to come out, I could return to our sitting room.

The use of my plimsolls could cause a problem when I had left them at school, which for the odd occasion did get me out of a punishment. Only when I outgrew a pair and my mother decided not to throw the old ones away did I learn that there was one readily on hand with which to punish me.

I did not bother fighting her or throwing a tantrum. When it was decided on the odd occasion that I had been naughty, the sooner I got the matter over with the sooner I could return to whatever I had been doing.

My mother was tall, and had the strength and physique to apply the plimsoll with force to cause real pain; fortunately when I was punished with the plimsoll it was more for show than for pain. I was told to lie face down on my bed; two or three hits were applied to my bottom. Once the plimsoll had been given, my mother left me alone. There was never any massive pain – just enough to bring me slightly to tears, which was to me more the anger of the punishment than the pain. I did not want her to see me in tears whilst she was in the room; when I had finished crying and had decided to be good, I was able to leave my room. On coming back into the flat, I normally had to say sorry about what I had done wrong and give a promise not to do it again.

The plimsoll was a punishment that seemed fair; it was the thought of my mother stopping my sweets and going outside that I was fearful of. When my mother decided to punish me with the plimsoll, it could easily be down to the way she was feeling at the time. In the normal way, my mother was one of the most easy-going adults one could ever hope to meet; these were on the days when there might be the odd short time to relax with a cigarette. On a day when she had run out of cigarettes, the most minor item of mischief could displease her. With the nearest tobacconist over a mile away, and funds always short, frayed tempers were a common occurrence.

Christmas was a disappointment. At the age of almost seven, I was growing out of the idea that there was a real Father Christmas. Whilst friends from school stayed indoors on Christmas Day and had their relatives visiting them, I was left alone in our flat whilst my mother worked in the main part of the house.

There were a few new toys from relatives, but as the items were sent by post to our remote location, they were of the smaller variety. My main present was a toy typewriter. The illustration on the box, when I had been allowed to choose it a few days before Christmas, made it seem that it would really work. On opening the box, the excitement soon turned to disappointment when it became clear that there were no real letter keys to press and each letter had to be selected by turning a wheel, then a single bar pressed to form the letter on paper. With a limited area that the paper could be printed on, the eventual things that were produced took too long for me. Total boredom over the toy set in when the single fixed piece of ink ribbon lost some of its ink. Parts of a line could be read but the centre area of each line became too faint to read. Extra special ribbons had to be purchased. The shops were closed over Christmas, and with them all in town, meant the end of that toy for the time being.

With just the two of us and a lack of money, a Christmas cake was a luxury we couldn't afford. For a treat, we had a Swiss roll with an extra layer of chocolate on the outside. Decorated by the shop with some green leaves it was disguised as a Christmas log. I loved chocolate so I was quite happy when my mother purchased this rather than the traditional Christmas cake. When it came to actually eat the log, it was very sickly; the covering was soft. This was not real chocolate but something based on cocoa powder and flour. We managed to get through about half of the log before it was put out for the birds and the local squirrel population, which would normally eat anything in sight – but they left the remains of the log alone.

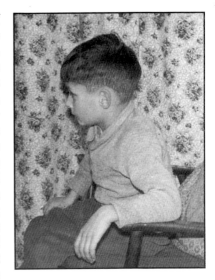

The local school was quite a long walk. At first my mother took me to and from school, but after a while I managed the just over a mile walk on my own. I shortened the distance a little by going along a muddy footpath that ran across a field. This was a route my mother would only take if it was very dry.

There was little traffic on the road that was next to the house. Local traffic knew to avoid this road at the time I went off to school, as a farmer would take his cows quite a way down the lane. Not having had much contact with animals, I found nothing really to be afraid of when I met them during my journey to school. If I did not make a fuss, they calmly walked past me. I found it easier to stand in the middle of the lane and let them pass me on both sides rather than be forced into the hedge.

My new school was similar to my previous schools. The English lessons were like my first school as the alphabet was back to twenty-six letters. Although it was not really a telling off by the teacher, it was an error on my part to use some of the extra letters I had learnt at my last school in the written work I produced.

For most of the time, I was quite happy at school. There was only one point when I had a few problems. The school was divided into three classes, one for infants and two for the juniors. This covered all the ages between five and eleven. Having just turned seven, I was still in the lower class of infants and looking forward to when I would move up into the middle class of juniors in a few months time. The older children had told me even more interesting lessons went on once you were in the middle class.

At the end of break, I had been chosen to take the hand bell back to the top class. The headmistress took that class, and would decide when the breaks would start. It was the first time I had entered her classroom. The instruction I had been given was that I was to put the bell on her desk.

Three of the boys from that class were already in the room; my attempt of trying to get the bell to her desk was thwarted when they blocked my passage for fun. In an effort to reach her desk, I made my way by walking between several desks. I nearly managed to get to her desk, but they pushed a couple of desks along the floor cutting off my route. I tried a second route around some desks, but again my path was blocked for fun.

I was on the opposite side of the room when the headmistress walked in. As she had entered, the other boys were still pushing the desks around the room and although I was not actually climbing over any chairs or desks, the angle that the desks were in made it look as if I was also pushing the desks around.

The four of us were brought to the front of the class. As the rest of her class filed in, we were led out to her office. There was a telling off; it appeared that we should know how to act indoors. It was easy to see we were all in the wrong, and needing to get back to her class, our punishment was over in seconds.

My friends had told me that the cane was given to any boy who badly misbehaved; I had imagined that you had to do something very naughty to be given it. All four of us were now given a stroke on one of our hands. I was too stunned with the suddenness of the punishment to think about crying. As soon as the cane had been given, we were sent back our rooms. I rejoined my class.

Our teacher did not notice that I was a few minutes late as she was busy dealing with some others in our room. I sat at my table and looked at my hand; there was a red mark forming across my palm. As it now stung, I started to cry. In time, our teacher came over to see what the matter was. I was not crying loudly or making a real fuss. If I had just received a little sympathy and told to be better behaved in future, things would have been fine. At first, my teacher thought my tears were due to one of our class hitting me.

As soon as I mentioned that the headmistress had hit me with the cane on my hand, matters worsened. I was now told to come with her and we went to the upper class. I was left to wait outside for a few moments whilst my teacher went to get the headmistress.

They were soon outside and discussing what I had done wrong to be given the cane. My teacher thought I was too young to be given such a punishment. All that the headmistress was saying was that she thought I had already moved up to the middle class and was no longer in the lower class. The matter was left like that; I was led back to my own class. Before we went in, I was taken into the girls' lavatory and made to wash away my tears. I was now told that when my mother came to collect me, she would explain why I had been punished. Once back in the classroom life returned to normal. I had almost forgotten the event by the time it came to going home time; the pain had really finished whilst I was being taken to see the headmistress.

It was only at the point we were all leaving the school, that my teacher asked if I would bring my mummy to see her. Most parents were waiting outside the school gates when we finished school. A few times a week, my mother did come to collect me; this was only when she had some time off work. On all the other afternoons I walked home on my own. I told my teacher that I was walking home on my own today. Now I was told to tell my mother about today and next time my mother came, she would have a word with her about my punishment.

The journey home was no fun, I was dreading telling my mother about what had happened today. On earlier occasions I had seen boys of my age receive a slap on the legs if they were naughty and a couple of older boys hit with a plimsoll, but until now I had never seen anyone caned. I knew my mother would think I had been very bad to be given the cane, even if I tried to tell her that I hadn't. If I then told her that my teacher wanted to talk to her about the matter, she would think I was still in trouble.

On arriving back at home, my mother was still in the main part of the house working, so I had even more time to think about what I was going to say. Eventually my mother returned; with the need to get me changed out of my school clothes and get my tea ready, I found I just could not tell her. By the time I went to bed I had really put the matter out of my mind. There was no pain and the red mark on my hand had long ago vanished.

School the following morning had returned to normal. It might be best to keep out of the older boys' way, as they would think I was to blame for their being punished. Almost as soon as my teacher saw me, I was taken to one side and asked if my mother coming to see her at the end of the school day. All I could do was tell her that I might be collected today. I was left to get on with my lessons. I knew this afternoon was one of the times I would be met at the gates.

When school finished I rushed out and managed to get my mother to walk away from the school as soon as possible. Often on the days I was collected, my mother would take me across the playground and out of the other gates that went in the direction of the shops. I was not looking forward to school tomorrow; my teacher might have even seen my mother waiting for me; I was going to be in trouble.

On going to bed, I was still worrying about school the following day. It was quite early the following morning when I woke up. If last night I had worried about what my teacher was going to say, I now had something else to worry about: my bed was soaked. I simply waited for my mother to come and get me up; I thought that my punishment would be the plimsoll. This was the first time I had wet the bed since we arrived here. Now I was seven I didn't think it would happen. There was a telling off from my mother about not getting out of bed in time, but I did not receive a smack.

The worst part was the bath I had to take. The hot water for the bath came from an electric cylinder. In the morning the water was always cold. To save money my mother tended to turn it on only for a short time in the late afternoons ready for baths at night. No time was spent to see if there was even the slightest amount of warm water; my bath was filled very quickly from the cold tap and soon over. With my mother having work to do in the main part of the house first thing in the morning, that I had now caused a delay by having a bath meant I was not in her good books.

The events of the morning were forgotten by the time I arrived at school. Again, my teacher asked if my mother would be coming to see her today. As it was a day I knew my mother would not be coming, I announced that I would be making my own way home. My teacher now told me that she would write a letter to my mother about the matter. I was dreading having to take her letter home, but nothing was given to me. On the way home I thought that my teacher might be sending it by post, so I was not looking forward to the next morning when the post would arrive. By the time I went to bed, I was worried about what my teacher was going to say about my punishment. Life was not going well; again I woke up to a soaked bed.

My mother thought I might not be very well; her answer was that it might be best if I did not go to school today. After a cold bath and clean sheets I went back to bed for the rest of the day. I knew I was not ill, but if it meant not having to see my teacher, things were better. There had been no post today, so everything went fine, if rather boring with the entire day in bed. My mother decided that I appeared to be well enough to go to school the following day.

Friday could have turned out better had I not wet the bed again. My mother had decided that there was nothing wrong with me; I must be wetting the bed on purpose. So there was a sterner telling off, and the time spent sitting alone in a cold bath was longer as a punishment. I was asked if everything was all right at school, and was it so that I did not have to go to school? I never had the courage to say anything about my teacher wanting to see her; all I said was everything was fine.

Once I had been given breakfast, I was given the benefit of the doubt and again let off school. Staying in bed for a second day was no fun. I was restless and bored. By the evening, I was wide-awake. My mother checked me all over; I did not appear to be coming down with anything. My night problems were put down to either laziness or not wanting to go to school. I was now warned that the next time I wet the bed I would be given the plimsoll.

The problems continued over the weekend. On Saturday as I did not have to go off to school, I should not have been afraid, but my bed was wet again. The time I spent sitting in a bath of cold water was much longer. Once dressed I was given the plimsoll; the scolding I received lasted the entire day as there was nothing wrong with me and as it was not a school day, I must be lazy at not getting out of bed. Sunday was a repeat of the day before. I was actually looking forward to returning to school and a reprimand from my teacher for not bringing my mother to see her.

On Monday morning after another wet bed, my mother decided to come to school in the afternoon and have a word with my teacher about me, and to see if there were any problems at school. With the need to get me off to school, there was no time for any punishment.

The afternoon came around and my mother was there. I waited outside the classroom whilst she went in and had a talk with my teacher. I could guess that my mother would now start to stop my sweets and going outside to play as a punishment for receiving the cane at school. Finally, my mother came out. It appeared everything was now sorted out, but I was a naughty boy for not telling her about my teacher wanting to see her.

As we left the school, my mother explained that now she had found the cause of my bed-wetting, she did not expect my bed to be wet after this. My mother could be firm; my plimsoll would be used for all future wet beds, even if it were a school day and there was not time to punish me in the morning, I would receive it when I returned from school. This final telling off seemed to be the end of the matter. I was happy that everything was now sorted out.

On the way home, I was questioned a little more about the cane; I was now asked if it hurt. All I could say was that it hurt and I did cry but I told my mother that it did not hurt as much as when grandmother had given me the cane. That I had been caned earlier was now news to my mother. I was asked to tell her where my grandmother got the cane. When I explained it was the one used to close the kitchen window, it was known that I was not making such things up.

It was now decided that as I was seven and the school could use the cane on me, this might be a further deterrent if I was very naughty. I could decide to either stay indoors or have the cane; my mother thought that the gardener at the house could soon find her one if it was needed. My only thought was that there might be a way of avoiding spending a day in my room.

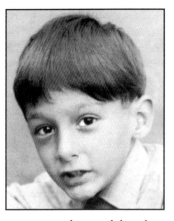

Odd little problems seemed to come my way. The house was covered in parts by a large creeper coming up from the ground at several locations. One point was outside our front window. The creeper had evolved over many years. A thick trunk about the size of my arm ran close to the ground. At first, it held my weight, and then it suddenly snapped. The damage was not apparent at first, but slowly the creeper started to die off. Soon a large area at one side of the house was clearly seen to be dead.

I decided to see how the radio worked. After taking out the many valves, I found that I was unable to get them back in the correct order. The set appeared to work but the sound was very faint and unclear. Another experiment was to set fire to a car tyre in the field. Although the flames did not spread to anything, the amount of smoke I caused was a bit of an annoyance. For each of these events I received the plimsoll and was in tears after every session, which for the level of damage I had caused was in my mind quite fair. I wondered how close I had come to the cane. I knew it was not just a threat; my mother had found a suitable one from the vegetable garden and kept it in our sitting room ready for when it would be needed.

Two other problems were not my fault. A couple of my friends decided that the metal swings could be given plenty of heavier use; the swings were soon a twisted pile of metal. The corrugated plastic panelling of an unused stable block was partly ripped apart in an effort to acquire a couple of sheets to use in a den at their home. I was blamed for these two events, as they happened on the same day. I found I had now reached a punishment beyond the plimsoll. I was taken to my bedroom; my mother spent a little while talking to me over these two events. Damaging these items was wrong and I had to be punished. I tried to explain that I had little to do with these events, but to my mother, as these were my friends and I had allowed them to come here to play, I should have made sure that no damage was done. In future, none of my friends would be allowed to come here again.

There was a choice given to me: either two days in my room with just books to read and no sweets, or the cane. I might have taken a day in my room, but two days was just too much. On telling my mother that I did not want to stay in for two days, I was left alone whilst she went to get the cane. She was only away a minute but it seemed to take forever for her to return. I was now asked how my grandmother punished me; was it any different to the way of the headmistress? On explaining that my grandmother had hit my bottom and the teacher had hit my hand, my mother decided that perhaps my grandmother was the best person to follow. Instead of standing up in the way I had been punished by my grandmother, my mother told me to lay face down on my bed in the same way as if I was having the plimsoll.

I was in tears, I knew it was going to hurt, but I was not going to stay indoors for two days. The two hits from my mother matched exactly the pain from my grandmother. It was one hit for each of the damaged items. My mother knew that the punishment had hurt, and instead of leaving me straight away, she sat on the bed and told me it was all over now, and I should now go back to being a good boy. I was now left alone to get over my tears. I was angrier that I was punished for the damage my friends had caused, than the pain from the cane. Soon I was out of my room; at least to me the punishment was over, and there was only a little more pain than the plimsoll.

At night, I was having trouble getting over the punishment. I was upset over the cane; to me I had not done anything wrong. During the night, I should have got up to visit the lavatory. I wet my bed – more to upset my mother, than being too lazy to get out of bed. In the morning my mother kept her word over if I wet the bed again – there was the plimsoll first thing on getting up. The following day was school and again my bed was wet. During my cold bath, there was a reminder that when I came back from school I would be punished.

If I was miserable during school, it was with the knowledge that I was going to get the plimsoll on my return. At the end of the day on my return home, I was given the plimsoll before tea and sent to bed as soon as I had finished the meal. From that night onwards, I knew that this was one battle I was not going to win and tried to be a good boy as had been requested.

The next time I went out to play, there was a reminder not to let any of my friends come here. I managed to get even with the two boys that had caused the damage. I was not forbidden from visiting them, so on a day they were not around, I went to one that had a den in his garden and caused a similar amount of damage. I opened a large party keg of beer that they had stored in their den. They did not have the intention of drinking it, but one of them had taken it out of their father's garage as a trophy. Emptying it onto the dry earth floor made their den unusable.

The next time I received the cane from my mother was after I had lit a few matches in my bedroom. I had not tried to set light to anything; all I was doing was seeing how slowly I could drag a match across the edge of a box before it caught light. In the normal way, I was not meant to have matches. If I was out of doors and at the bonfire that was fine; if I burnt myself that was my own lookout. Indoors it was wrong and I knew it. I might have got away with it had I not struck the matches shortly before it was time to get up. On coming into my room my mother had noticed the smell from the recently struck matches. It was quite easy for me to tell that it was not going to be the plimsoll.

Once my mother had removed the matches that remained, I was left alone for a short while before she returned with the cane. If the punishment was to hurt more today it was because I was still in pyjamas. The ritual of lying face down was soon requested. To my mother my crime was worse than any previous matter; today it was three hits with the cane. I had thought there were only going to be two hits, so I had moved slightly after the second hit, when the third one hit at the top of my legs. I was crying in agony.

It was easy to see my mother was still cross, the telling off over the matches now followed. I was now told to get up and have my morning wash. As today was a school day, the delay I had caused meant that there was only time for a very quick wash and breakfast before leaving for school. In a way, getting the punishment over so quickly had made me forget about the pain for a short while, but once out of the house I could still feel the stinging as I walked to school.

By the afternoon everything was back to normal, and when I met up with my mother outside the school gates, there was a reminder about not playing with matches. Once that was over, the matter was at an end. A reward of a small bar of chocolate was purchased for me once I promised not to light any more matches indoors.

At the age of seven, I was confident to be out on my own. Our isolated area gave me courage to explore alone. From the grounds, I could travel in three directions. The main one was to walk up the long tree-lined drive; with its neat gravel surface there was little scope for play. A route through the farm and down the farm paths led to the main wood. Originally, this had been part of the grounds to the house but had been sold off many years before. I was however allowed to use the path, but as it did not lead to any interesting areas, it was seldom taken.

The farm used the third entrance. This small private lane was in a muddy state almost all the year. Part way along the lane was a small market garden, growing vegetables and flowers. This also contributed to the mud, only on the days I was out at play did I venture along this route, as it was a quicker exit from the grounds of the house. I had only made little contact with the man who ran the market garden. There was a German Shepherd dog that roamed around. From an early stage, I learnt that although the dog was there to keep guard, he was quite friendly when the owner was around to keep him under control.

On one occasion I was making my way down the lane when the dog bounded up from the distance. I was not afraid and knew not to run off as the dog might attack. The owner was nowhere to be seen. The dog did not bite but its large powerful mass soon had me on the ground. There were no snarls or biting from the dog, it just tried to keep me on the ground. I was eventually allowed to get up. I decided to return home but the dog seemed to have other ideas. By size the dog was larger than me: when outstretched, the paws came above my shoulders. I could feel the claws digging in every time I tried to move away. The dog tried to grab me again. Finally, when I was far enough away from the site, the dog returned home.

Arriving home in a muddy and bleeding state, it looked worse than it really was; my mother could not understand how there were so many scratch marks on my shoulders and across my back. If the dog had attacked me why did I not have any bite marks?

Shortly after cleaning me up, my mother went to visit the owner of the dog to find out what had happened. On her return, it seemed the dog had just been playing; it was my own fault for just wearing a thin T-shirt. When I was going to use the lane, it might be best I wore my duffle coat for more protection if I was going to play with the large dog.

For several nights, I did have nightmares over the dog, but this might have occurred as it coincided with a play on the radio, that was read over several nights, about The Keeper of the Dead, who had the body of a man and the head of a dog. Our isolated house did not give much reassurance to a seven-year-old boy that, with its many passages and rooms, Anubis was not lurking in wait for me. I started wetting the bed for several nights over the fear of leaving my room. There followed the scolding from my mother, the plimsoll and the cold baths, but later I seemed to get over the problem and did not mind the dark passages of the house.

It was some time before I had the courage to venture down the lane again; then it was simply luck that the owner of the dog was around when I did decide to go in that direction. I was reassured that the dog was only playing; I now found out that the dog was behaving in a way some male dogs did. On later occasions when I was alone and the dog came up to me, I stood perfectly still. The dog putting his paws on my now protected shoulders soon finished his antics and I was left alone to continue down the lane.

Providing I gave my mother an idea of the location I was planning to visit, there were few restrictions, other than if I went too far it would be a long walk home. Friends in the village of my own age were fun to be with, but as most had families that took them out, I was often on my own. The local beach was about a mile away, so was within walking distance; there was little going on when the season was quiet, so I had most of the small pools and the beach area to myself.

At the far end of our lane, a wood was slowly being cleared in preparation for a small housing development. Mechanical diggers and bonfires were a magnet for a small boy. If I did not get in the way my presence was tolerated; if I was encouraged to help, it was to drag the smaller branches that had been cut over to the many small fires that were continually burning. The best treat was to be lifted into the bucket on a tipper truck and driven around and over the more bumpy areas of the site. It depended on the weather as to what state I returned home in. The clothes and myself were washable.

The wood had a large amount of unwanted tyres. These varied in size from the normal car up to tractor size. A few were used during the salvaging of the timber; the unwanted ones were ideal for encouraging the damp branches and waste wood to burn easily. This secret site was only revealed to a few of my friends.

One dangerous activity we took part in was to each select a tyre and roll it out of the wood and onto the lane. A steep hill then took away all the major effort of propelling the tyre in its downward direction, and if we were careful it took only the odd nudge to keep it out of the ditch and trees. The lane was little used and we never encountered any vehicles coming up. If there had been traffic, we would have been able to spot it and take full control of our own tyre. It was only when we were near the bottom of the hill and could see that there was no approaching traffic that we let our tyres out of our control. A small bridge with a stream running beneath was our target. If we had the tyres positioned correctly they would hit the edge of the bridge and then bounce into the air. The competition was to see if one's tyre could then go over the wall and into the stream below. Often the tyre bounced back onto the road and needed to be physically thrown over the small bridge. Our tyre play ended when the houses were starting to be built and the tyres were all used up.

Most of my free time was taken up at the farm near to the house. I soon became interested in how the dairy side of the farm worked; it was a small family farm and within a short while became accepted as always there. They had a son who was in his late teens.

My favourite activity was to be allowed to ride the pony at the farm; this had been the boy's when he had been younger. Until I started to ride the pony, it had not really been ridden for some time but it soon accepted me. The farm also possessed two massive carthorses; these were mainly used for pulling carts at the farm for many years. The two horses were now almost in retirement, however they were useful when the tractor became bogged down in the mud and needed rescuing, and during harvest time when the big hay wagon needed to be moved.

Steering the tractor along the lane was another treat. I was tall enough to be able to reach the pedals, but my lack of weight did not enable me to have full control over them. One other draw for me to the farm was to be allowed to play with the toys the boy still possessed. A clockwork train set would be set out on the concrete yard and could keep me amused for some time, and compared with the few toy cars I had at home, this was wonderful.

Watching chickens being killed and having their innards removed might have upset other children who did not live on farms, but I quite enjoyed watching such activity and helping. Collecting eggs from some more remote areas of the barn was something I was soon quite agile at. Helping mucking out the cowshed was another activity that I took pride in. Raking the straw from the drain gully might have been a little dirty, however, my mother had one set of clothes for me if I decided to visit the farm.

The move from infants to juniors at this school was quite easy. We moved into another room with a different teacher rather than actually changing schools. Some of my friends now found sitting at traditional desks in rows rather odd but it was a form of education I was already used to. Having a master teaching us was a way of encouraging us to behave.

The only major injury I managed to achieve was at the start of the afternoon break. I was the first onto the metal climbing frame. At one end, there were low bars that you could climb across, this then continued to a high single bar that took you to the end of the frame. Originally, the high bar was designed to have ropes or other equipment attached, rather than the difficult movement we had to complete to enable us to swing hand over hand along its length. My attempt to climb along the bar after a short shower meant part way along I lost my grip. The sensation of going headfirst was all I remembered until I awoke with what seemed the entire school gathered around me. I was carried into the school, and the various cuts and bruises were sorted out. All I could think of was that concrete was hard. If they had left me alone I would have been quite happy, but the headmistress thought it necessary to telephone my mother about the accident. I was let out of school early and as soon as we arrived home I was put to bed.

If the adults thought I was a little odd, it was that I did not use the words 'Mum' or 'Mother' either to talk to or about my mum, but addressed her as any adult might. This was down to not being told that I could go back to the words that any ordinary child might use.

CHRISTMAS 1964

The decision to send me to a new school came about owing to a number of events happening at the same time. In December, I realised that there were some family problems. My mother had to return to London for a day to see her parents. My grandmother was ill and needed to be looked after; my mother went up to see how everyone was. For me it was a normal day at school; I would have liked to have gone up to London with her. In the evening, it was a real treat to be allowed into the main part of the house to have my meal although when I did go to bed, I felt a little lonely on my own, but being allowed into the main part of the house had made up for it. School the following day was fine; my mother had returned by early afternoon so life was back to normal. From what I was told, it appeared my grandmother was now out of hospital; two aunts were taking it in turns to see to her needs. It was hinted that we might have to move back to London at some time in the near future.

The deciding factor as to my future life occurred at school. I was reasonably happy, although I was not in any way brilliant at lessons; I was beginning to settle into my third school. Now I moved up to the middle class. Perhaps our lessons were more difficult, but these could be more fun now that we had a master teaching.

A few of us spent our time annoying others but that was part of the fun. During lessons, we thought it fun to see who could get each other in trouble, just minor things, but enough to keep each other alert. If we went too far we knew there would be severe punishment, but for minor incidents, having to stand in the corner or do extra work was as far as it went.

If I were in trouble at school, it was usually for fighting. My height made me a target for every smaller boy that wanted to prove he was the best at fighting. In the normal way, I would do everything to get out of a fight. Running off was possible up to a point, but the confines of a playground meant that escape was impossible.

When I became involved in a fight, my fists played little part in my defence or for hurting my opponent; I was more apt to kick any foe or wrestle anyone to the ground. This was more for defence than causing any injury; if their fists were not in use, then I was safe. If I had an advantage over my foe, it was the size of my hands. I had an extra-wide hand span and it was easy to lock both my hands round someone's neck until they gave in. None of my foes ever managed this trick. Had I put my wide hand span to good use, it would have been on the piano, but there was no one who wanted to teach me.

If I was thought not to fight fair, it was using any method to win or draw. If a foe happened to put their arm or leg across my mouth, then there was a simple means of quickly removing it.

Teachers often put a stop to fights. For those that I lost I made sure it restarted at some later point. To the adults my size made me look like a bully, but I did not have the strength of those that were shorter.

The most recent of our deeds had happened during the last lesson of the day. With two of us mucking about for fun, my punishment was to stand in the corner, whilst my friend was sent to wait in the corridor. There was no other punishment given to us; as it was an art lesson, missing that was thought enough punishment.

At the end of the lesson, everything returned to normal. With the room tidied up, and final prayers said, we were released into freedom. The pair of us had a little pocket money so the intention was to head to the sweet shop to pool our funds to buy a quarter of sweets between us.

On going into the cloakroom to get my coat and boots, I found that my friend had spent his time in tying the belt of my raincoat to the metal coat rack. This was merely a delaying tactic that enabled him to gloat over his actions as he left. It was not a case of simply doing the belt up once around the rack – it had been carefully threaded several times around the pole using the full length of the belt and the hooks on my raincoat. Eventually freeing my coat and putting it on, I went after him, announcing what fate awaited him. For sport, he was a short distance outside the door, in readiness for the chase.

Having half a playground's head start, I eventually found him waiting just beyond the school gates. The headmistress and our teacher were in the playground and witnessed my blood-curdling threats of violence as I pursued my victim across the playground.

Had the headmistress needed an explanation as to my recent action, our teacher might have mentioned that we had both been punished for some wrongdoing and up until this point we had been separated; I was apparently now going to even up the score. If our teachers had been at the gate end of the playground, they would have seen us happily going together to the sweetshop. With no further view of us from their vantage point, they could only wonder if I ever caught him up.

The sweets purchased, we spent a short while dividing the spoils up. There was enough of the bag to enable our two shares to remain in reasonably clean condition for the duration of our walk up the main hill. Often I did not go this way, as it was longer than my normal way up the footpath and across the fields.

A mouth full of sweets and the rest put safe, we set about our normal antics. We paid little attention to our surroundings; that traffic was using the road next to the pavement and grass area we were on was simply out of our minds, I was now busily threading the belt of my raincoat back into its proper location. Due to the more important matters of sweets, this had been delayed until now.

My friend was simply trying to annoy for fun. As I started to thread the belt, he would try to pull the original part out. Eventually the task was completed and the buckle done up; no amount of tugging could release the belt, pulling the belt and me round in circles was all that could be managed. The grass bank that we were on was quite damp, so only a little effort was needed to turn me into a type of roundabout.

It was not a fight but both of us were taking turns to grab each other; there was one final tug at my belt, the clip at this moment gave way and the belt slid out of the fixings around my coat. My friend went with it; nothing serious in our minds happened, and he ended up at the edge of the pavement, not even making it into the road.

A bus driver coming down the hill thought my friend was going to go into the road and decided to stop very quickly. The bus stopped a good distance away from us; neither of us was really going to take much notice of the bus stopping had it not ended up at a slight angle, preventing cars from going up.

From the driver's cab came a telling off. Had we ran away, that would have been the end of the matter. With the cars that were trying to get up the hill now hooting at the bus driver, we stayed around to see if more events would unfold.

A small crowd soon formed; my friend was too busy wiping the mud off his coat to see the driver of the bus approaching. I did notice and beat a hasty retreat, leaving him to get the telling off. It was not really an act of cowardice; it was sensible in my mind to avoid trouble. Once at the top of the hill, I slowed down and then finished my sweets before returning home. My only thoughts were for tomorrow and asking him how much of a telling off did he get.

During tea, there was a knock at the door. My mother opened the door; it was the headmistress and someone else. I was eager to find out what it was all about, but as the adults wanted to be alone, I was sent to my room. Eventually I was brought back. It appeared I was being accused of trying to push another boy under a bus, although it seemed he would not admit I was trying to push him into the road. Several people had seen us struggling a short while earlier, and the driver of the bus had seen me at the side of the road letting the boy fall.

Three adults against one was unfair. I was never very good at explaining things at the best of times; now being accused of something I had not done, sent me into a rage. As they were not able to get any sense out of me, I was sent back to my room. The adults continued to talk about me for quite some time.

Finally they left. My mother tried to explain what she had been told. If I tried to put my side of events, it appeared that there were many others who had seen things a different way. Two of my teachers had witnessed my going for the boy, and several other people had seen us fighting. It would be best if I admitted what I had done, and get the matter sorted out. My final demands were that my mother should talk to my friend, and get his side of the events; he would be able tell her what had really happened. In my mind, we would go to school tomorrow, my mother would ask my friend what happened, and that would be the end of the matter.

Events however did not go as I expected. For two days I did not go to school, and at the weekend I was not allowed to go into the village. Other than visiting the farm next to where we lived, I was not allowed my normal freedom; even at the farm, I could sense that there was something not right. For most of my time I sulked indoors at not being believed. The headmistress and another adult paid a couple more visits; I was only talked to for a short while, and as I did not want to change my story, they gave up trying.

Monday came and I was again not sent off to school. On asking questions about when I was going to return to school, all I was told was that it would be when things were sorted out.

By the evening, events were starting to change. There was the hint from my mother that a different school might be best for me. As this idea had been proposed some time earlier, I agreed that I would love a change of school; if they were not going to believe me at this school, then I did not want to go back.

Eventually I was sent off to bed. The following morning I was still quite happy with the idea of a new school. During breakfast, it was explained that today we would be going into town to see about finding me a new school. Asking where it would be and how I would get to it. I was fobbed off with various excuses.

Mid-morning we set off by bus. As it was a school day the town seemed quiet; I was taken to a large building, there was a long wait before we were seen. First my mother went off to talk to some adults, and then I was brought in and questioned as to what had happened when my friend fell into the road. Until that moment the day had gone quite well. I now started to get angry and upset. I tried to explain that he had not fallen into the road. We had been playing on the grass bank and he had only landed on the pavement.

After a time my mother went in to see them on her own. Eventually she returned. All I could ask was when I would be going to my new school. There was a truthful answer of tomorrow, but first we would go home where more could be explained to me. I was eager to start a new school.

When we returned home a few more things were revealed to me. My mother spent some time explaining to me how my grandmother was ill, and that soon she might have to leave here and would have to look after her. Returning to the flat in London with me running about was not possible; my grandmother needed a large amount of quiet.

BOARDING SCHOOL

The way the words "boarding school" were arrived at I could not really work out; there seemed to be something else mixed in with the idea of boarding school. All that I could understand was that the recent event had something to do with the school I was now going to join, and I would stay there until I was eleven.

There was the hint that the other boys I would be at school with also had some little problems before joining the school, so I should not tease them or upset them in any way. Going to a different school did not seem to be such a good idea; for the rest of the day until I went to bed, I spent my time begging to stay and pleading that I would be good.

The next day arrived and events were on the move for me. From a book that had been read to me some time ago, I had thought that you left with all your clothes and a school uniform; all I was taking with me were a few toys. It appeared that a school uniform and everything else I would need would be waiting for me. In a way I was quite happy; shopping for school clothes had never been one of the best ways to spend a day.

I was reassured that it would soon be the holidays and she would visit me. That normally at holiday time, one went home from boarding school, had not crossed my mind. My thoughts were more on what the other boys would be like.

My mother had arranged for someone to collect us and take us into town. The moments up until I left the flat were spent being reminded to visit the lavatory, wash my face, and clean my nails. Finally, the car arrived. I was not scared about starting at my new school, but the sudden decision for me to go had been a little upsetting. For most of the journey, I cried. On reaching town, I had to try and make it look that I was not afraid. We returned to the large office that we had visited the previous day.

Some time was spent by the adults explaining what my new school would be like. Most of the boys were aged between eight and eleven, and a few boys that were almost eight. As my birthday was a few weeks away, there would be plenty of boys of my own age to play with.

From what I had understood, I could guess I was in some sort of trouble. Over the years, my mother had always threatened that if I was a bad boy, there were schools that you were sent to until you were very good. The adults tried to explain that I was not going to this school because I was bad; they thought that I might find a school like this a happier place, as there would be boys of my own age to be with all the time.

My mother would not be taking me to the school; it was best if I was collected by the staff and taken to my new school. There was a hug from my mother and I was told that soon she would be able to visit me. It all depended on how much improvement my grandmother made over the next few weeks.

I was off to my new school. Other than the driver I was the only one in the small van. As a treat, I was allowed to sit at the front instead of the seats in the main part of the van. I might have seemed quiet and sad. In an effort to cheer me up, I was told that the boys no longer wore chains and our clothing no longer had arrows painted on them. It appeared that this was a joke.

I was told that now the school was just like an ordinary boy's boarding school. A short time ago, it had been run on similar lines to a Junior Boy's Approved School, but recently it had become more relaxed as to whom it took in. The rules were the same: no going out of the grounds and I should obey the instructions of the adults; if I followed those two simple rules then I should find my stay all right. We arrived at the school after a short ferry crossing; I expected to see a school surrounded with high stone walls or barbed wire and a strong gate at the entrance. There were none of these. Fields and hedges surrounded the large building and even the entrance had no gate, simply a long drive, similar in length to where I had just left.

I was taken through the main entrance where a lady who introduced herself as Matron met me; I might have looked a little scared of my new surroundings. I was reassured that the place was not as bad as it seemed; there would be some boys of my own age to make friends with. I was now left alone with Matron.

The first thing was to have a look at the possessions I had with me. It was explained that a few items like knives and cigarettes were not allowed. It was mainly the older boys who seemed to have those, but to make it fair all of us had to follow the same rules.

Now I was taken to a small side room. If I ever wanted to find her, this was where I should first come. When she was not on duty, there was another lady whom I also should address as Matron. Any problems other than matters to do with lessons, I should come to see either of them first.

My bag of toy cars was put on the table, sorted through; there appeared to be nothing that I should not have. Next Matron asked what I had in my pockets. One by one, everything I possessed was checked over; my mother had done a thorough job of removing any non-essential object from my possession before we left. I was now told that I could leave my bag of toys and raincoat here for the moment as I was just in time for lunch. When that was over my clothes and which dorm I was going to be in could be sorted out. I followed matron along a corridor and was shown where the boy's lavatory was. There was a mention that a good wash of my hands was required as an inspection was often made before we sat down to meals.

Soon cleaned up I was escorted to the dining room; an orderly queue was forming close to the door. I was taken past the queue; several boys of around my age were near the head of the group. Matron singled one boy out and suggested that he should look after me during lunch, and then bring me to her afterwards.

The nearest boys soon asked my name and how old I was. Within moments it was worked out that I was the third youngest: the three of us would become eight the following month. The main conversation was on the food. Most days it seemed to be all right, Mondays were the worst with liver at lunchtime.

My main question was how many boys there were at this school. I was now told that in our lower form there were eleven; with me it would make twelve. In the middle form there were about fifteen and the upper form had eight. It was best to keep out of their way as they could bully at times.

Everyone wore grey shirts with grey pullovers. I stood out a little – although my jumper was grey, I had a white shirt on. The main conversation turned to what I had done to be sent here; eventually they persuaded me to tell them that the adults had accused me of trying to push a friend under a bus. I was asked was there much blood; they seemed most disappointed when I explained that my friend had fallen onto the pavement and the bus had stopped some distance away.

Those that were close explained why they had been sent here. One had set fire to a barn, another kept running out of schools, one of them did not get on with his parents, and there were several other reasons that seemed similar to mine. The adults did not believe what we ever told them, and did not like the mischief we got up to. The two boys that were younger than me had come here a month ago. They told me that they liked this place better than ordinary school.

I soon settled into the school and was quite happy; that I was going to be here for the next three years was not really upsetting, as I knew I was going to gets visits from my mother.

At night, I shared a room with five other boys of my age. Life was fun, and Matron was far more relaxed over our behaviour than my mother would have been. Lessons were a little stricter, and possibly our movements around the building and grounds were rather too restrictive; but there was still plenty of excitement.

Within a few days of my arrival, lessons finished and some of the older boys left to go on their holidays. Christmas was enjoyable with just twenty boys. We did get up to some mischief for which we were punished. I managed to get the cane on two occasions by the time lessons started in the New Year, but was equal to most of my friends over this matter. To me everything seemed to be fine. The Christmas holidays with other boys to play with had been far better than last Christmas, as I had received several presents from the school as well as my mother.

In the second week of term, Matron told me that I was going to leave and return to my mother. I was taken to see the Headmaster; he seemed to confirm that I was to leave the school. He hoped I would be able to settle back at school and that during my short stay here I had been happy.

A flood of tears by me was not something that had been expected by the Matron. To return to my mother was something I did want, but I was happy here; there were friends around me all the time, and apart from the older boys who could be bullies at times, life here was fun.

Matron took me out of the room, explaining that I would have to gather up some of my clothes to go home with, and that there were the toys in my locker that needed to be collected. My locker was dealt with first. Everything was neatly packed into a small box. I was asked if I had borrowed toys belonging to any of the others or if any other boy had something of mine, but every toy that was mine was inside the box.

In the dorm, I was now told to change into my white shirt. A small suitcase was next to my bed. Matron now started to fill my case with a selection of clothes from the drawers. I was told to take my best raincoat from the wardrobe; she wanted me to look smart when I returned to my mother. Whilst Matron carried my case downstairs, I was left with my box of toys. I was taken to the main hall. The car would be ready to collect me soon.

Compared with ordinary school, it seemed we were expected to act in a much more responsible manner, but life was not that bad. There seemed almost the challenge that although you did not aim to be naughty, there was fun to see what you could get away with. Apart from being one of the youngest and having to keep out of the way of the older boys, it had been quite good. If I had stayed there for more time, I might have found the lessons the worst part.

The reason I could leave the school was down to my version of the events that happened before going to the boarding school were now believed. A lady who had been in the sweet shop when we had both purchased the sweets had seen that we were happy together. When she found out that I had been accused of fighting and I had tried to push the boy into the road, she had spoken up and mentioned that we had left the sweet shop on good terms, and were sharing the sweets out.

The information of what really happened emerged during the first few days of my stay at the boarding school. It was decided to leave me there during the Christmas holidays, as it was not certain that my mother would be able to look after me, as she might been called back to London at very short notice to look after her mother. If my mother was soon going to return to London to live permanently, it was thought best that I now left the school.

On returning to my mother. It was suggested by her that I did not tell anyone about my few weeks away. If I was asked about not being around, I should say I had been on holiday and leave it at that. On returning to the school in the village, there were now a few weeks of what seemed ordinary school. There were changes in my free time; I was still allowed to walk to school on my own. After school I was now always met at the gates by my mother, and had to walk home with her. Going out to play with my friends did not happen now and none of them came to visit me.

At school, I was not very happy; I missed the fun of boarding school. During lessons, I did not really take much interest in what was going on around me. At playtime, I was kept indoors, and allowed to read books of my own choice, whilst the others were out at play. My unhappiness with school resulted in a couple of wet beds at night, and back to the plimsoll from my mother. There was the warning that now I was eight, she might have to think about using the cane instead of my plimsoll if I wet the bed.

During my time at boarding school, my mother had prepared for our return to London. Throughout our stay, we had accumulated quite a few possessions in excess of the two cases we had arrived with. As our return journey was probably by coach and train, our possessions needed to be reduced to a similar amount.

If my mother had been ruthless with my things, it was with the thought that I had either grown out of many items of clothing and toys or they would have little use in London. There was never the case of my clothing or toys having any major value; in many instances they had come from the local jumble sales. Our distance from the centre of the village meant that it would be difficult to pass items on. The bonfire at the end of the garden took anything that could be burnt; with the isolation of the house, refuse collections were always a slight problem.

The few metal cars I had left here had been put safe whilst I was away. I did not really miss the small number of other toys or books that were too bulky to take back to London. There was one item of my clothing that I was angry about that was missing; it was that my mother had put my riding boots on the bonfire, as they would not be needed in London. My anger resulted in a trip to my bedroom and a couple of hits with the plimsoll.

Once the clothing I brought from the boarding school was added to the clothes that were ready for my return to London, there was now a selection of best and school clothes, and one set of respectable play clothes. On my last few visits to the farm, I managed to ruin the set of play clothes together with my school shoes and a duffle coat. The day before we left, after a few final hits with my plimsoll, I was made to take all the clothes I had ruined down to the bottom of the garden and arrange one final bonfire. Such a major clearout of my clothes and possessions was not really needed in the end. Instead of travelling on our own, an uncle came over to take us in his car.

RETURN TO LONDON FEBRUARY 1965

I was happy at the age of eight in returning to London; soon I was settled into a new school. The large size was a little frightening at first, simply being one of the youngest but there were plenty of things to do, and I was quite happy for most of the time.

I was in trouble with one of the teachers at lunch break. A few of the older boys had decided to fill the sinks in the outside lavatory block with water and let them overflow. The plugs to the sinks had long ago vanished; all the sinks plugholes were filled with scraps of paper to stop the water running away. When the sinks partly filled, the paper would start to rise, allowing the water to run away. Extra pairs of hands were needed to keep the basins filling. I had come out of one of the cubicles and found myself with the instruction to help them.

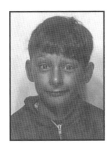 As it was a chance of mischief, I became an easy member of their gang. With all the taps running at the same time, the flow of water was not that fast, slowly the sinks at the far end started to overflow first. The older boys were hopping about trying to keep their shoes or plimsolls from getting soaked; like the younger boy at the next sink, we did not have these problems as we wore wellingtons. We were too busy watching the others to notice a teacher enter. If we were unlucky, we were the nearest to him and had continued to hold our wads of paper in our sinks as he walked behind us.

The six of us were removed from the lavatories in seconds. It was a quick march to the main building and the Headmaster's office. Waiting outside the office took forever; the teacher had gone inside to report our activity. The older four were trying to frighten the pair of us, mentioning that he normally gave out harsh punishments. Our conversations ended at that moment and we were beckoned inside. There was little chance given to us to explain our actions; as we had all been caught flooding the floor, there was little we could have said to clear our names.

The instruction to hold out each of our hands was given by the Headmaster. I was the second to be dealt with; it was one stroke on each hand. We were soon in tears. The older ones did not reach this stage, but as soon as they had been given the cane, it was clear to see it had really hurt. There was one final instruction for us not to be caught messing about again and we were sent on our way. The four older boys rushed off, probably to boast to their friends about their latest deed. The two of us younger ones headed to a quiet area to be out of attention of any of our friends, so that we had a chance to hide the fact we had been in tears. We were still looking for trouble and headed back to the lavatories to see how soaked the floor was. There was little to see as the slight slope of floor had solved the problem of the water that had overflowed from the sinks, I had made a new friend.

At afternoon lessons in my class, I was able to show off the red mark on each of my hands. My status was going up in their estimation. To be given the cane in the first year of primary school meant I was high up in the league of crime. When I returned home, I did not say anything to my mother about getting the cane at school.

Living conditions in the flat were not ideal for a small boy, who was perhaps a little energetic and at times could get in the way. I thought everything was running smoothly and I was quite happy to have come back to London, but this did not last for long. My mother announced that I was going to live in the country with other boys and girls of my own age; I was told that the new boarding school would be friendlier, as I would be living with just six other children as part of a family.

I don't think the words 'Children's Home' were ever uttered; if they had, I might have taken immediate notice and made more of a fuss. As I was told my aunts and uncles lived quite close to my new home and they would be able to visit me, I did not offer any protest. I was even looking forward to the move.

THE NATIONAL CHILDREN'S HOME

ARRIVAL

N.C.H. HARPENDEN.

The day came for leaving London. My possessions fitted into one suitcase. The main content was clothing; I was taking both play and school clothes with me. For the journey, I was dressed in my best clothes. A few model cars that I had been given for my eighth birthday, plus a few comics and the odd book took up any space that remained in the case; it would be too heavy to carry if I had put all my books in. These I would be able to have later. There was no fear of leaving. It was explained that in a month or so I would be able to have a visit, and a short time later, there would be some holidays and I might be able to come back to London for a short stay.

It was quite a walk to the station with my mother carrying the case. We were heading off just after lunch, which would give me a little while to settle in before my mother had to return. Once on the train, we had most of the compartment to ourselves. As I was going to live in the same town as my three sets of aunts and uncles, having visited them before, I knew roughly how long a journey to expect. When I had settled in at my new location, I would probably be able to go to my aunt's and uncle's for tea occasionally, as they would be living quite close.

During the journey my mother told me it might be best not to tell the other children that I was going to live with, about the various schools I had attended, and possibly, it was best that I did not mention anything about where I had been during the Christmas holidays.

Eventually we arrived; it was a short ride by taxi to my new home. Having been told it was called Highfield, with all the excitement, I never noticed the sign at the front that read Children's Home and Orphanage.

On my arrival, it looked like a large park surrounded by houses. Once we had visited the main office building, I was now taken with my mother to the flat I was going to live in. Each large house I was told had four flats in each. I would soon get to make friends with many other boys and girls who lived in the flats. If I wanted to know which flat I was in, it would be very easy for me to remember, as it was the first upper flat at the end of the row. I was introduced to a lady who seemed almost as old as my grandmother, and should be addressed as 'Sister' rather than 'Miss'.

As this was a school day, all the others from the flat were at school. The Sister gave us a short tour of the flat, and then I was shown the bedroom and the bed that would be mine. I would share the room with three other boys who were slightly older. They would be able to show me where everything was kept. As well as the boys there were also three girls who lived in this flat; I would meet everyone later.

From the bedroom window, Sister pointed across a large grassed area to where some swings were, and suggested I go over and play for a short while, while she chatted with my mother over a cup of tea. It was put in such a way as not to really offer any alternative. If Sister wanted to talk to my mother without me around, I knew it would give my mother the opportunity to tell her about my temper and behaviour.

Before I left the flat, I was shown where the boys' bathroom and lavatory was. Sister mentioned that it was best to go before going out as it saved coming back later and dragging mud indoors. I was soon down the stairs and walking across the neat grass. I was quite happy playing on the equipment alone; in London, the parks I could go to were quite a long walk away – having come to a place where there was a park so near was great.

Quite a high slide, although not the highest I had ever been on, was the first item to conquer, followed by a roundabout and some swings. The metal rocking horse and the bars were not bothered with at this stage; the climbing frame then occupied me for most of the time. I was not really bored, but I thought I should be going back. I looked at a small building next to this playground; from the sound, I could guess that this was the school for the youngest children.

Heading back across the grass, I met my mother starting out from the flat. I was told that she had to get back to London now; I should go in now, as Sister had told her that the others would soon be back from school and they would want to meet me. She would visit me soon, so I should be a good boy and do whatever Sister told me to do. After a hug and a kiss, my mother headed off down a path and was gone. I was sad, but I was a big boy of eight and I was not going to cry. I headed up to the flat where Sister was waiting. I was on the verge of tears, but none came. It was not fear or disappointment, it was that everything was so different from how I imagined. That there would be almost two hundred other children here was not something I had expected; I thought I was going to live with six other children.

It was suggested by Sister that I might want to change into my play clothes as the others would be going to change out of their school clothes when they returned. My case was unpacked; the clothes were checked to see that my name was inside each item. Sister showed me the drawers that I could use. A few toys and books I had with me were left in my case; these could be put away later. I was told that my bed had a rubber sheet on top of the mattress. I was pleased about my bed already having a rubber sheet on it, as it saved having to ask Sister if I could have one. During the train journey today, I had been reminded about the few problems of last year, and if I was

Wakefield House Flats 1 & 2

asked, did I wet the bed I was to say that it did happen. I decided that as the question had not actually been asked, there was no need to say anything.

There was a slam of a door somewhere in the flat, followed by someone running. The door opened quickly and a boy of about my age rushed in. Possibly he did not expect to find anyone here, as the running became a walk. I was now introduced to Lenton.

If I had any fears about starting a new school where others might tease me over my lightly tanned complexion, I need not have had any worries. Lenton had similar looks to myself, although his hair was in short tight curls. Sister now suggested that he show me around the flat until the tea was ready. For the short time while Lenton changed into his play clothes, I was questioned as to where I came from, how old I was and did I like fighting, plus a range of other matters. I was asked if I had brought any toys and if Sister had already seen them; I pointed to my case and mentioned that I had been told that I could put them away later.

Sister had quickly put away my clothes. All that had remained in the case were my toys and comics. I was led back to the day room and shown where an empty locker was, and my toys were soon put away.

Sister would explain all the rules to me. I was given a few hints: no knives, cigarettes, matches, money, food; you could keep sweets, but don't complain if they go missing. There were shouts from the main corridor; I was informed that the others were back. We returned to the bedroom; it was easy to see that the other two boys were a few years older than we were. Soon I was told their names, and who could beat up whom, but this last fact seemed to be argued over slightly between them.

Lenton suggested that we go and see how soon tea would be ready; if we finished early, there might be time to go outside so I could be shown where everything was. He knew he did not have to do washing or wiping up and it was doubtful if Sister had put my name down this soon on the list. In time I would be doing my share; washing up was better than wiping up, but we all took a turn at each.

Both of us headed off to the bathroom. Lenton hinted it was best to make sure you went before you sat down at the table. Although Sister did not actually ban you from leaving the table to go to the toilet, you might find on your return that your share of any cake or pudding had been given out. It was best to try and sit through the pain rather than leave the table. It was also necessary to make sure your hands were clean; you would be sent back if they were not to her liking.

Almost everyone appeared together. I was now introduced to the two girls who were sisters. I would meet the older girl later and, as it was the helper's day off, I would not meet her until the following day. A place at the table had been left for me; this would be my seat, unless Sister decided to change our positions. Before the meal started there was grace. It appeared that each of us took turns at each meal to say grace; my turn would soon come, and as the grace was very similar to school, I did not think I would have any problem when my turn eventually came.

At the side of my plate was a neatly folded serviette inside an orange ring the shape of a rabbit. Each of us had our own individual rings, with a different design or colour. The serviettes were to last for several meals.

Normally tea for me was a quiet affair. For most of the time my mother was busy; I had the meal on my own. When the other adults sat down for tea, if I was having my tea with them, I was expected to be quiet and eat my meal. Here it was different. Other than odd comments from Sister over not talking while your mouth was full, there were conversations going on all around me. It was not really like school. In a way it was meant to be friendlier than that, but having to now live with six other children was strange. I was used to having bread and butter with some spread to go on it followed by cake if I had been good. Tea was now a lavish meal; we had a cooked meal as well as the tea I was used to. Sister made the comment that I would soon be fattened up a little. A disappointment was being given a cup of tea to drink; this was one item which I did not really like.

The boys were asking if I could be shown round the grounds after tea. The older pair it appeared were on washing and wiping duties, so it would be left to Lenton to show me around for a short while. There would not be much time as it would soon be dark, but I might get some idea of my new home.

As tea was finishing, Sister mentioned that I really should have a play coat for going outside; the raincoat I had brought with me was rather too good for play use. I could use that for the moment as long as I did not roll about on the ground or climb any trees. Lenton was now questioned as to where he was planning to take me. "Everywhere" was his reply. Sister seemed to accept that there was no real point in telling him where I should not be taken, as he was bound to show me that first. The meal was finally finished; the two eldest boys set about clearing the table and starting the washing up. There was the hint from Sister that if they were quick, there would still be time to find the pair of us outside.

There had been a light drizzle during tea, however it had not been heavy enough to postpone the tour of the grounds. There was the instruction from Sister that it was best if I was given a pair of wellingtons to go out in; if Lenton was going to show me around, he was bound to find mud. I was taken to the far end of the corridor. Lenton was there before us, and from a side cupboard he pulled out a pair of wellingtons and put them on. It seemed as if I had been here long enough to fend for myself.

Sister indicated that at the far back of the cupboard she was sure there was a spare pair that should fit me for the time being. I knelt down and reached to the back. Two pairs of boots came out; one was ordinary boys' boots, but too small for me, the others were for a girl. I showed Sister the boys' boots and remarked that they would be too small and that the other boots were for a girl. My only reason for telling Sister this was that I thought they belonged to one of the girls in the flat. In a rather cross manner I was questioned to whether the larger boots I had hold of would fit, and what size shoe did I take. Within moments, it was found these were the correct size for me. I was now given a lecture from Sister that I should be thankful for anything that was given to me.

It was easy to tell that the boots were for a girl; they were shiny and the shape of the toe was different from that for a boy. The biggest giveaway was that the lining was a tartan design rather than simple cream cotton. Soon I had them on my feet. Sister pinched the ends of the toes, remarking they would be all right for the moment. I was sent out with Lenton.

I was now told that Sister could get cross at times over the smallest thing. I did not really mind wearing girls' wellingtons; they were a very comfortable fit compared to the short heavy dull boots that many of my school friends wore. I always chose the taller shiny style wellingtons as they were ideal for my long legs. There was nothing wrong with these boots except for the tartan lining.

I told Lenton I had already been over to the swings by the school. It was decided that I should be taken around the back of the flats and then we could work our way all round the grounds. The older two boys never found us; it was almost dark when Lenton decided it was time to go in. Normally we would be given a set time to go in at. The big clock on the office block was the one to use. All the Sisters went by this clock. Even if you had a watch, or the television told a different time, if you were in the grounds, the clock on the block was the correct time.

We arrived indoors; Sister seemed pleased that I had been happy going out and looking around. I was asked if everything was all right. Possibly, she had expected me to be in tears for not having my mother here, but as I had gone through this same event a few months ago, I was not going to burst into tears here. I might feel a bit rotten but with girls around, I was not going to show how I felt.

Now Lenton introduced me to one of the many chores that would make up part of my daily life. Shoe cleaning was until now not something I had really had to bother with very often. My first introduction to it in earnest had been at the school I had stayed at during the holidays. At the end of the day our school shoes and other items had to be cleaned to high standards. Until then, I had never been made to clean my shoes and boots; on many occasions I had given them the final shine, but my mother had never trusted me with an open tin of polish. Both our play shoes and school shoes had to be given a good polish; Lenton mentioned that if you did not do a good job Sister would make you do it again until she was satisfied.

We finished at around the same time; it appeared that my shoes would pass inspection. Lenton told me the worst thing was trying to get a shine on play shoes after you have been outside playing football on wet days. The leather was often too damp to allow you to get a shine and you would get a telling off for not wearing your wellingtons. If you had been playing in the woods, every bit of mud had to be cleaned off your wellingtons before coming inside. There was a trough of water near the back door and a stiff brush; they had to be completely clean, as you needed to wear them for some of our indoor chores. An old towel was in the shoe cupboard for drying them off before putting them away.

Our chore over I was now told it was time for supper. We headed into the kitchen; some of the others were already there. I was now told that supper could vary. It might be a few biscuits or some cake; often it could be toast or something similar. For me toast and Marmite was fine; the others had a more sweet tooth and were eager to delve into the jam and chocolate spread. The drink we were allowed was milk. This we could have either cold or hot; if you were having it hot then chocolate powder or instant coffee could be added. I easily chose coffee, but made entirely with milk I found a little rich. I was more used to having it made with hot water and a little cold milk added. I realised that mentioning any preference at this point would soon get me into trouble.

Sister now judged that it was time for getting me ready for bed. Lenton was disappointed as for the next few days he was not going to be grouped with the two older boys for bedtimes, but with me until I became settled in the Home. There was slight questioning by Sister when I used the word dormitory when referring to the bedroom. She now asked me if I had been away to boarding school before coming here. Knowing what my mother had told me about not saying anything about the boarding school I had stayed at during Christmas, I got over the problem by telling Sister that when I first started school, my mother had gone to work at a school that took boarders. I was not actually told off, but it was suggested by her that it was best to use the word bedroom in front of the other boys.

Once in the bedroom, Sister explained that she had originally intended for me to start school on Monday, but as she was going to be busy on that day, I would have to be taken to school by her tomorrow, so that I could be shown where the school was and introduce me to my teacher. I should put my school clothes ready. Lenton spoke up and mentioned that he could take me, but it

Highfield main block

appeared I was going to the same school as most of the others, rather than to his school. However, Sister announced that she had been told to take me to the annexe part of the school rather than where the other four were.

We were packed off to the bathroom; I had brought a flannel, toothbrush, toothpaste and a towel with me. Lenton soon pounced on my tube of toothpaste and begged to use it. He explained that the Home provided toothpaste but it came in tins as a solid block, you had to wet it to get any of the paste onto your brush and the taste was horrible. Toothpaste in a tube was an absolute luxury; I was warned that the other two would use my toothpaste as well. It might be best not to say anything to Sister as she might take it away from me for being greedy. I was quite happy to share my toothpaste, but I was a little cross to see the amount that was spread across the full length of the brush. If all three were going to do this, the toothpaste would be gone within days; my mother had always made me put just enough on the end of the brush that would clean my teeth.

Eventually we returned to the bedroom, Sister was going through the drawers that had my clothes in. I was told that I really had everything I needed, but over the next few days, she would take a few measurements and add a few more play clothes to my drawer.

At night, I had been used to being told when to go off to bed, and then going to sleep. Even at the boarding school when it was time for bed, we went to bed, a final check was made by one of the staff that everyone was actually in bed and that was that. Here it appeared that prayers had to be said, the counterpane was folded down to the bottom of your bed and you could get in. Sister tucked the sides of your bed in so that no bedclothes were loose. I now found that once the bedclothes were tucked in, it was almost impossible to move. I was wished a good night by Sister. As this was my first night, I might feel a bit lonely, but I had Lenton for company and the other two would be joining us soon. The lights went out, and the door finally shut.

Lenton explained that when Sister tucked our bedclothes in, it was known as a cuddle. If I was uncomfortable, it was all right to loosen them a little. He mentioned that once the lights were out, we were meant to keep quiet but if you talked in whispers, everything was normally fine. A small glass panel in the wall was connected to Sister's room; this allowed her to hear everything that was said in this room.

After the events of the day I was tired and was soon asleep. The other two boys came in later but I stayed asleep. At some point during the night I did wake up; everything seemed so odd for a few seconds, then I remembered where I now was. It was the grunts and snores of the other three that made me think I was back at the boarding school. From what I had seen so far, this place seemed a bit tame, although Sister seemed strict and would not tolerate any wrongdoing. There did not seem to be the activity of daring to do wrong things or the punishments that were threatened at every moment, that I had noticed whilst I was at the boarding school. Other than the occasional noise from the other three, it was generally silent. I missed the background noise of the London streets. I was not really on the point of tears, but how long I was to be here had never been explained. If I had been at the boarding school I knew I would have left at eleven; here it looked as if you stayed until you left school at about fifteen. After wondering about the events of the following day for a short while, I went back to sleep.

Before coming to the Home, I had been used to getting up when I woke up. If it had been too early for breakfast or the like, I would have read my comics or amused myself until it was time to start the day. I was told that here, we could only get up at the point that Sister told us to get up.

My first morning in the Home started with Lenton calling my name. His main question was how I felt; it seemed he was disappointed that I did not spend the night crying, as he would have enjoyed teasing me. There was little time for conversation; Sister entered the room and turned on the lights. It appeared I was her main concern; there were questions like had I slept well, and was I happy. Confirmation was given by Lenton, that my night had gone without any problems; it appeared that I would survive. Sister now left to see to the girls.

The boys explained the daily events to me. First you pulled back your bedclothes so that the lower sheet remained to allow your bed to air for a short while. There was no need to pull your top sheet or blankets off your bed unless they had come loose during the night. There was a joke made, that this was the point when Sister would see if your bed was wet. This was aimed at one of the others rather than myself, who admitted there had been the odd problem a few years ago. It appeared that Sister would not be pleased with you, as it meant you would be late for breakfast with the need to have a bath.

There was no need to bother with your dressing gown unless it was cold; we headed off to the bathroom. As today was my first day I was given the privilege of using the lavatory first. This was however so the other three could get at my tube of toothpaste without having to ask me. Soon we were all washed and dried and we returned to the bedroom. It was easy to dress first then make your bed; this way you could put your pyjamas away without disturbing the bed.

Sister liked our beds to be made in a certain way; Lenton was pleased that I had come, as it was easier to make a bed if there were two of you. If you made a good attempt and had the counterpane on nice and evenly it would normally pass Sister's inspection.

Bed making had never been a chore I had ever bothered with when I lived with my mother. At the boarding school, we did not have a counterpane; the grey blankets had to be straight at the first attempt so that a coloured stripe on the top end was in line with the pillow.

I was now led to the kitchen for breakfast; I seemed to be treated now as one of the group rather than something strange that had appeared for tea yesterday. I was introduced to the helper who had returned after I had gone to bed the previous night. It was explained that I should follow any instruction that I was given by her. On Sister's days off, she would be in charge. I took my place at the table; the meal was started with grace. It seemed my turn would come soon.

Until coming to the Home, on a normal school day I had been used to either Kellogg's, toast or bread and butter, with possibly Marmite, marmalade, or if there was an unfinished jar of meat or fish paste; to drink either milk or squash – if neither were available I was quite happy with a glass of water. At the boarding school, our breakfasts were more or less ready for us, with little actual choice available. I was offered either porridge or a cereal. If I now made the first mistake

Girls' side

of the day, it was asking for Kellogg's. This resulted in my second telling off since my arrival. With our family having adults in the majority the only packet of cereal on the table had been Kellogg's cornflakes. Occasionally there was Shredded Wheat, but that miniature straw-like bale had never appealed to me. On rare occasions a variety pack of cereals might have appeared, but once finished the next would be a long while appearing. I had been used to calling the cornflakes 'Kellogg's' and with no other item on the menu there could be no confusion. I now realised that several other large packets of cereal, were also made by Kellogg's. Soon I was provided with a bowl of cornflakes. Once finished there was now a cooked breakfast; these I was only used to at weekends and then in place of cereal. Bread or toast now followed, with a wide variety of spreads. Most were sweet and even jam came out at this time of day. I was pleased to see Marmite was put out again. I was more or less happy with breakfast. There was the thought that on the following days I would be able to work through the range of other packets, most of which I had never seen as full size packets on the breakfast table.

The only item to ruin breakfast was tea. If there were a hot drink, I preferred coffee. For a small boy coffee might seem an odd drink, but as long as there was a little sugar in it I was happy with it either white or black and real or instant. Why I was the only member of my mother's family not to like tea was a mystery to all: everyone it seemed even from a very young age liked to drink tea, and wherever I have lived the teapot seemed to be the most important possession. The mug of tea that was now provided at breakfast ruined the meal for me.

During breakfast there were continual reminders about the items that it was necessary to take to school; for the older ones it was homework and for everybody there were questions such as was it games or PE today. When breakfast was over, the two eldest girls were on washing and wiping up. It appeared that my turn along with Lenton would be at tea.

I was told to go into the dayroom and read a book whilst the others were packed off to school. Lenton came with me to the dayroom. It was explained that he was one of the lucky ones; several of them were taken to school each day by coach and were driven back at the end of the day. He gloated that he did not have to walk to school in the rain. A light drizzle had started early and looked to be around for the entire day. Both of us could hear Sister demanding that the others put on their raincoats properly with the buttons done up before they left the house. The pair of us were left in peace for a short while. I was shown some of the toys that Lenton had in his locker. Once you put your toys in your locker they were reasonably safe, only Sister or the helper really having the right to go through your things.

Lenton gave me a piece of advice. What went on in the Home was not to be mentioned to friends at school or parents, and what went on at school was not to be mentioned once you were back at the Home. Try to have two different lives – that way you would stand a better chance of keeping out of trouble.

Finally, Lenton was called to get ready; I was left alone in the dayroom. There was a large bookcase next to the emergency door, which led through into the next flat. This door was to remain firmly closed unless there was a fire. The books on the shelves were rather boring; several girls' storybooks and a few boys' books of war stories. No real storybooks or comic annuals really took my fancy; I managed to find a 'Jennings' and sat down to read it.

Possibly my quiet behaviour was not normal in the flat. Sister soon came to see where I was. My preference if I was not at school was to be left alone. Whenever I was out with friends, trouble or other problems seemed to happen. I was told to visit the lavatory and to make sure my hands and teeth were clean as shortly I was to be taken to my new school.

A, B, & C.

At the point we left the flat there was only a light drizzle. Sister intended to take me to my new school and to get my admission sorted out. They had already made enquiries about me joining the school. Having some idea on the results from a previous school it had been decided, with the choice of an 'A' form and a

'B' form. It would be the latter I would join; there did not seem to be a 'C' stream. Owing to overcrowding, a few classes were situated in the annexe of the school, quite some distance from the main new school. Had I been attending the main school, Sister would have given the job to one of the older boys to take me to school on Monday and to see I returned with them at the end of the afternoon. Sister was not even sure if any others of my age from the Home were at the annexe. If I was the only one, then some arrangement would have to be made for Monday when I officially would start.

A little way into our walk it decided to pour with rain. I was fine, the raincoat I had brought with me, and the wellingtons Sister had found, kept me dry. I resisted splashing in puddles, but Sister seemed to be concentrating on our journey to watch where her feet went and soon ended up soaked without any help from me. I made a mental note of roughly our route; it seemed easy enough. Once we had arrived at the end of the road, we followed the next road down, then crossing over we went up a slight hill and carried on walking, eventually coming to the school. Sister explained that she thought this was the quickest route; if not, others would soon tell me. There was one rule to follow when I did start school. At the end of the day when school finished, I was to come straight back to the Home; there was to be no visiting any friends' houses, and even when I arrived in the Home I was to come straight indoors.

We entered the school; from the outside, it looked like an old village school. Sister had timed our arrival perfectly; the bell for the start of morning break was just being rung. Within a short while, a teacher came out to see us. It appeared that my arrival was expected.

It was explained to me that I would be staying for school lunches. On a Monday morning when the lunch money was collected for the week, I should simply tell my teacher that I was from the Home; there was no need to bring any money with me. I would not be alone as there was one other boy from the Home that was in the class I would be joining.

Sister asked the teacher if the boy was here today, as she would like a word with him about escorting me from the Home on Monday and seeing that I arrived back at the end of the day. The next question Sister asked was on what day PE and games took place. Sister was now told that as this school did not have any grassed area, we did not really have games. There might be a short PE lesson in the playground, but it depended on the weather. If it was fine, that lesson could be on any day so it was best to keep some PE clothes handy. Sister decided that it might be best if I took my PE kit in on a Monday and just returned it on a Friday, which would mean I was not left out of any lessons. I was now told that when the weather was fine there were also swimming lessons; as we went to an open-air pool the weather was the deciding factor. If I did not know how to swim I would soon pick it up. Apart from short doggy paddles in the sea, I had only been taken to the swimming pool on odd occasions.

We were left alone whilst the teacher went away to see if the other boy from the Home was here. Within a short while, a boy of my own age was brought in.

I was now introduced to Edward. Sister asked him if he could come to my flat on Monday to bring me to school and see that I arrived back with him. From his expression, I could see that it was not going to be a problem. The teacher suggested that it would be nice for him to have a friend to come to school with.

Sister mentioned that she was not really looking forward to the walk back with me. The teacher now suggested that I might as well stay, if there were no plans for me; at least it would make sure that Edward could show me the way back when lessons finished. I did not seem to have any say in the matter; Sister seemed to think it was a good idea. The teacher told me that lunch for me was not going to be a problem; there was always plenty sent down from the main school.

It was now suggested to Edward that he first should show me where the boys' toilet was, and then where I could hang my coat. We headed down a small corridor. Edward asked me when I had arrived at the Home. He told me that he had not said much in front of the Sister, as she was known to be one of the strictest Sisters at the Home. He would make sure that he called for me first thing on Monday, as he did not fancy the telling off that he would get if he forgot. We went outside just as the bell was being rung and the few boys that were outside were ushered in.

The boys' lavatory was quite primitive. It was at one side of the playground. Edward commented that on wet days it was best to make sure that you did not have to leave the room in the middle of the lesson. If you ran across without your coat you would get soaked, and as the urinal part was mostly open to the sky you will also get soaked unless you used one of the cubicles. We stayed outside for a little longer. Edward told me that there was little point in getting back into school straight away as we were still in the morning period and it was all written work; had I arrived in the afternoon then things would be different.

It was great being at this school; most afternoons we did not have difficult lessons. As we did not have any of the equipment or spare rooms like the main school, if we did art lessons, everything had to be brought out of cupboards and put away at the end. In the evening our school was used by adults for their

Boys' side

62

lessons, so we spent the last part of every afternoon clearing up. If we finished quickly, we were often let out a few minutes early.

Eventually Edward decided that it was time to return. I was taken into the classroom; coats and belongings were hung up on the back wall. The teacher introduced me to the others. There was only a small number in my class; it was not really cramped but the desks took up most of the room, with just odd tables at one side and a blackboard on an easel at the front next to a main blackboard. Edward had gone back to his own desk; I was now given a desk at the only remaining space on the other side of the room.

There was the instruction that for the moment there was not any point for me to do written work, as they were just finishing off a subject. Looking around the room there did not seem to be any set uniform here. It was mostly grey shirts with a pullover or jumper; these were mainly blues and grey shades, but there was nothing really to suggest a set style. I seemed to fit in with grey shirt and blue jumper.

From what the boy next to me was wearing it seemed to prove that no high standard of clothing was demanded. Other than the last school in London most of the schools I attended seemed to set a level that we should attain in both design and neatness. The boy whom I now shared a desk with had a shirt that was cream but had a faint blue check woven into its fabric. Both the collar and cuffs were well frayed; the jumper was a fairly rough coarse grey wool which showed the signs of darning at the elbows many times. From the way Sister had inspected my clothes, I did not think I was ever going to be allowed to dress like that.

Although the teacher was talking, my partner at the desk wasted no time in asking my name and telling me that he was called Bob. Having been to several schools, I had become quite used to working out within a very short while who my close friends would be. Whilst Edward had been quite nice to me and I probably would become his friend, it was almost the moment that I sat down next to Bob, that I worked out that he was going to be one of my close friends. I was like a magnet and seemed to be able to attract trouble, and I might have guessed that with Bob sitting alone, possibly the teacher had a good reason why he should have a desk to himself.

I tried to pay attention to what the teacher was saying, in the hope of catching up when the next lesson started. If Bob wanted to gain my attention, there was a light kick on my shins; it was not spiteful or painful as they were well protected – this was done to get my attention without the need to speak. By the time the lesson ended, I thought that I had managed to understand the work. Talking started immediately, and books were soon put away. Within moments we were allowed our freedom. The teacher now told me that she would see me at the start of the afternoon lesson to sort out any books I would need.

Bob asked if I was staying to school dinners and, as soon as I replied yes, it was decided I was going to be his partner during lunch. We went through to one of the other classrooms that were slowly transformed into the dining area. Large benches were placed together and a large waterproof cloth stretched across; the stools we were to sit on were now placed at regular intervals. Bob pulled me to one side; it appeared that there were ideal positions where you could sit without any table legs getting in the way. Another boy came and sat on the other side of me. Soon names and a number of facts had been exchanged between us. I felt quite happy about the move to this school, from what I could see it was not that strict.

DAILY LIFE

My bedtime was as soon as I had finished supper. There was a final visit to the bathroom and a check by Sister that I had cleaned my teeth, and I was straight off to bed. The other three would normally follow an hour after supper. Once in bed, I was soon asleep; often the older boys would wake me up when they came to bed, which in a way showed it was a pointless exercise sending me to bed early.

There was always the fear of wetting my bed during the night. I wondered what Sister would say in the morning and what the punishment would be. With my mother it had been my school plimsoll at the age of seven, and the threat of the cane now I had reached eight. I wondered if Sister would use the slipper or the cane.

To prevent any chance of an accident, I found it best to wake myself up late in the evening and pay a visit to the lavatory. This was the only way I knew of preventing it occurring in my sleep. At around five or six in the morning, I would also pay another visit. For my first six months in the Home, this routine worked and there were no accidents at night.

Shortly before Christmas and my ninth birthday, Sister seemed to object to my evening visits to the lavatory. If she found me on my return from the lavatory, there was a minor telling off about my forgetfulness for not visiting the lavatory before going to bed. I did protest but was never believed. If I was caught before getting to the lavatory, I could not convince her that I had been at the correct time and now needed to go again. On every occasion I was sent straight back to bed without being allowed to visit the lavatory, often with comment that I would have to learn to go at the correct time. If I had argued with Sister over her sending me back to bed without visiting the lavatory, it would have been the slipper.

Trying to get to sleep with the knowledge that I needed to go for a pee was impossible. I would lie awake trying to work out what I had done wrong, and eventually wet the bed when I could not hold on any longer. In the morning I was told to go and have a bath, and put my sheets into soak; there were no other punishments, which I found strange.

Once I reached the age of nine, bed-wetting now regularly happened about once a week. I tried to plan my visits to the lavatory after I knew Sister had gone to bed, but often I did not wake up in time. In the morning there was never a telling off or the slipper if I had wet the bed.

On the nights I did not have an accident, if I was caught by Sister visiting the lavatory shortly before getting-up time, I was always allowed on my way; to her this was a good idea that would prevent a wet bed. The two different reactions from her was something I could not understand.

Stripping my bed and going off for a bath was the most embarrassing matter; the older three boys did not really tease me. As they were at different schools, I had no worry that they would ever tell my school friends about my bed-wetting. They were glad that if Sister were focusing her attention on me, it would get them off any minor items of trouble they might be in.

Once I had finished my bath and put my sheets into soak, I needed to get a damp cloth and wipe down the rubber mattress protector on the bed. With these tasks I was a little late and any chores I should be doing would still have to be completed before school. To save time I had to fold up my blankets and counterpane and put them on the side chair. When I arrived home from school later in the day, I would be able to use my own free time to make the bed up with clean sheets. A reminder of an accident was that the bed remained in its stripped condition for the entire day. If friends had been allowed into our flat, it would have been embarrassing. In other flats, the Sister could use this as an extra form of punishment.

The morning wash was another moment that as the fourth and youngest boy I did not fit in. Two sinks meant that two could wash at once, the third could visit the lavatory, and they would then swap over. Eventually when all three had washed, dried and cleaned their teeth I would get a chance to use the sinks. This was the other reason for my visits to the lavatory first thing in the morning before they were awake, as I was not going to be allowed to use the lavatory until all three of them had made use of it; I knew that on many mornings there would have been a desperate need. Whilst Sister did not punish me over wet beds, standing in soaking pyjamas in the middle of a puddle on the floor would have brought some form of punishment.

As they returned to get dressed and make their beds I was left alone. This slight delay meant that from this point until breakfast, I was delayed in every task and chore I had been set. Before breakfast Sister would check to see if everything was to her high standards. If the bed was not made to her requirements, everything would be thrown onto the floor and you would be made to make the bed to her standard while she watched over you. Sister also would make an inspection of the bathroom, to see that flannels were correctly hung up, the toothpaste had its lid on, the soap was in the correct position, and that there was no scum line around the sink. This gave me a chance of getting into trouble; as I was the last to leave the sinks, any scum line was down to me, even if it was in the sink I had not used. After my wash, extra time was spent cleaning the second sink so as not to get into trouble.

The other little problem that affects boys is their aim at the lavatory bowl. I have to admit that I was not accurate on every occasion, but now as I was apparently the last to visit the lavatory, I was responsible for every mess. My excuse that I had not used it after them, failed to get me pardoned. All the others said it was like it when they used it; Sister often having witnessed my earlier visit, now believed them. Having been blamed for this after several occasions, I realised that the older boys were doing it just to get me in trouble; on all my future visits to the lavatory, I remained in seated mode. I left the lavatory with the seat down and with no wet patches on the floor to coincide with Sister passing. Eventually I appeared to be given the benefit of the doubt over future spills. There was a comment from the Sister that I should learn to pee in the bowl like a boy rather than in a girl's fashion. It was impossible to win.

Breakfast was never really a battle for me. I accepted that it was long, drawn out and noisy. I soon became used to the cooked breakfast on the days that Sister provided one: tomatoes on toast, bacon and other items. On certain days, it was either porridge or hot milk over an oat type cereal. At the end of breakfast if not on washing and wiping up duty, you were free for a few moments once your set cleaning chores were over, to amuse yourself before finally getting ready for school.

On several occasions, it was down to having to finish the mug of tea rather than the large breakfast, although possibly with a lighter breakfast I might not have felt so unwell, had me visiting the lavatory to be sick. With all the morning rush and the need to get seven children off to school, little attention was paid to a small boy disappearing for a few moments. I was quite capable of being sick and getting over it without drawing attention to myself. Possibly if I had allowed attention to be focused on me, something might have been done over having to drink tea. Staying silent meant that having been sick, I would be starving until school lunch several hours later. I was more afraid of Sister finding out that I had been sick after eating one of her breakfasts, than the actual event.

Once all our chores were finished, we could put the final touches to our appearance. My hair was that of the average schoolboy; other than for the five seconds after a comb and brush had been put through it would look anything other than perfect. While the girls could sit down and take time to brush their hair, boys it seemed had to achieve perfection in moments. To Sister, I was a new challenge; it was perhaps some years since she had to wrestle a comb on a boy. The other three boys and the boy who had recently left before my arrival all had close curly-cropped black hair; with my ordinary mop of hair I was a challenge for her. With a little time, my hair could look neat. My mother never had allowed me to have long hair, however she did allow the top of my head to be well covered, often choosing Italian barbers, who liked to take longer than normal, if the parent simply did not want an economy short back and sides to prolong the time between visits. Sister however did not seem to wish to give the slight extra amount of time that my hair really needed.

Within a short time of my arrival, I was despatched to the carpenter's shop at the Home, where it appeared a few boys were still dealt with for haircuts. I was given the option of sitting still for him or having a pudding basin put on my head. I sat still; the result however very much resembled a pudding-basin cut, possibly achieved after many years' experience. As well as the front, back and sides losing hair, the top of my head also was cropped quite severely. This was possibly one of the major differences my mother noticed on her first visit to see me.

CHAPEL

The Home having a religious theme on a Sunday was something I now had to become used to. Other than going with the school to a Harvest Festival service or a Christmas service, actually going to church was not something I had ever done. There was a good chance that Sister had been informed of this when I had first arrived. There was also a good bet that my mother would have explained to Sister that I might cause a nuisance over such a matter, and I would find a quiet service difficult to sit through.

Administration building and Chapel

Before my first visit to the Chapel for Sunday service, Sister took me to one side and had a quiet chat. I was told that on Sundays the service could last an hour to an hour and a half. She knew of a few boys in other flats who found it difficult to sit through such a long service without becoming bored or finding the need to visit the lavatory. Once we were seated in the chapel, she did not like us to disrupt the service by making a request to leave. I was told quite firmly this would not be allowed; she would also not expect me to cause any fuss if I needed the lavatory. It was for this reason that some younger members in other flats were provided with waterproof pants to wear under their trousers on Sundays. There were also the odd few boys of around my own age in various flats who wore them as well, just in case there was ever an accident during the service.

As she was unsure of my behaviour for such a period, it was suggested that for my first visit to the chapel, it might be best if I also made use of a pair. Once the service was over, if I had proved that I did not need them, I would not be required to wear them again for chapel unless I thought it was necessary. At the end of the service if there had not been any problems, I should take them off and tuck them at the bottom of my drawer. At the age of eight, I thought I would not have a problem, but as this was a request from Sister, I would not make a fuss. If it had been from my mother, I would have refused, as not since the age of five when I had been on a long coach journey was it thought that I might have needed them. Sister did not embarrass me in front of the other three boys; I was given a pair, and told to go into the lavatory to change.

I was not too sure that I could last through a long service. Sister was trying to make sure I did not have any problems; it was possible to see that this was not a punishment, but something that was done to help me. What Sister did not explain at this moment was what I should do if I did have an accident. During the service, there was this thought in my mind the entire time.

The service in chapel went without incident. On returning to the flat, there was the hope I might find a moment to change out of them. As I was a younger one, I was due to go to Sunday school when lunch was over. I needed to remain in my best clothes, whilst the older three boys changed into play clothes. I did not get the chance to change out of the waterproof pants until teatime. Over the next few services, I did put them on for each visit, just to make sure I could last out the service; after the first month, I left them in the drawer. There were a few services in the next few months where I wished I had worn them, but it was just luck that I managed to hold on and did not embarrass Sister. At the age of eight, I should not have had such problems; it was just living here that made me so uneasy over so many matters, for some reason since coming to the Home that I found I needed to go for a pee much more often.

PUNISHMENTS

Extra chores were an ideal form of punishment. If set a chore when our favourite TV programme was on, even if the chore itself was useless, we soon knew not to repeat our bad behaviour. As a younger one in the flat, some minor physical punishments were also used as a way of keeping me well behaved. When you reached senior school age Sister did not bother with the slipper; restricting your privileges was felt a far better way of controlling any poor behaviour. The older three boys seemed to always fall into the age group to lose privileges.

Sister was quite kind in not embarrassing me in front of others when it came to such punishments. Often whilst the others were all watching TV, I would be called out of the dayroom. I might escape with a telling off or some chores; if not

I would be escorted to the bedroom. The events of my bad behaviour would be explained. Sister was never angry with me at the time that I was punished, but it was easy to tell she was not pleased with me.

The first time Sister gave me the slipper had been about a week after my arrival; a minor argument and I was soon alone in my room with Sister. I was in total fear of the punishment. I had not expected to wet myself, and I just could not help it. I was expecting it to hurt far more than a spanking from my grandmother when she had only used her hand, and with Sister picking up a slipper, I had expected far more pain.

Once given the slipper, I was told to go and have my bath, as it was almost the time for me to go in any case. Nothing further was said over the matter, my tears proving to her that I knew to be better behaved. The only real difference I found was that unlike a spanking from my grandmother, there was the lack of any reward from Sister to make things better.

This punishment had been two days before a visit from my mother. I expected Sister to tell her about my behaviour, but nothing was said to my mother when she came, and even when I returned at the end of the visit, nothing was mentioned about either event. I soon realised how kind Sister was: once I had been punished that was the end of the matter. I knew not to say anything to my mother about having received the slipper if I wanted to keep in her good books. Now I knew what the slipper from Sister was going to be like, I had no more fear, but knew if I had done something wrong the matter would soon be over.

During other punishments, if I was in my pyjamas that was all right; if I was in trousers, these were normally to be taken down, leaving me in underpants. It was not necessary if my behind was not well covered for her to put that much effort into a hit, and it stopped us having additional pairs of underpants hidden under our trousers to lessen the pain. Often either two or three hits were all that were ever done; they were enough to make me cry. Had I not cried I could bet that the next time the slipper was given, it would be with a little more effort; once over I was left in my room. That was the end of the punishment and nothing more would be said. When I felt like returning to the others I could, but it was recommended by Sister that I went and washed my face first. In a way I did not really mind the odd hit with the slipper given by Sister; they were not as painful as school punishments and with no chores set, I did have more of my own time to enjoy. When my tears had finished, we would be friends again.

I was given the slipper on odd occasions when Sister found that the insides of my wellingtons were damp. The Home possessing no ponds or such areas where you could wade in water, meant that unless I came up with a good explanation I must have been out of bounds. I was not going to admit the hiding places where I had found interesting adventure areas with water; the others would soon find out. Although they had been here longer than I had and would have been past these places, they did not seem to realise their potential. The was an area under the Administration Block with its flooded cellar to explore; in the grounds there was the area at the far end of the disused railway cutting where a small pond formed after heavy rain and a small pond was located at the back of the cemetery if you climbed the fence onto the railway line. These were all places that if waded in, could risk water going inside your wellingtons. All were out of bounds, so I should not have been there in the first place; that would have meant the slipper from Sister or the cane from the Governor. Accepting Sisters punishment, when her thoughts were that I might have been playing with the gardeners hosepipe in the out of bounds orchard area, meant a few light hits with the slipper and the ability to keep my play areas secret.

One of my major crimes was daft. Near to the carpenter's hut there were a few sheds, most containing grass cutting and similar equipment. One of the sheds was used by the nursing Sister to store her car, and as I knew that the only thing in this shed was the car, as it was locked there was no point in trying to get in as there was nothing interesting.

A couple of younger children had been around and had been playing with the padlock and chain. How the chain snapped in my hand I did not know, but I was left holding a broken chain. With no reason to go any further into the shed, I let it go. It was decided that it might be best if we were not around. It was a day later when Sister tackled me over the matter. There was little point in trying to get out of the punishment; there were two other children, who could put the blame on me. Soon I was in my bedroom and receiving the slipper. It did hurt, but it might have been worse had I tried to put the blame on the other two.

During the period that Sister looked after me, the number of occasions I received the slipper from her would have been around a dozen, and as this worked out to less than once a month, she must have been quite tolerant of my behaviour.

When Sister ever wanted us to behave, she would tell us how the Home was run when she first arrived. We were told that in those days there was the Girls' side and the Boys' side: the two groups did not really mix. The boys had the larger woods to play in and the girls had the smaller woods at the back of their flats; each group did not go into each other's areas unless they wanted to risk serious punishment. Even today, the woods were still called by their original names. When Sister started, she took on a group of boys; it was only in recent years that our flat became a mixed group. We were told that the large hall that we now used for recreation was where the school was. With everyone leaving at fourteen this school was for ages 5–14; the small nursery school was originally the laundry building.

Any boy that was up to mischief was severely dealt with, either in her flat or would be sent over to the Governor. Most preferred to take what was offered in her flat as punishment rather than risk being sent over for an alternative decision. When Sister first started, it appeared that many minor matters that if committed today would get us a few extra chores, would have originally been punished with either the slipper or the cane. Once you reached the age of eight the cane was the more regular form of punishment, which she gave to the boys in her flat.

We asked Sister if she could tell us what she would have caned us for, if we had been in the Home when she originally started. A list was soon forthcoming: everything from missing clothes, lying, stealing, taking extra food and even if you wet the bed the staff were instructed to use the cane. There was a comment made, it was that perhaps a few of the old rules might be brought back for us. If this slightly frightened me, it was that I would now be caned if I wet the bed.

Compared with the other three boys, I had seven years of freedom before coming to the Home – seven years of contact with the outside world. Sister had brought up boys for many years, and what they did, how they acted, and in many other ways there had been little change.

One minor thing seemed to bring us into conflict. I was always on the move; when I was out at play whatever I was up to, was always at a rush. Until I arrived at the Home, to help my agility if the weather was reasonably fine, I tended to wear a pair of baseball boots. The advantage over the slip-on type of plimsoll was that they did not fall off, and when compared with the lace up plimsolls, baseball laces were long and strong; broken laces on plimsolls and their unmanageable knots were always an annoyance to me. Originally, when I had arrived at the Home, I did not have my baseball boots with me; given the lack of space several of my preferred items of clothing had been left out of my case. Until my first visit back to London I had managed without them, however Sister did not normally let you use school plimsolls in the grounds unless it was completely dry; in my mind there was a need to bring them to the Home at the first chance I had. On returning from my first visit, I had thought there would be nothing wrong in baseball boots; they were nothing out of the ordinary, simply the standard type that many of my friends and myself had worn for both play and school use. They were only slightly more expensive than a decent pair of plimsolls – certainly only a fraction of the cost of a pair of shoes.

For some reason Sister took a dislike to the boots I had brought back with me. They were neither new nor tatty in any way; possibly, if I had them the other three would soon demand them too. If it was a case of money, then there might be a saving if shoes were not worn out so quickly. All I could seem to find out was that she was cross that I had introduced something new to her flat that she had not chosen herself.

It was never a case of actually being forbidden from wearing them in the grounds, but a rule now seemed to be invented. Before I went outside in them, I had to come to her and ask permission to wear them. This was one of many rules that were invented without any real explanation why they were there. To me it was a waste of time having to find her each time I wanted to go outside to play. On most days in the grounds, I wore wellingtons simply to avoid having to find Sister; it also saved me from having to polish my play shoes. The baseball boots were returned to London on the next visit and were left there. There never was the request from the other three for such items; their choice on most days was football boots.

Going to Christmas and other parties should have been happy events. It was true that they could be fun, but travelling there and back was always the worst part. Often it was a couple of hours' journey by coach and to help prevent travel sickness, I made sure that I did not eat anything before the journey. Often we set off early in the afternoon; other than breakfast, if I had eaten lunch I made sure it was only the minimum I could get away with.

On the coach to make it fair, if you had a window seat to the event, the rule was that you would swap with your partner for the return trip. I normally tried to get a seat as near to the front as possible; most of my friends would head to the rear of the coach. There was always the instruction that if any of us felt sick or needed the lavatory, we should come and see the staff at the front of the coach. For anyone that ever had problems, going to the front did little good; we would usually be on roads where it was impossible to stop or almost at the location, and we would be told there was not long to wait. Part way into the journey I would start to feel a little unwell. It was never the case that I felt I was going to be instantly sick. It was made worse if one of the others came to the front announcing they felt ill. With little chance of the coach stopping they would stand perched at the front, slightly swaying in the aisle. This was normally enough to make them sick. If they could only have been sick in the rear seats, the stench and sight would not be affecting any of us that were already suffering from weak stomachs.

The other event would be someone announcing they needed to go for a pee. Again, the coach would not be stopped; they would stand there hopping from one leg to another ready for the coach to eventually stop so they could be the first off. On almost every journey, there was someone unable to wait any longer. The result was a puddle on the floor or on a seat; this would make everyone around also think they desperately needed to go.

I was in trouble after a party soon after my arrival at the Home. On the return trip, I had sat in a damp seat after someone had an accident on the way to the party. When Sister saw the state of my trousers on my return to the flat, I was blamed for this act; there was no point in arguing the matter, having already found out that arguing with Sister resulted in the slipper. I accepted the punishment of having to wear waterproof pants under my trousers for the next few months on all coach outings, and on a few visits outside the grounds with Sister. At the age of eight, I was rather embarrassed at the demands by Sister. In an odd way I was quite happy, as there was not any fear of an accident occurring, which would have brought teasing from the others, and a possible punishment for causing embarrassment in front of Sister.

Nosebleeds at the Home whilst not actually getting me into trouble could cause a few problems. If I was out at play, I normally found somewhere quiet to sit down, and then would wait until they finished. As I often had two handkerchiefs with me, it was possible to control where the blood actually went. With plenty of experience over past nosebleeds, I knew that it was best to get the handkerchiefs washed out and to get them into salty water to stop the blood staining them. To Sister I was a little bit of a nuisance in having to have such matters dealt with.

If a nosebleed occurred in the flat, I would normally be sent out of the dayroom or the kitchen to sit on the hard chair in the hall, as this was a quiet spot. A nosebleed could easily be over in ten minutes or so, and once any mess was cleaned up, I was free to go back to whatever I was doing before the nosebleed happened. A nosebleed during a meal presented a couple of extra problems. Most of those sat at the table preferred me to leave their presence as soon as possible. With a major nosebleed I could quite accept such a feeling; a minor nosebleed and there was a little reluctance on my part to leave the table. I might be lucky and the remains of the meal could be saved on one side for my return, but on many occasions the best parts of any meal were not available for my later return. Had any adult thought I was having nosebleeds to get attention, missing the best parts of my meals was not something that I would voluntarily do.

Nosebleeds during the night did cause problems. Although I did not normally sleep through a major nosebleed I was reluctant to get out of bed. Often having a handkerchief did solve some of the bloodstains; however normally both my pillow and sheets were often badly stained. I could normally work out how bad a nosebleed was by how fast the drops of blood came out. I found it more comfortable to lie on my side. Trying to block my nose or the like did little good; it might delay the nosebleed for a time but it never actually stopped it. If I had a major nosebleed, I would get out of bed and sit in the hall. If it was late at night or shortly before it was time to get up I would often find some attention from Sister. If she was not around, I was quite happy to sit for half an hour, when normally it would finish completely.

The morning after such a large nosebleed normally did bring a telling off. There might be some spots of blood in the hall; I would have tried to wipe up as much as I could, but with only a dim light and not wanting to bend over, there was always the evidence. My bed was normally the more revolting sight; although it did not frighten the other three, the blood-soaked pillow and sheets first thing in the morning might have been something to wonder at.

A bath first thing on getting up, followed by the encouragement to wash out my pillow case and sheets in the bath once my bath was over, was the only

Harpenden hospital

73

punishment. There was not any scolding over the state of my bed; there was little point in suggesting that I should have knocked on her door during the night. If I was having a nosebleed there was no way it could be quickly stopped. Often I was sent over to see the Nursing Sister, but by then the matter was over and little more could be done.

Having a rubber sheet on my bed kept the mattress from being stained with blood. After a while, my pillow was given a similar treatment. Instead of an inner pillowcase the Sister made up one made out of an old rubber sheet, and when it came time to sorting out my blood-stained sheets and pillowcase, the pillow could easily be cleaned. Others might have been upset over nosebleeds, but having always suffered from them; I did not really take much notice.

It was quite easy to displease Sister. As many of my journeys to and from school were on rainy days, a raincoat was always needed for the mile walk. My school raincoat was almost new; it had been given to me when I left the boarding school, so unless I suddenly grew by a large amount it would last at least a year or so.

What I was unhappy about on rainy days was putting something on my head. A school cap was almost useless if it rained; once sodden it would take ages to dry out. Sister thought my head should be covered; her solution was to provide me with a waterproof hat that could be tied with a cord under my chin. I have always hated anything under my chin. I did not actually refuse to wear it, but on coming home after school with my hair wet, it was obvious that I had not bothered to put it on. After a couple of complaints from Sister, it was clear to her that I was not going to wear it.

Punishments from Sister could be odd; I was now told that if I did not want to wear the hat, I would be dressed like a girl and have a hood on my coat. In the mind of Sister this would be the worst ever punishment a boy could be given. I did not object; as my play coat was already in the girl's style with a hood, I had little problem when I was given an almost new navy raincoat with a hood attached. I was not really a sissy, but having to wear some items of girl's clothes had never been a problem to me, and if they were similar to the design that a boy might wear, I never objected. That the coat buttoned up the wrong way did not matter; I had never learnt to do any coat up the boy's way. If I ever wore a coat that buttoned up in either direction, I had always found it more natural to do it up in the girl's fashion, as this was the way I been shown by my mother at an early age. The punishment Sister had given to me was something I was quite happy with, going to and from school, my head kept dry, other boys did not even tease me.

In a way, there were a couple of advantages. As Sister had provided me with girl's wellingtons, if I wore this coat with the hood up, as I had fairly fine features as well as being tall and thin, it was very easy to mistake me for a girl unless you were very close. Adults would pay little attention to a girl as they were seldom up to any mischief. My original school raincoat was now reserved for Sunday or best use. I had never liked the metal chain that was used to hang the coat up as it could rub on the back of my neck.

I annoyed Sister again over my clothes when it was time for a couple of us to have a new pair of wellingtons. Several of our garments came directly from the main administration building. On occasions, we were taken into the town, if there was nothing of the correct size in the stock at the Home. Sister probably still had a memory of my first objection to the boots I had been provided with on my arrival; if I was thought to be of good behaviour now, it was the treat of me actually getting some choice in what was provided, rather than the standard system of if it was the correct size it was yours. Most of my friends would have chosen the heaviest rugged looking boots available. It might be that at the age of eight or nine they wanted to show they were grown up. That it was impossible to run in the heavy short boots and that walking for any great distance was tiring made little difference to them. With two of us needing to be sorted out, I allowed the older girl to be seen to first; I could bet there would have been a telling off if I had put myself first. When my time came, I requested the same item; even the shop assistant suggested that there were some more rugged styles for boys. I was not put off. My new boots were of a similar design to the girl, but did not have such a pointed toe. That they were knee length and very shiny was to me all that mattered.

One treat was to be allowed to keep the box that the boots came in, although no time was wasted changing back into my shoes; I was allowed to put my shoes in the box to take them back to the Home. I did not mind that the box clearly stated 'Girls' and had an illustration of a girl in a raincoat and boots on the outside of the box; that could soon be covered up when I constructed something with the box once we were indoors. There was a comment from Sister on the way back, as to why did I have to be different from all the others; it was something for which a reply was not really required. I stayed silent, simply happy that I had been given a choice and had a good solid box to play with.

It was easy to be told off for minor matters even if they were not your fault. The cat that lived in the flat took to spending most of its time in our bedroom during the day. As there was little reason for us to be in our bedrooms during the day, it was actually the quietest place in the house. My bed was the usual resting place for the cat. When the cat vacated my bed, there would be an impression on the counterpane of where he had been resting. Sister occasionally inspected our rooms at odd points during the day, and would then find fault with the appearance of my bed. Rather than correcting the slight problem, I would often be called to put the matter right.

The cat seemed to have a quite peaceful life. If there was too much noise there was always the outside if it was necessary to get away from us. Another favourite place to sleep was in the vegetable rack on the floor in the kitchen; even if there were a few potatoes already there, a comfortable position could be made. During one meal, the cat suffered an urgent case of the runs. As the cat headed outside, Sister made the comment that if he did it again, she would be taking him to the vet's to be put down. This was not really the best conversation topic for mealtimes. Most were quite upset that Sister should have such thoughts on how to treat the cat, but something we could see was not an idle threat.

In the winter our rooms were quite cold; although there were a couple of radiators, the size of the room made it difficult to keep warm. Hot water bottles were available for anyone who wanted them. Just before we went to bed there was the ritual of getting Sister to fill them up, and it was up to you to make sure they were securely fastened.

Most of the bottles had a top that folded over the end. Once secured, they remained sealed until the following morning; the older ones grabbed these first. A few of the bottles were in the traditional style with screw stoppers and no matter how hard you tried to do them up they often leaked slightly. The bottles were in good condition, but the small washers on the stoppers were almost perished.

Part way through the night they would leak. Early in the morning you would wake up slightly damp; kicking or throwing the bottle out of the bed was the only solution. When it was time to get up, Sister often understood that a damp area in your bed was not something to really become cross about; if it was only slight, there was no need to change your sheet, and leaving your bed to air during the day, it was soon dry.

Sister told us that if we did not press on the hot water bottles they would never have leaked, so little was done about any replacements, and if we had damp beds it was our own fault. I preferred to have a damp bed rather than to challenge one of the older boys for a water bottle that would not leak. On the nights I wet my bed, it was not worth mentioning that the hot water bottle leaked. To end the problem of getting a leaking hot water bottle, I brought my own from London. It was much older and made out of metal; when filled it was boiling, but wrapped in an old pillowcase it was fine.

CHORES

Although it was not slave labour, the chores that I found that had to be done for Sister certainly made it seem like that. Our morning chores started with our bedrooms. The floor had to be clean and any mats near our beds had to be in a tidy position. There was little in our room to become untidy. As all clothes had to be put away and our beds made, the lack of any other personal items in the room meant that any polishing and cleaning we did was quite easy to complete.

Most of the flooring in the flat was linoleum; this was easy to keep polished to the standard Sister required, if we put some elbow grease into it. There was the modern electric polisher that was powered from the mains. For most of the time, we used a heavy mop type polisher. This appeared to be a device which would put us in good stead if we joined the Navy when we left the Home; Sister had this route planned for many boys who had been in her care.

Washing up and general cleaning duties were part of everyday life. Some of these were done before school, and the others were completed before we went out to play once school was over. Our Sister had designed chores to make us responsible for keeping things clean; often however some of the regular cleaning chores seemed to be designed to keep idle hands occupied. If anyone ever was foolish enough to utter the phrase that they were bored, chores could soon be found. When we were free, it was best to get out of the flat; if we ever appeared to be unoccupied, a chore could be found.

In our flat most of Saturday morning was occupied with cleaning. Only if you had made good job of your chores were you allowed to spend a short while outside before lunch was started. Looking outside, most of our friends did not seem to have these long chores first thing on a Saturday morning and were happily out at play. For chores, the four of us boys were normally given the heavier dirtier chores to do, whilst the three girls were given lighter chores of washing and ironing of clothes. I was quite happy over most of the chores that were allocated to us.

Once a week the floor area of the corridor needed to be thoroughly cleaned. This was often the final Saturday morning chore, so it was in our interests to make a good enough job that it would pass Sister's inspection and allow us freedom outside.

During the week the hall, bedrooms, kitchen and day room floors were given a quick polish to keep them looking clean. The Saturday event was far more thorough. First came the damp mop through, followed by a dry mopping. Once everything was dry the final polish with the heavy bumper mop was made; this final part was the worst chore. On most occasions the two older boys took on this chore. To Sister if one boy had put a good effort in for a few minutes, he was allowed a short rest whilst the other took over. The easiest job was the dry mopping of the floor. The boy who was slightly older than myself claimed this as his right, and I was left with the damp mopping of the floor. This gave the biggest chance of getting told off if anything went wrong. I was quite happy with the task; once it had been done I was more or less finished with chores and might get my freedom before the others. The others disliked the damp mopping because a bucket had to be filled with water and disinfectant added. To them the stuff stank too much; it was a smell that I had become used to.

If I had wet the bed, a capful of the disinfectant had to be added to my bathwater. My sheets could then soak in the mixture during breakfast. My next task would be to give them a final rinse and take them outside and hang them on the washing line, and any chores I would have done after breakfast were to be done after tea.

It was difficult to know if it was down to cost or Sister's idea that cleanliness was next to godliness, that we were given such a powerful disinfectant to use. The thin black treacle-like substance might normally be used for the cleaning of drains, but one small capful in a bath of water or two capfuls in a bucket of water was enough to give everything it touched a very clean aroma for many hours.

Sister knew of its powers, and we were never to wear our slippers when we were mopping the floor with the disinfectant in case we spilt some over them. Like the mornings I put my sheets into soak, it was required that wellingtons be worn. Sister could embarrass me on those mornings, by not allowing me to change back into my slippers before I went in for breakfast, as I would soon be returning to the bathroom to rinse out my sheets. When I arrived at the breakfast table in wellingtons, everyone knew the reason.

The mopping of the floor with the damp mop was quite easy. There was never the need to get the floor very wet; as long as Sister could see the odd damp patch in the hall when she passed, and that there was enough of an aroma in the air she was happy.

The only ones in our flat who managed to get out of the first chores in the morning were the two older boys who had a daily paper round. For some odd reason the Saturday papers always took longer to deliver. If there had been no extra chores on a Saturday, there might have been the possibility of asking if I could have been allowed out of the grounds to visit the local cinema, but as nothing like this had ever been allowed in our flat, the request was never made.

Sunday morning also brought major chores. For the first part of the day our normal play clothes were worn; the major chore of the day was fresh sheets on our beds. Once a month there was the ritual of turning your mattress over and re-fixing the rubber sheet to the mattress with the ties. If you worked as a pair such tasks could be completed far more quickly.

Only when all the chores were finished was it time to get ready for chapel. Hands, nails, hair and face were all items that had to pass as very clean, and with the need to make sure we were perfect, we were often ready long before it was time to leave the flat. No play was allowed at this point as we were bound to get in a mess. The worst event that could happen at this point was to get into trouble; having to sit next to Sister during the service owing to your bad behaviour was boring.

When Sister thought it was the correct time, we all set off in an orderly group walking together. A few of our friends from other flats were able to make their own way to the chapel. To Sister a major crime was to cut across the grass to and from chapel.

If our Sister was rather restrictive over our behaviour, it possibly went back to the period when she originally started at the Home; the grounds were divided by an invisible barrier. The girls were in flats on one side of the grass, the boys on the other. There were also separate play areas, the two groups did not mix. On a Sunday they were allowed to walk round the paths in controlled groups. It appeared that if there were brothers and sisters from the same family, there might be slight contact allowed at this point.

During one church service when The Governor was giving a sermon, the rather religious works gave way to a short talk on rhymes and similar light-hearted matters. We were set the task of thinking up our own rhyme; we could bet that the following week a few of us might be expected to give him our own rhyme.

Later at lunch Sister asked whether we had yet thought one up. An older boy came up with his own version or possibly one that he might have heard at school. 'Desperate Dan the big fat man fries his knickers in a frying pan.' This was perhaps not a rhyme to recite in front of Sister; that he chose to utter it on a Sunday and that it was meant to have some religious merit brought an instant rebuke from her. Most of us were either laughing or choking over our meal. The rest of the meal however was now conducted in silence; it appeared we could not take such things seriously.

The day room had to be neat and tidy before we left for school. Any toys left out risked disposal. Comics and the like if they had been left out would find their way to the utility room. Unless the owner was very quick at retrieving them and putting them into their locker, it was easy to find they were placed in the sack, ready for the weekly collection for the incinerator.

With the amount of rubbish that could be generated by each flat, normally only the items that could not be burnt were put in the dustbin. Once a week the groundsman would come with a tractor and trailer and collect everything burnable from the flats. As this was normally a school day, it was impossible to see what Sister had actually decided was rubbish.

During the holidays as our building was the first to be collected from, it might be possible to be picked to help; eventually after the twenty flats were visited, the load would be taken to the orchard. A disused greenhouse that was now down simply to low brick walls was used as the incinerator, rather than any special device. As most of the rubbish was in sacks or boxes it was possible if you were quick to empty them out as you threw them onto the pile; a few useful items happened to drop at the area where the eventual fire would not reach. For a second chance, it was possible to toss any item you really wanted outside the brick walls to be collected later.

The staff decided that this area was out of bounds, but they could not supervise it all the time. Rich pickings of items that a Sister thought unsuitable could often be made; rainy days gave the best chance of making a find; a slow smouldering pile might last for several hours, giving us a chance to wait until the coast was clear. The threat of the cane from the Governor if caught, did little to stop our foraging. The cane was a minor price to pay for the chance of finding treasure.

Normally there were never any useful things to be found in the dustbins at the Home; it was worth however taking the occasional look. If a Sister had confiscated a penknife or other item, there was always a chance that it might be put in a bin rather than finding its way to the incinerator. During one of my odd searches, I found that one of the Sisters had chucked out almost the entire contents of one boy's locker. These items might have been put in the bins, as they were due to be collected the following morning, rather than for the incinerator, which had been collected the day before.

Finding that every toy or book was smashed or torn up was a disappointment. Normally if someone was in a rage, it might be possible for a few things to be damaged, or there might be a general clear out of worn-out items. Everything seemed to have only recently been smashed; it looked as if they were smashed at the point of going into the bin rather than at an earlier time.

As the flat was at the end of the row, there were no overlooking windows; with the weather damp there were few outside to witness my exploration. My rummage through the bin showed that even to me there was nothing worth removing. I moved onto the next bin in the hope of finding something that might still be sound. This second bin was full of clothes. I took a few out in the hope that there might be something underneath. The clothes were all for a boy of around my age or slightly older. Nothing appeared to be damaged so I could not think why the Sister should chuck these out.

79

With my regular problem of getting into trouble over play clothes getting either soaked or dirty, I decided to take a few things. If I was ever outside and needed more protection these would come in handy, without the need for going indoors to get some more clothing. Selecting a raincoat, shorts, wellingtons and a jumper I headed off quickly before being seen. I could have taken a few more things, but I had to make it appear that I had not been through the bin. For most, there were few hiding places available for items that needed to be kept dry. I had the ideal hiding place in the flooded cellar under the Administration Block. Although it was possible for any of us to get inside, it appeared I was the only one to venture any distance into the darkness. Having hidden a torch inside that had never been found, I regarded the flooded cellar as mine. Soon these clothes were added to my other items I would not have been allowed indoors. The items might come in useful if they could keep me out of trouble.

It was several years later before it was explained to me why the entire contents of a locker might be thrown out. Very occasionally, there was the death of a child at the Home. If there were no relatives of the child that wanted any of the possessions, normally the entire contents of the locker belonging to the child would be thrown away. This prevented any squabbling over the possessions. It was also thought of as unfair that such items were divided up.

In a similar way, the clothing was also disposed of. Although the names in a garment could be erased, it was often thought that other children would be able to recognise the items, and might be upset at having to wear the clothes of a dead child. In past years when we had all worn very similar items, once a name had been removed, the garments were sent back to the Block for later re-use, as it was thought that the origin of the garment would not be known. In later years, when we had more individually recognisable garments, it was always thought best to remove all traces of the child, to prevent other children becoming upset.

During my time with Sister, I went with her on a few afternoons out to the common on a Saturday. These were often not with the entire group from our flat, but with another Sister and a few of her younger members. Both the Sisters were of the older Sisterhood, so the two of us from our flat could expect almost the same restrictions and required behaviour; the girl slightly younger seemed quite happy to be taken out with me. The older ones possibly thought themselves lucky either to be able to stay in the flat under the control of the helper, or outside in the grounds with total freedom. These were about the only occasions where I saw the inside of another flat, and was soon able to make friends with a boy of around my own age who was selected to go on these outings.

The layouts of the flats were similar; the boys' bedroom was one single room of five beds. As my friend was the eldest, at least he had some extra privileges. He told me that for the last four years he had slowly made it to the eldest. Before we left to go on the outings, the pair of us were allowed a short time to play quietly with the others, whilst the two Sisters had a break with a cup of tea. I was shown round the entire flat. In a way it was surprising how both the Sisters could choose almost the same items to display on the walls and shelves. If we had exchanged flats, we could expect that our lives would have been identical. Both Sisters gave their flats the status of not where to live, had there been the chance to swap flats.

The only difference between our bedrooms was that on the wall in his flat there was a large chart with each of their names, followed by a row of stars, similar to the ones used by our schoolteachers to add to our workbooks when we had presented good work. At school, I possessed very few stars; here the chart was full mostly with green stars but there were red stars in places. Thinking that here, the Sister awarded red stars for good behaviour in the flat, I asked my friend why his name had so few of the coveted red stars, and his row was mainly green. He was embarrassed at explaining the reason for the chart, but knew that I would not tell anyone else of our age group about it. The chart was Sisters method of keeping a track of who had wet their bed. Each morning Sister handed out the stars for them to stick next to their names, green for a dry bed and red for wetting it during the night. Now that he was eight, a couple of hits with the slipper were also given on those mornings.

I was different from the others in the flat, by having a suit as well as a blazer; the others only had blazers. Sister had originally brought back the suit from the main office. The suit was not new but there was little sign of any real use. In Sister's mind, with our mixed sizes, there should be the possibility that it would fit one of us. The older three boys took one look at the suit and decided that it would not fit them, simply for having two pairs of short trousers rather than a single pair of long trousers, which at their age they decided were deserved.

They need not really have worried when I was given the task of trying it out for size – it was clear that it was designed for a tall thin boy. Until this moment, Sister had always complained about my odd shape, and that none of the clothes that were ever to hand ever seemed to fit me. My mother had found the same result when we shopped for my clothes; most of my shirts and trousers were taken in before they were presentable for wearing.

The suit was a light brown, with a very faint lighter brown and green cross hatch design woven into the cloth. It was easy to see that this suit had not been purchased from an ordinary store. The label neatly sewn into the jacket showed that it had been hand-made for its original owner; it came with an extra pair of trousers, this proving that it was designed to give long service. In the manufacture there seemed to be plenty of extra material to let out as its owner grew. The suit was one of the occasional items of clothing that were donated to the Home when outgrown. I was happy to have such a nice garment; the other three did not tease me over the short trousers – they were relieved that it fitted me. Had it not then Sister would have made sure one of them were the correct size for it.

Most Sunday visits to chapel I wore the suit, and on the visits home to London. Once out of the grounds of the Home, it would have been very difficult to suggest that I lived in a Children's Home. The local shops seemed much more tolerant of me, if I was dressed in the suit, than on an ordinary Saturday when small hordes of us might descend. Once I arrived in London the suit would generally be put away until the moment it was time to return to the Home; the areas where I wanted to play were not locations where a suit or any good clothing should be worn. With the ability of my mother to let down the hems, sleeves and waistband when I eventually put on extra weight through the quantity of food at the Home, the suit still fitted and lasted for several years.

The older ones in our flat often managed to sneak into dry places when Sister put us out in heavy rain. In a way, I preferred getting soaked outside than to being under Sister's feet in the flat. Sister was a little tired of me returning to the flat, either soaked to the skin or half drowned, and provided me with a waterproof playsuit to go outside in. I was the only boy of my age with one; it was the younger children that were normally provided with such clothing.

When the younger children wore these play suits they were always quite loose in design; with my height it was an exact and very snug fit. The playsuit actually looked quite smart compared with our ordinary play clothes. If the trouser part ended a little short, it did not matter if I wore them inside my boots. When Sister first provided me with the playsuit, almost everyone in the flat teased me by saying I looked like one of the characters in a recent *Dr. Who* episode. It was made of greenish dark grey cotton that was thinly coated on both sides with rubber; it was in one piece and buttoned up at the back. Once you were inside, you always needed someone to do it up. If you wanted to get out of the playsuit, it was possible if you were agile enough to undo the buttons. If you ever needed to go for a pee, getting out of the playsuit quickly prevented your pants becoming soaked. A few of the younger children hated their playsuits for this very reason.

Once outside I was quite happy to go off on my own. Often I might be the only one in the grounds, but I was quite happy. When it was time to come indoors, I was not now told off, as I had normally managed to keep dry.

On occasions, I was thought to be responsible outside the Home. Having gone swimming quite often, at some point I picked up a verruca on my foot and was sent over to the nurse. I was given a note with an address of where I should go for treatment. At the age of eight, I was thought old enough to go there on my own. After reminding Sister I was going to be late home, I made my visit after school. After a few sessions, the verruca was finally removed and I went back to swimming again.

The other matter when it was thought that I was old enough at the age of eight to look after myself was on trips to the dentist. I made one first trip escorted all the way; from that point on other than one visit where it was necessary to give me gas when a tooth was taken out, I made my own journey to and from the dentist. There was not any fear, other than knowing that at some point there might be some pain and discomfort. The only part that I really disliked was having a rubber bung put between my teeth to stop me closing my jaw whilst the dentist's fingers were too close. Once over, I returned to school. In a way I was reasonably happy with a trip to the dentist, as it got me away from the Home and trouble at school.

A few items in the flat were part of another era. The soap that was used at the washbasins or in the bath was a basic type. Normally designed for the washing of clothes, it was thought good enough for our use. The triple green block of soap had the word 'IBCOL' impressed across its length. Once broken up, it showed only part of its origins. The smell was not off putting; I can vouch for it simply having a soap-type flavour, when a chunk was inserted into my mouth by one of the staff for swearing. It could have been a worse punishment if we had used carbolic soap, but the taste of this green block was enough to stop my indoor use of certain words.

Toilet paper was similar to the type found in most public conveniences of the time. I had originally been used to a quality Izal hard paper or even the newer soft toilet tissue. Sister however managed to supply us with paper that seemed to be polished on both sides; we found it more use for putting over a comb and blowing through. It was a partial failure for the intended use. It was not that soft toilet tissue was an unknown product in the flat. A roll was kept under Sister's close watch in the end corridor cabinet. This was for our use when we had a cold, and not for us to use for the original intended purpose. None of us dared sneak a few extra sheets for comfort or cleanliness.

Until coming to the Home, bath time had generally been uneventful. Getting into the bath, getting rid of any dirt, and out again had really been the limit to the actual event. I had learnt that if I did not remove any dirt within a few seconds of getting into a bath, my mother holding the flannel could also remove dirt in seconds.

Sister did not really have the time to supervise the baths for everyone. The youngest girl could generally be looked after by her older sister; the two oldest boys were old enough to be sensible without making too much of a mess, and until I came, only the boy slightly older than myself had needed any supervision at bath time. All knew that if Sister was busy in the bathroom, more freedom existed for everyone in the flat.

My arrival seemed to spoil this event for them. We could now watch out for each other; if one of us did manage to drown the other, then it would be quite easy to find the culprit. If there was any mess of spilt water then we would be equally guilty. The idea that Sister had was whilst one was undressing the other could be in the bath. When he was out of the bath and drying off the second one of us could be in the bath. Once finished, the scum line could be removed and everything left clean for the older two boys.

Spending any length of time in the bath had never been something I had ever been used to. When I was very young I might have seen the odd plaything to keep me happy, but from the age of four, a bath was simply there for getting clean. My mother had no additional time for creating any fun. Any recent dislike of going for a bath was down to my mother supervising my baths in cold water after I had wet the bed at the age of seven.

At odd moments, Sister even made our baths more fun by adding a foam mix to our bath water. It was not something that she would have ever bought, but as each flat had been given several bottles of a new play bubble mix for children, we were all allowed to try it out; she supervised the amounts that went into our baths. Other than that, we were generally left alone once it was thought we would behave. Once the bottles of foam were finished, we went back to the green blocks of soap and the never-ending scum lines around the bath.

Two small boys can have odd ideas of fun, most of which neither Sister nor my mother would have approved of. In my mind it would be difficult to work out which would bring the worst form of punishment. With Sister it would be a telling off, followed by either the slipper or extra chores: for my mother it would be the plimsoll and cold baths.

At our age we knew there were two ways of spelling the word 'bath' one had four letters – and the other had a silent 'p' in it. We each took it as a competition of who could do the most; when we had finished our bath and were allowing the water to run away, was normally the point of any competition. It was everything from climbing onto the laundry basket and seeing how far across the bath you could reach, to lying in a drained bath and how far in the air you could achieve. Both of these games took courage on our part; our bath area was behind a door, but the door was never locked; Sister passing could come in at any moment, and if not Sister than even the helper might be around to catch us.

Since Sister's original arrival, there had been a few modern additions to the flat. In the dayroom, there was a television for our use. Squabbling over which channel to watch, was not allowed. Normally the older ones would choose the programme to watch. Once switched to that station, the set tended to remain like that for the entire evening, unless a good reason to turn over to the other side was agreed upon, often only then with Sister's approval.

The other modern device was the telephone. Normally only ever used by Sister or other members of the staff, it remained quiet for most of the time. When it did ring, it was often due to someone's misdeed that had now been found out by one of the other Sisters, who was ringing to make a complaint. The use by us of the phone was rare. For us to receive or make a telephone call something very urgent had to have occurred; talking to relatives or friends on the telephone was simply never done by us.

CHRISTMAS

This was meant to be a happy time for all. It was true I did like most of the activities, but I might have wished that I could have returned to my mother and there were just two of us. In the Home, there were plenty of activities organised and whatever age we were, we had to show that we all believed in Father Christmas. Had an older child tried to convince a younger child that he did not exist, there could have been two unhappy children for the holidays. Presents were well organised; on Christmas Eve we had a visit from Father Christmas who presented us with a main present each. The following morning we had a selection of other presents. These might come from relatives, friends or to a few children that had few close relatives, simply from the Home.

There was no child that really had more than any other due to family circumstances. With a number of aunts and uncles, on odd occasions, I seemed to get more than the others did, but as soon as they saw that with my Christmas presents, I also received a selection of Birthday cards, any jealousy ended at that moment. If they divided my pile in half to make up for the two events, what I was actually getting for Christmas was often far less than they were receiving. One matter that kept me occupied for some time after Christmas was writing thank-you letters.

During my stay in the Home, I continued to keep a diary. At Christmas, I always received a small pocket diary from one of my aunts. The first one had been when I was almost seven; from then on a pocket diary always arrived at Christmas. There was always a small amount of money tucked into the first page. As the diary was quite small and my writing was not that neat, little could be put in each day's entry. Although I did not add something every day, most weeks I could add a few words.

At the start of the diary it was mainly on the presents I had received. By the time school started, it was listing those that I disliked at school and what the punishments had been that week. This I wrote in a coded form to stop either Sister or others working out how bad I had been at school. Their punishments could also be recorded. When the holidays came and I was allowed to stay in London, a list of the films that I had seen took up most of the entries. To the others in the flat, my diary was of little interest. With me not writing about them or my friends, they could not see the point of keeping a diary in the Home. Every year the diary was slightly different in the theme; the only item that was the same each year, was the London Underground map, which I slowly memorised.

The other three had various toy guns, footballs and types of toys that to me were very uninteresting. It was one matter I was never bullied over, or found any of my possessions had been taken by them. There were continual arguments over missing toys. It could take a small object that was part of a larger toy to become mislaid, before either a squabble or fight started. On occasions, some of the arguments could result in very childish behaviour. At these times I was not involved. During Christmas, the two older boys were bought identical compendium games sets. Toys like these took co-operation from at least two of you to have any fun. I was the only boy to like solitaire; I could often end up with one ball, but never managed to get it to end up in the centre. Sister tried to treat these two boys identically whenever possible, and as they were the same age and had spent most of their time in the Home together, they had grown up more like brothers.

It took only one odd item in one of the games to become missing before the argument started between them. Each now decided to attack the other's game to make them identical with an item missing. Cards from the sets were ripped in half, counters snapped, small models damaged. It took some time for two games sets to be reduced to useless mess. As the boys were older than me, there was little I could have done to make them see sense. If one had merely accepted part way through the destruction that they might be wrong, then some of the sections in each set could have been saved. When Sister eventually found out what was going on, life for all of us for some time was under a cloud.

The only other disappointment during Christmas was at Sunday school. A few of us had thrown a few small bibles to each other for fun. The resulting punishment was two strokes of the cane on our hands. The punishment was given by the deputy governor, the same man who a week later dressed up as Father Christmas and asked us all if we had been good this year.

One of my aunts as part of my Christmas presents had provided me with a selection of obsolete blank paper from her office. Multiple carbon sets and the like were to me fun to play with. For the other boys as I was happy with such items, it proved to them that I was odd. At one point I exceeded this by getting an office typewriter for my birthday. This had also come from my aunt, when her office had changed over to electric typewriters; the old heavy manual machines were no longer required. The object stayed at the Home only until the first visit to London where it could be kept safe. With some encouragement, I might have been taught to type in the correct fashion, but my style soon evolved with one finger doing all the work. I had fun with the typewriter: with a two-colour ribbon in the machine and time, a picture could be created.

One of my birthday presents was a simple camera. Not really a toy, having basic features, it was possible to get fair results if subjects stayed still and there was enough light. Returning to the Home I brought it back with me. I managed to use up one roll of film outdoors during the snowy weather. It was put away ready to take back to London on my next visit. The roll of exposed film stayed safe in the locker but the camera did not. As it did not have any film in it, some of the others now thought of it as a plaything. It was not long before the small plastic lever that you pressed to take the picture was broken. If the adults wondered why I became upset at certain times, it was over these types of matters. On a later holiday in London I managed to buy another camera which was not taken to the Home.

I could be mean. At one point I returned from London with part of a bar of Ex-Lax chocolate. Knowing full well what it was for, I removed the outer wrapper and left the few squares of chocolate wrapped in the silver foil slightly hidden in my locker. Within a few days it was gone. I never did find out who had stolen it.

Comics were sent to me every fortnight. My mother purchased a few cheap comics, rolled them into a small bundle and then sent them by post to me at the Home. The other boys in the flat were quite friendly for the period of getting to read the comics.

The ideas I had for play could at times annoy the adults. In the day room, there was a doll's house; this was something for the girls to play with. With only one girl of suitable age, the doll's house sat on the top of the boy's lockers without much use. Over the years any furniture inside had disappeared; the girl not having any dolls that fitted inside showed little interest in it. Only on close inspection did I find that originally, this had been a doll's house from the luxury end of the market. In each room was a small bulb fitting to give the illusion of electric light. In part of the house there was a battery compartment and at the side of the house several switches to turn the lights in each room on and off.

The bulbs had gone missing and the switches had become broken. This was down more to the design rather than rough play, and parts of the wiring were also missing. Repairing it for the girl was something I would have been quite happy to do, providing I had been given the parts, but as I would have to provide my own bits to get the house to light up again, there was a little reluctance on my part to repair the doll's house.

I experimented on an idea of my own, to insert a small switch into the front of the house. In the normal way you would have set it to turn the light on when the front of the house was open. I changed the idea to make the light come on only when the front of the house was closed. It was worth sacrificing an almost dud battery, just to cause annoyance.

In the tidy life of Sister, if the front of the doll's house were even slightly open, it would cause annoyance. I rigged the house so that during the day the light was out. Only when we all went to bed and Sister made her final check of the room to see that everything was in order, would my plan come into action. She would simply close the front of the house; at first the light going on was probably not noticed. Only when the main light to the day room was turned out would the light in the doll's house glow and then flash when the bulb had been on for a few seconds. I only had to set the trap once; the following day I found the wires pulled away from the battery, my small switch having been missed.

In my experimentation to find out how things were made, I decided to find out how a golf ball was constructed. I knew that just under the outer white coating was a long length of fine elastic. The quietest place I could find to take a ball apart was in the bathroom. To speed up the removal of the outer coating I had selected a fork to pick the white pieces off the outside. Within a few minutes, the ball was in a state for the elastic to be unwound. Soon I became bored of the slow process of unwinding the elastic, as it did not come off in one length but in annoying short lengths. To speed the process up of getting to the end of the elastic, I sunk the prongs of the fork into what remained of the ball. Without warning, the ball suddenly leapt out of my fingers and appeared to attack me, spraying a fine sticky substance into my eyes and over my hair. The ball then set off around the bathroom at great speed, showering the entire area with a mixture of bits of elastic and a whitish spider's web.

I made a retreat from the bathroom as the ball was still in full flight. My eyes stung. I made my way to the kitchen to seek help. One of the older girls attended to my face, washed my eyes clean, and generally tidied me up. Eventually I returned to the bathroom. Apparently, I was not the first to find that the centre of a golf ball may have a small amount of liquid rubber solution. Having pierced it with the fork, the rubber solution was under great pressure as it still had elastic wrapped tightly around it. My face was the first point for the solution to hit. It took quite a while to clean the bathroom up. Surprisingly I did not get in any real trouble; it appeared that I had learnt a lesson over such activities. It was thought that I had managed to make the worst mess in experimentation of undoing a golf ball than anyone else had achieved.

For most of our free time in the flat we got on with each other. There were a few squabbles and fights, but there was nothing very serious. If there had been a falling out, by the following day everything was back to normal.

Some of my activities might have seemed to be nasty, but in the main, I was allowed a little freedom. My room-mate who was slightly older than me, had a slight problem with one of his first teeth. His second front teeth were all in place; he always had a happy grinning smile. One of his minor first teeth was loose. In time it would fall out, but it was in such a position that when he ate it hurt. The Sister suggested that if it did not fall out in the next couple of days, he would be off to the dentist; this was something that he was dreading.

Alone in the dayroom with him, I looked at the tooth. It was quite loose; I offered to pull it out. At first there was a bit of reluctance, but my suggestions that it might save a visit to the dentist and that if he handed the tooth over to Sister there might be a reward, made him agree. I announced that on the count of three I would pull the tooth out. Having lost most of my first teeth, I knew how easily they came out. I started the slow count, and I pulled out the tooth just as I was saying two, and surprised him over my action. There did not appear to be any pain. The tooth was later presented to Sister. I don't think it was mentioned that I had helped it out, otherwise I could bet that I would have been in some form of trouble.

FALLEN OVER – AGAIN

The Home was a relatively safe place for children. If we followed the rules, and did not sneak out of the grounds, there was little chance of any road accidents. A slow speed limit was set for vehicles travelling around the grounds. With very few cars around, there was little chance of injury.

Tree climbing was not really forbidden. If you were out of sight in the woods, there were few adults to make any comment. Cuts, bruises and a few broken bones did occur at odd times, but as children went, we were possibly less likely to be injured whilst in the grounds of the Home. For those that were taken to school and back by coach, they were the most likely to be injured in the road when outside the Home, due to having little experience of road traffic. The majority of us had the same chance as ordinary children on our way to and from school. Older children supervised the younger ones, so all were normally safe. From the age of eight most of us were thought to be wise enough to walk to school without any supervision.

Other than playground injuries, all my injuries were in the grounds of the Home. Branches had a habit of digging into me, concrete and tarmac paths met most parts of my body on regular occasions. Minor scratches and the like I normally paid little attention to until it was time to go inside. With more serious injuries excluding nose bleeds, I would head back to the flat well before the time to go in, so that Sister could decide if it was a simple wash of the cut or to be sent over to the Nursing Sister for a little more work.

Not all my injuries were my own fault. Some of the older boys seemed to have a death wish for the rest of us, and it was thought fun to lay traps for the unwary. In the woods various pits were dug and covered over with sticks. Never deep, they could have caused a broken or sprained ankle if encountered at speed.

Most of these I recognised before any accident occurred. A rope tied to a tree branch was to me irresistible, I soon learnt it was wise to really tug the rope to see if it was securely tied or just lightly fastened, so that once you were part way up you fell.

Running down a path on a slope, I encountered what I took to be bushes with a small gap to get through. It was only when I reached them and due to the speed, it was impossible to stop, I found odd pieces of barbed wire were mixed in with the bushes and across the gap.

My knees and the surrounding skin took the full force. The pain was fierce, and some of the cuts were deep. There were several long scratches and open cuts. I limped back crying to the main part of the Home; it was easier to go directly to the Nursing Sister as the small hospital was on the ground floor. I did not feel like climbing the steps to our flat and then being sent down again a few minutes later.

The Nursing Sister thought the injuries looked horrific. It took some time to clean each cut. Soon into the cleaning session it was decided to stand me in the shower and spray warm water onto my knees in an effort to remove the dried-on blood and to see exactly how many cuts I actually had. Finally, I was returned to my flat with several soft bandages around my legs and knees. Once Sister saw them I was confined during my free time to the flat for several days. I was however fit enough for the walk to and from school. Bandages finally off, I was released to go on my active play again. Around this time I started visiting the Nursing Sister for regular tetanus and booster shots.

During the summer months our free time could become a little boring. When one of my friends found a wasp's nest that was buried into the ground, it was something that needed more investigating. I knew that a wasp could sting, but as yet, none had ever bothered me. It was only a short time after prodding the underground nest with a stick, that one took its revenge. When I had recovered from the sting and my tears, I decided that the nest needed a little more action; once it was flooded, there were no more problems from that nest again. I left them alone from that point onwards. Any wasp that dared settle anywhere near me from that moment on, had little future.

OPEN DAYS AT THE HOME

Once a year the Home held an open day for members of the public. Those living outside the Home were given the chance to come and see how the Home worked. Our friends from school also attended as many activities for children were laid on specially.

During the summer months, various sporting events were organised. Some of these were by the various schools in the area – the grounds at the NCH were thought of as neutral. To a few of us from the Home, the schools invading our Home were slightly resented. If our teachers attended, we were now meant to cheer for our school, rather than our flatmates who might go to other schools.

To our friends the Home seemed so wonderful. There was a play area with climbing equipment, there were smooth roads and paths to cycle and roller-skate on, a football pitch, woods and a host of other interesting areas. All of us tried to explain it might seem a wonderful place for one day, but live here for years on end and it might be thought of in a different way. For us it was life in an open prison; there was nothing physically stopping us from leaving the grounds, except for the knowledge of the punishment we would receive when caught.

NATIONAL CHILDREN'S HOME, GIRL'S HOUSES, HARPENDEN.

Our friends from school had arrived, and were happily playing on the equipment. A few of us from the Home had some far more important matters. If it was dry and hot there were always plenty of drinks purchased from the refreshment stand. Our targets were adults who had purchased small bottles of pop. Few realised that they had paid a small deposit on the bottle. If we saw they had finished their drink and had some litter around, we simply went up and asked if we could clear up for them. Possibly thinking this was some form of chore the Home had set for us, they happily allowed us to retrieve the empty bottle and other items. If you had courage and were polite, the Open Day could be very lucrative.

At the end of the day when the visitors had left, if we were near to the refreshment area, we might be allowed to finish the remains of the cake without having to pay. Often this treat had been after our own tea, so there was an actual limit to the amount of cake we could eat. When we had finished the nice soft parts of the sponge cake, the hard-burnt edges became something to throw at each other once we were out of the Sister's view. The birds would soon finish any bits that fell on the ground.

On one of the Open Days, my mother and cousin had decided to come up. On this occasion I did not have to resort to collecting bottles, but had treats almost forced upon me. Several of the flats were open to visitors for tea, and this brought in extra funds to the Home. Those of us who lived in the houses that were serving teas were not welcome back whilst the teas were in progress. Our teas were known as 'bag teas'; these consisted of a brown paper bag containing sandwiches, a biscuit and a piece of fruit. At some point we were to return, collect our tea and make ourselves scarce until it was time to come in at the end of the day.

It had been fun spending the afternoon with my mother and cousin; I should have returned to collect my tea. My mother decided that the pair of them would have tea in one of the flats and to save me running off I might as well join them. To have tea it was necessary to purchase a ticket at a single location. At that point you would be allocated the flat to visit. This system made it easy to regulate the numbers of visitors going into any single house. There was no actual choice of flat; I was dreading our tickets being made out for my flat. Although my mother and cousin were paying for my tea, what Sister would say on my arrival for this proper tea I dared not think. Thankfully, we were allocated another flat for tea. The tea was very nicely presented for the guests to admire; possibly visiting adults thought our meals were always this nice. To me there was the pleasure of squash to drink with my meal rather than a mug of tea.

Finally, it was time for my mother and cousin to leave. Saying my farewells after a day of fun was in my mind far worse than when my mother normally left after a visit. I was unhappy but I did not show it at the point they left.

Eventually I returned to the flat. Instantly I was in trouble from Sister. She was cross that I had not returned to collect my bagged tea. I tried to explain that my mother and cousin had visited and I had been taken out to tea in one of the other flats. At this point, I was made to sit at the table and eat my bagged tea. With it being a little while since my full tea, I managed to get through it after showing my feelings. I did not bother with any supper a little later when it was time for bed, which for me came quite early. It was so easy to have a pleasant day ruined.

If Sister wanted to keep me out of mischief, sending me to bed was an easy option. Our bedtimes were earlier than many of our friends that we met at school. During the summer, having to lie in bed awake, whilst there was still plenty of daylight outside was boring. On the evenings that I was sent even earlier, living at the Home became really unbearable.

One event that was organised to raise funds on the Open Day was to belt the living daylights out of an old car. This was aimed more at the men. Some of the older boys might have liked to have a go, but actually paying to use a sledgehammer was not worth the money. During the day, the old car was reduced from a car that was too worn out for the road to something that had dents in every part imaginable and not one piece of glass remaining intact.

Once the Open Day was over, the car remained where it was first put; it was out of the way on a piece of waste ground. Eventually the groundsmen would take it away to the far side of the woods, where a small dip in the ground seemed to be the location for all manner of rubbish that could not be burnt.

To children an old car was a plaything. Soon the more careful ones had swept out the car of its broken glass. With the car sheltered by overhanging trees, it remained dry. At some point, it became my climbing frame. I did not indulge in sitting in the driver's seat pretending to drive. I climbed up from the inside and sat on the partly open metal sunroof. I was quite light and the thin metal roof could quite easily hold my weight. With the various men pounding the car the sunroof appeared to have become jammed in this partly open state, allowing a small thin child just enough room to crawl up through.

The roof decided to slide back into the fully open position. I fell forward; my mouth now took the full force of the top front rim of the car. This was a part of the car that was still undamaged; my mouth also had little effect on the car. The blood from my mouth and nose covered the top of the car, the seat, the front shelf and even the bonnet. As well as my regular nosebleed, I had managed to cut both my upper and lower lips and taken a good sock to my teeth. For many friends of my own age, this would have merely loosened their remaining first teeth. I was well ahead of them, my second teeth had appeared quite some time ago, and taken together with my height, it could give me the chance to appear older than I really was.

Some friends escorted me back to the flat. Sister was perhaps a little sick of my continual injuries. If my friends expected to see Sister concerned over my injuries and to be sympathetic, they saw her at her best. I was quickly whisked inside. Apparently, the telling off could be heard through the closed door and even when they had reached the ground outside the flat.

My face really ached, after swilling my mouth out with several glasses of water and mild disinfectant. Sister decided that a good sleep with a hot water bottle next to my face might take the pain away. The next day, there was a slight telling off for the blood on my pillow and sheets, but her mood compared to the day before was mild. I did not appear to have broken either my nose or my chin. In her mind, I was fit enough for school. Friends from yesterday eventually caught up with me; other than finding out if I had managed to break any bones, the amount of blood I seemed to drip around had given them the impression that I was very badly injured. Most were surprised at how Sister had reacted. All I could do was explain that this was how Sister normally acted; that I was returning too often with injuries might have been the true reason. Had a different member of our group had similar injuries, they might have been treated in a more sympathetic manner.

Once everything healed up, there was little to see any sign of me trying to chew through a car. My chin never did fully develop, and my front teeth remained pushed slightly back, but not eating my crusts at an early age might be another cause.

THE TARGET

One afternoon I had been outside at play with a friend; we had stopped by one of the trees on the main grassed area in the Home, facing some of the flats. Suddenly I felt a sharp pain in my knee; it was so sudden that I simply fell down. On getting up, there was blood coming from the inner part of my knee. The bet was that someone was quite close to us, with either a catapult or small toy gun that originally was meant to fire soft plaster pellets, and having run out of those, something like a small piece of flint was now used as ammo. The bushes were the most likely hiding place, but none of our enemies could be found. Escorted over to the small hospital, it might be best to get a plaster put over the cut; although the blood was not spurting out, there was a small constant trickle. The Nursing Sister was out, however I was soon attended to by one of the other staff. It was best not to say much about the cut being caused by something like a catapult, it would only cause problems. As the cut was clean, once the blood was wiped away, and a plaster put over the cut, all seemed fine. I headed back to the flat, my knee still stinging.

Sister was more unhappy over the blood that covered my sock than the cut to my knee; she remarked that for once, it was not the front of my knees that I was damaging. I was accused of climbing a tree to end up with this type of cut. It was best to let her have her own ideas of the injury; if I said that I thought one of the boys in the next block of flats had a catapult, she would have soon been on the warpath. The cut healed; there was a small lump under my skin which I took to be the remains of the scab. For some odd reason, once the scab had completely faded away there was still a little lump.

The adults only started to take more of an interest after I had been for several X-rays as part of our growth study tests in May. A morning off school meant several of us were very willing to be measured, weighed, X-rayed, photographed and generally prodded, every three months or so.

Later the Nursing Sister, the Governor, and the local doctor became interested in my knee. They found I had a small piece of metal in my knee; their solution was that I ought to have whatever was in my knee out; it appeared to be a gun pellet. The little hard lump was really just below the skin; I expected the Nursing Sister or the doctor just to remove it like a splinter. However, I was taken to a hospital in the next town for more X-rays. It was December before they decided they wanted to take the gun pellet out. It was originally expected that I would have a local anaesthetic, but from what the Nursing Sister told me, and the attention I received, it appeared, I was going to be given a full anaesthetic and put completely out. To the Nursing Sister this seemed far too much bother. I could guess that if she had been allowed, a small cut with a knife and the pellet would have been taken out in her hospital.

The most annoying matter was that I had to miss breakfast, however as my appointment was quite early in the morning, I would be back at the Home for lunch, but would probably miss afternoon school. I did not have any worries over the operation; I was more interested in what else was going on. The most painful part of the visit to the hospital was to have an injection in the rear. This really hurt; this one was not to put you out but to relax you. Then I was taken on a trolley to the operating theatre. I was afraid that the next injection was going to be even more painful, but there was just a minor prick in my arm, and I was told to slowly count. On waking up after the operation, all I wanted to do was sit up, but the hospital staff kept pushing my head down and telling me to lie still; it seemed to feel like I was rolling over. When I was allowed to sit up, there was nothing to see as the cut that had been made to the side of my knee was covered up with a bandage. It seemed I was lucky having the Nursing Sister with me, as she would be able to see that the cut healed properly. On our way back to the Home, I was told that there had been four stitches to keep the cut closed. I was not to go out playing football or to run about for the next couple of weeks; swimming and other such activities were also forbidden. When the cut had healed a little more, the stitches would be taken out; until that time the cut should be kept dry. I would have a fresh bandage put on when we arrived back, but as soon as possible, it would be best to let the air get to it.

I had a souvenir of my hospital visit. This was a clear plastic container, with the pellet that had been removed from my leg. At the point we had left the hospital this had been taken from me; apparently the Governor wanted to see it.

When I did get to look at the cut, it was far larger than I thought it would have been. It was just over an inch in length. There was no real pain; it was just stiff to walk on. It was easier to keep the leg almost straight and hop on it; the cut was just on the point that the knee bent. This was the first opportunity that the Nursing Sister had to see the cut. Her comments were that she could not understand why they had made a large cut; she could have made a small cut and pulled the pellet out with a pair of tweezers, possibly not needing to put any stitches into my leg at all. But I would be able to show my friends my latest battle scar. Soon I hobbled back to the flat accompanied by her, not having eaten since the previous evening; I was more concerned with wanting something to eat rather than resting. It was decided that it was best if I went to bed and was still for the rest of the day. I was soon washed and changing into my pyjamas before I could offer any protest. Eventually some soup and bread was brought to me. It was thought best that I only had a light meal at this stage. Once finished, boredom encouraged me to have a nap. When the others returned, as I was wearing pyjamas and the cut was covered up, there was little to show off. At teatime, I was allowed out of bed, then for the rest of the evening I was allowed the most comfortable chair.

The next school day was missed; it was felt that perhaps walking to school was a little too much for me. There was a visit to the Nursing Sister; the cut seemed to have healed enough to allow it to go without any covering, but again there was a warning not to play football. On returning to school, the cut and stitches were enough proof for the teachers to allow me to miss games lessons for the rest of the term, which disappointingly was very close.

At Christmas, there was a change to our bicycles. I had brought my own bicycle to the Home; this was now rather too small for me. The two oldest boys were getting a new bicycle each; this was partly paid from their paper round and in part by the Home as their Christmas present. As part of the deal, they would pass their two old bicycles down to two of us; these would now become our presents from the Home, and we would give our bicycles to the two younger boys; this deal seemed to work out the best for all.

Slowly my tastes in food changed. At tea and at other meals, I found the sweet spreads were actually to my liking. Marmite and peanut butter were still high on my lists of preferred tastes though. I was the only one who liked to put the OXO spread on my toast. Normally it would be used in gravy, but to me it was similar to Marmite in style although everyone else found it too salty. If you were the last one to scrape out the jar of any item, it gave you the privilege of opening the next jar. On starting the next jar of spread, it was the custom to engrave your initials into the top of the spread before taking the first spoonful.

Until coming to the Home, trips to the dentist had been quite a rare event. Losing most of my first teeth before the age of six, there was never any real chance for any decay to set in for most of my teeth. The few first teeth that were still in place soon started to decay within months of my arrival. If sweets were to blame, it was the increase in cheap boiled sweets, rather than the smaller quantities of more luxury sweets from my mother.

POCKET MONEY

Saturday was the most important day of the week. Our mornings were generally occupied with indoor chores. At the end of lunch, pocket money was given out. Deductions for items like Church, Cubs and any stoppages for breakages, Holiday fund, Christmas fund, School events and the like were kept back. The amount of money you received depended on how old you were. It was thought that the older you were the more money you needed. Try to explain this idea when an older boy is scoffing a large amount of sweets in front of a smaller boy, and it appears unfair.

Most Saturday afternoons any money left once the deductions had been made would be spent on sweets. Until this point in time whilst I had been with my mother, sweets came at various periods during the week when I was good – not vast amounts but just enough to make me willing to behave at times.

An organised trip to the sweet shop was the normal way of spending our money. Age group–wise I was in the middle; the older ones were allowed to go off as a group. I was grouped with the younger girl, and taken by either Sister or the Helper to the sweet shop. The apparent reason for this was that at eight, I was thought too young to leave the Home on my own. That I went to the annexe of the school either on my own or with one other boy, and we had to cross various roads on our journey to and from school did not seem to count. Until my arrival, the younger girl had often been taken out by her older sister, but my arrival now made it worthwhile to allow the older girl her freedom to be with her own age group.

When you did get to the sweet shop you spent all your money. There was no use for actual money at the Home. Sweets purchased, you returned to the Home. I soon found out that it was best to eat all the sweets before tea. Older boys finding that you had sweets might arrange an unfair swap or decide that you were offering them the rest of your sweets as a gift. To the older boys one of your large humbugs was equal to one of their fruit pips in a swap.

Eventually I was allowed out on my own to the sweet shop. Although there was a busy main road that we had to cross, a pedestrian crossing made the matter reasonably safe if we were alert. The older group was not really something I wanted to be involved with, from what I had learnt, it appeared on occasions some of their behaviour would not have pleased Sister. If I had been with them, I could easily guess that I might be the one landed in trouble.

The other reason for often being able to be on my own was the older boys' love of football. Special trips to a nearby town to watch a league match, and a treat they willingly used the majority of their pocket money. Only on one occasion did I let the adults talk me into going with the group. Most of my pocket money was taken from me to pay for the entrance fee. Eventually we arrived at the ground. Being taken in the small van was never my favourite way of travelling. With only a small amount of money left, I decided to buy some sweets to give me some pleasure while standing in the cold watching a football match that I had paid for. The sweet shop near to the football ground was quite busy, so there was no time to waste on choosing how to spend the remaining money. Cheap boiled sweets were possibly the best value. My odd taste in sweets was often not my friends'; Winter Mixture was possibly the most revolting choice I could make, and few wanted to make even poor swaps for my sweets.

I chose a plain cough sweet marked at 6d on the jar. As I was in a rush, I had not noticed that instead of 6d per quarter these were 6d per ounce. As I had asked for sixpence worth, there was no problem for the assistant; although there were only a few sweets for the money, they were strong. At the Home, I was one of the only boys of my age to be able to suck a Victory V lozenge to its end, without either crunching it up or spitting it out. If older boys tried this trick on me, I was quite happy to accept their free sweet when they liked to tease younger children. Asking for a second one normally upset them. Today's cough sweets were strong, not hot but just full flavour. During the match I slowly went through my purchase. It was not necessary to eat another one as soon as one was finished, the taste stayed in my mouth; there was a nice numbing sensation.

Eventually the match ended, we were taken back in the van, and returned to the Home ready for tea. I could actually name the local team that we visited, but as to who they played was forgotten. From that point on, if there was ever a suggestion that I could go and watch football, it was something that I opposed. It appeared that if you misbehaved during the week, you were not thought good enough to go and see the football. If only I had known that rule on the Saturday I was selected to go and see the match.

During the summer, I spent as much time as I could outside. If this was spent alone, it was more by choice rather than lack of friends. One of my favourite areas was near to the small cemetery; this was too far from the main area of the Home for many to bother with, so I could be left to my own thoughts. The quiet solitude was broken only by the sound of a train passing. If it made me feel sad, it was because the trains were heading in the direction of London, where I would have preferred to be. The other sound that seemed to carry for miles was the sound of an ice-cream van. Whilst in London it was a regular treat to have an ice cream from one of the many vans that passed. In the Home it was wishful thinking.

At the side of the administration block, a flight of steps led down to a cellar that was always flooded. The depth of the water depended on if it had recently rained. When I had first arrived, as a torture by the older boys, I had been made to go down the steps and into the water, then to walk into the cellar whilst the door was closed behind me. Eventually I was let out. This was a game according to the older boys. On the first trip inside, I was a little frightened as the only light that came in was from the gap around the closed door. There was the threat from the older boys that if I ever got them in trouble, they would bring me down here and shut me inside.

During my stay, I had found this a place of refuge; the water was normally only a few inches deep at the entrance so it was easy to go inside and hide. Few of my enemies were ever prepared for wading in water, even if it was only a few inches deep. When the water was deeper than normal, cold water running inside my wellingtons was not as bad as meeting ones foe face to face. The water was always dirty and stagnant. On leaving my hiding place I was occasionally in luck in finding that waste washing water was running from the laundry room. This was far nicer to wash with as it was often warm, rather than the cold water from the tap that the groundsman used. No attempt was made to solve the problem of the flooded cellar; to me it was simply a lucky place few others would venture into by choice

Our Sister had rather an old fashioned view of how the flats should be run. Her ideals were those of the early 1950s. There was nothing wrong in this as we were well cared for; however by the 1960s, the idea that we should integrate more with the outside world was now slowly coming to fruition. Perhaps children in other flats did have more activities outside the grounds, but for our flat and a few others that were run by the older Sisters, life had not changed that much over the last decade or so.

On a Sunday, our Sister believed that any play should be quiet and respectful for that day. Although we did go out to play in the late afternoon, any ideas we had of activities that most children were allowed, was discouraged. The older children in the flat were trusted over such matters, however the wearing of football boots and the like for active play was not allowed. The younger members of the family were really too young to obey such a directive. If our Sunday afternoons needed occupying, then Sunday school once afternoon lunch was over, kept us in order. During my time of torture of Sunday afternoons spent with a small group of other children in the administration block, it was possible to look out of the windows and see the majority of the children in the Home happily out at unrestricted play.

MY GIRLFRIEND

To us children some of the staff could be quite odd over rules and punishments. I had been out at play in the grounds during the afternoon and had met up with a girl of about my age from another flat. We both must have been about eight. I had been at the Home for a few months and generally knew the rules that we had to follow.

Playing with a girl would not have been the normal way of passing the time. We must have been bored with things to do, and had just chosen each other's company to pass the time. As the weather was dull and showery, there were few other children about. We were wearing identical brown raincoats. Originally these had been smart school raincoats, but now rather shabby; they had been classed as play clothes by the Sisters who looked after us.

It was mid afternoon; we must have been passing the time before going in for tea. Not really soaked, we had slowly made our journey around the rear of the flats, and had ended up at the side of the administration block. Neither of us was up to mischief of any kind. For me this form of play was quite sedate. A small flight of three steps led up to a side entrance; this had a large porch awning. The reason for our choice was that it gave a little shelter from the light shower of rain.

Most of our play was hopping from one step to another, and then trying to do two steps at a time. Our final part of this form of play was to jump onto the ground. There were no large puddles that would get us soaked and only a small film of water splashed very slightly when our wellingtons landed. Had we both been rolling on the ground even with our play clothes, I could understand the staff getting cross. Our coats were clean, we had not attempted any rough play, they might be a little damp, but we did not have any mud on them. One of the Sisters came out of the door; it was easy to see that in her mind we should not have been playing on the steps, but to the pair of us, we could not really see what harm we had done or that we had broken any rules. She was one of the older Sisters. I did not recognise her from being in charge of one of our nearby flats; all I could do was think that she must be from the flats on the other side of the grounds.

If we had been playing in an area where we shouldn't have been, the reaction of the staff would be to send us on our way if we had not really been up to mischief. The Sister beckoned us inside and as we entered both of us pulled down the hoods of our coats; as we were now sheltered there was little point in having our hoods up. Instantly was a telling off, that she did not want to see our faces. To comply with her wishes we put our hoods up again, although our faces were of course still visible. Now the pair of us were questioned as to what we were up to. All we said was that we had been hopping on the steps; neither of us could really have given any other reply. If I had done something wrong, I could be sure that the Sister in charge of me would soon be told, but at this moment I could not think what rule we had broken. Both of us were now taken down a passage and into a side room. This was a laundry room with a selection of sinks for washing clothes. There was a small alcove at one side of the room; we were told to stand there. Width and length-wise, it must have been about four foot square; there was just enough room for the pair of us to stand against the wall.

The Sister was not telling us what we had done wrong. We were told to stay there in silence. Questioning a Sister over such an instruction was simply something we never did as it could easily have meant the slipper. We stood and waited for the next instruction. The Sister now walked off leaving us alone.

If she was going to contact our Sisters over our behaviour, she must know which flats we were from, as neither of us had been asked our names or which Sisters looked after us. Knowing we might be in some form of trouble we waited. Neither of us spoke. If the Sister was close, we might be in the wrong for talking. We waited what seem to be ages, but in reality, it might have only been five or ten minutes. The Sister came back. The only instruction we were now given was that we were to sit on the floor. There was no telling off, just this odd request. We sat down together in the small alcove. Nothing had been said as to how we were to sit. For comfort as our coats were damp, we sat with our legs straight out. The Sister apparently was satisfied that we had complied, and went off again.

Until this moment, I did not know the name of the girl I had been playing with. It was Helen. Once Sister had gone, we talked a little about ourselves just to pass the time. We now asked each other what it was all about; all I could think of was that the Sister was probably waiting for my Sister to come, so that our mischief could be reported. It was just that we did not think we had been up to any mischief, in the normal way. If you were in trouble, you would be accused of a wrongdoing and it was up to you to try to get out of it.

Other than being told to keep our hoods up, stand in the alcove and then to sit, the Sister had not said anything else. We were left alone for a slightly longer period. My only thought was that it must be getting near teatime, and that I would be in trouble if I were late. If Sister were coming over, then my only lateness would be if she delayed coming over.

The Sister came back; Helen asked 'can we go now please?' It was polite and the way it had been said, I did not think would get us into trouble. There was a simple reply of 'No, I've told you to stay there.' We were left alone. Not knowing the layout of the room or adjoining passages, I did not want to move away from our alcove, and if we did try to leave, whatever trouble we were in would only be made worse. The Sister came back, looked at us without saying anything and went off. What trouble we were in I could only guess at, and why had the Sister not wanted to tell us what we had done wrong.

Both of us were fidgeting slightly, although the alcove was big enough to sit in, we had damp raincoats and were sitting on a cold floor, it was uncomfortable. Helen told me she would soon need to go for a pee, and asked did I think the Sister would allow her to go. From the window we could see that the light was fading, although it was not yet dark. I knew teatime had now passed, and after sitting on this cold floor, I too would soon need to go for a pee.

This room had a few lights on, so that it was not actually in darkness. There was nothing really to be frightened of; it was just that the Sister had been so odd with us. On her next visit, we both asked if we could be allowed to visit the lavatory. We were not crying with desperation, but she might have guessed that we really needed to go. She just told us to stay sat down.

Disobeying a Sister for any reason was never worth it; the one rule you always had to follow was obeying a Sister. All we could do was sit and wait. Sister passed a few minutes later but said nothing. Now I knew I needed to go, I was on the point of getting up to see if I could find a lavatory or the way out, when

Helen asked me to stay. I mentioned that I was starting to get desperate; Helen seemed to agree that she would not be able to wait much longer. I had not really been very keen seeing what was beyond the alcove; asking me to stay only made up my mind that I should continue sitting here.

Helen was fidgeting, and then came the announcement that she had done it in her knickers. This was the limit of my waiting. I could not hold on any longer either, but I was too afraid to move from this spot.

We both held hands. The trouble we were in was slowly getting worse; it was a joke between us, that the floor was a little warmer now. The Sister paid us another visit whilst we were in tears. We did not know what our punishment was going to be. This was odd; the Sister did not say anything and just left us. Our tears now became a full-blown crying event. If one of us started to stop crying, the other one soon started the other off again. The only noise we heard was a door slamming somewhere in the building. If this was our Sisters coming to punish us, our crying now became a howl. It was neither the Sister nor our own Sisters, but the Governor. His first question was, why were we sitting here. All we could tell him was that we had been told to sit here by one of the Sisters.

Both of us were helped up, each of us was shaking, it was partly from the cold and partly about the trouble we were in. All we were told was that it might be best if we now returned to our flats. I expected to be let out of the building to make my way back to my flat and face the reception from Sister. The Governor now escorted us out of the building; I looked up at the clock it was now after seven. We had been in that laundry room for over four hours. The Governor was asking each of us which flats we were in, then both of us were taken to our flats.

I waited on the doorstep as Helen was ushered into her flat. She was crying in front of her Sister and trying to explain that she was sorry that she was late and we could not help wetting ourselves, as the Sister we had been with would not let us leave the room to visit the toilet. Helen then went further inside the flat. The Governor had a word with her Sister and then came back to me.

Now alone, I started to cry again. I was told that I was not in any trouble, and Sister would probably give me a nice warm bath when we got to the flat. When we arrived at our flat he had a quick word with Sister whilst I stood in the corridor. Eventually he left. I was worried about what Sister had in mind for me. There was no telling off; her main comment was I ought to get out of these wet clothes. I was taken straight to the bathroom and stripped off. There was not any way that Sister could not spot my damp underpants and trousers, but nothing was mentioned. A warm bath was run, once in it I was left alone while she went to get my pyjamas.

I expected some of the others to come and gloat over the trouble I was in, but only Sister returned. It was thought best that I went to bed. I was escorted to my bedroom; I expected that I would now receive the slipper. I was then asked would I like something to eat? This was odd. If I were in trouble, the last thing Sister would be offering me would be something to eat. I nodded; I just did not feel like talking at this moment.

Left alone I was soon in tears again; I could not think what I had done wrong. Sister returned to bring me some food and comfort me. I ate a little, but I did not seem to have an appetite. It was not that I was afraid of Sister, but I just could not think what I had done wrong earlier in the day. Sister comforted me a little more and told me to get some sleep. The other three came to bed later; apart from visiting the lavatory late at night, I stayed asleep until the following morning.

In the morning it seemed like a bad dream; the other three on being woken by Sister rushed off to the bathroom, and I was left alone for a quiet talk. It appeared that we had not done anything wrong; we should forget about it. I was told that the Sister we had met could be a little forgetful at times; she had retired a few years ago and now came over at odd times just to help. She might have forgotten why we there in the first place. None of the others asked me about why I did not turn up for tea yesterday; I could guess Sister had told them not to bother me. Eventually the day started as normal, and noisy commotion ruled the flat once again.

Later I met up with Helen. She could not think what it had all been about; the only part we were happy about was that we had not been punished. I told Helen that Sister did not blame me for having wet my pants, and did not seem to mind. If something like that had happened in front of my mother, I would have been in serious trouble. I would have been back to cold baths and the plimsoll as punishment. Sister seemed to realise that it was not my fault on this occasion. I knew that if it happened again, Sister would request that I wear a pair of waterproof pants out to play, as I still was not trusted on long coach journeys by her. Helen now told me that when she first came to the Home a few years ago, her Sister had made her wear them every day when she went to the nursery school. Only when she started infant school did the Sister think she was old enough not to need them.

The pair of us often arranged to meet up when we were out at play. We would take ourselves off to the remote parts of the grounds. We seemed to share some bond; it was not something we could explain to each other. Sitting down and just trying to work out how things went on at the Home seemed to take up most of our time. Allowing other children from our flats into our time together was something we did not want. I did not really think of her as a girlfriend; at my age such things were thought to be soppy. Helen brought my sheltered life over the ways that boys and girls could act more up to date. It was possibly for this reason I wanted to keep such meetings secret from the other boys in my flat. If they had found out and told on me, the punishments I would have received would be unthinkable. Helen had no reason to tell anyone in her flat that she met me, so our happy times were kept secret from everyone. As we went to different schools, there was nothing else to link us together.

THE GOVERNOR

Almost everyone at the Home was afraid of an encounter with the Governor. It was not the case that we were always caught by him doing wrong deeds. He had the ability to be at any location where you were up to mischief or simply doing a minor deed that you knew was wrong. Some of the Sisters and Houseparents sent their children straight over to him when in trouble. The Sister I was with never sent anyone to the Governor unless it was very serious. Having been in the Home longer than he had, it was thought that with her experience she had a better idea of how we should be controlled.

With my agile and fast movements, I was often in a position to spot the Governor and depart the site of any crime before he descended. Often a clue to his whereabouts was to keep an eye on where his car was parked, if it was located other than by his house, it meant he was in the area – not the best time to be found in the orchard or near the incinerator. If you were a younger boy, the small cane or baton that he often carried with him, gave a clue to what you could expect, if you were caught committing a crime that did not warrant serious punishment. A quick very light swipe and you knew not to be caught at that activity again.

My first real encounter with the Governor had been a few months after my arrival; a group of older boys had decided to make a raid on the local outdoor model railway club that was next to the grounds of the Home. This was run by adults, for the enjoyment of adults, and we were not invited.

The model railway club was located on a plot of land that at one time had really been part of the estate of the Home. A disused railway cutting separated the two locations, and although this was really out of bounds, we used this as a wild play area where few staff from the Home were ever likely to visit.

To show that we were not welcome in the club, a tall gate was padlocked shut when not in use. Surrounding the club area was a fence with barbed wire; this was in a way odd for something in the Home: it would have been thought that any fences would be used to keep us in not to keep us out.

For a challenge, the older boys had decided that if adults wanted to keep us out there must be a good reason. All that could be viewed from outside the fence were lengths of concrete girders with lengths of railway track. For the inquisitive, there had to be something very special for the need to keep us out. If damage was done to property in the Home, it was quite easy for the adults to work out the most likely persons responsible.

Possibly recent war films of prisoners escaping from camps were the basis for the event. The older boys took pride in finding ways over the wire. A few of us younger members were used as lookouts, and if any adults were spotted we should shout out a code word to alert those inside the wire. Had any adults been spotted, shouting out something would have brought far more attention to us than had we just been thought playing in the vicinity. Eventually the older boys emerged. They had found the hut where the members met. Nothing worth removing had been found except for a small amount of loose change. The money was now divided up according to age and deed. We were quite pleased with our share of the spoils and soon made ourselves scarce. All of us knew that if our Sisters found money on us, there would be many questions as to how we had come across it. Pocket money on a Saturday was soon spent and apart from church money or money for cubs, there were very few left with money after Saturday afternoon.

That particular day was a club day. Originally designed to teach and inform, it had turned into a meeting place where the latest records could be played and the older ones could show off the latest dance craze. For the eight to ten year-olds, it was more of a place to cause a nuisance. The club was the one place where you could spend money in the Home. A small tuck shop that sold fizzy drink and a few sweets catered for the lucky few that still had a small amount of money. A few things were offered at less than the normal shop price, but few of us ever had any money left to take advantage. Together with a friend, we had soon spent our money on a bottle of fizzy drink and some sweets. We stayed around, as when you returned the bottle the deposit money was given back enabling more sweets to be purchased; if we had not been greedy we would not have been found out.

At what moment the Governor had been informed of the deed we did not know. Picking the very day that the model club had its meeting was not the best idea of the older boys to mount the raid. Had it been done the following day then it would have been several days before the matter became known.

With the grounds being generally deserted, the Governor had come across to the hall where the club was held. If the day's takings were up, he soon found it out. Grabbing one of the older boys, who was the least likely to have any spending money, soon brought forth the names of his close accomplices.

One by one the gang formed, and he managed to round up most of those who had been involved. The normal rule was that you did not split on anyone, but it did not apply if you were an older boy telling on a younger boy, or by dropping someone else in it your punishment might be slightly less.

All of us were marched outside and formed into a line. From where we stood, we could see that the others who had been in the club had come to see what was in store for us. They kept at enough distance to be not really in view, and even the Governor knew they were there. Possibly them watching our punishment was the worst thing that could happen. The shares of the money were soon worked out until the missing amount was accounted for.

Several small scraps of paper were now handed to us. The figure of money we had stolen was written on each. These were to be handed to our Sisters when we returned indoors; this amount would be deducted from our next pocket money, and anyone failing to hand the slips in would lose twice the amount the following week or for however many weeks it took.

The punishment was not yet over. Each of us now received a whack across the palm of one of our hands with his baton, and was given the instruction to go and return to our flats. All of us seemed to have the stick in a similar manner. It did not hurt; we did flinch when the blow first landed, but there was no pain. Our audience was made to think that we were severely dealt with. None of us let on that it did not hurt; we let the others think we were just brave over the matter.

The thought of returning to the flat was not a happy one. Losing pocket money and getting even a light whack was one thing; having to admit to Sister what you had been up to and the punishment that would come from her would be far worse. The older three boys from my flat had not been involved in this crime, and having seen them witness our removal from the club I could guess that Sister already knew I was in trouble.

There was little time wasted by Sister over the questions on what I had been doing. The story that I had not actually been into the model railway was believed; however it was just stupid of me to take the money off the older boys. Sister thought losing next week's pocket money was a just punishment; I did not argue at this moment, that the Governor had only requested the missing money be returned. It was thought that for the next month I should miss going to the club.

SCHOOL

In the second year of junior school, our old building was closed down. We now joined the main school where two new classrooms had been built in the playground to take us. One activity at school that occupied a large amount of my time was the swapping of possessions. Minor swaps would be amongst friends, and then other boys in the same year would be involved, followed by boys older and younger. Often the item you were acquiring was not even the thing you wanted, but if you could provide the person that you were finally swapping with the item they were looking for, it made the deal. After Christmas was one of the best times to do any exchanges. I was wise enough to avoid any of the swaps that involved large toys or items that were easily identifiable. Marbles, cars, puzzles, pens and the like could easily pass around the playground several times before getting completely lost as to who really owned them. Often it was easy to witness a few that made stupid or unfair swaps. A few days later, a parent would be up at school trying to find the culprit that had their child's best possession and demand that it be returned. Some boys had toys that were of little interest to them, and offering money rather than a swap I did quite well. At the Home my locker often had the toy items changing quite regularly. If I had any doubt over a recent possession, taking it back to London for a few weeks often let things cool down a little.

One of the reasons for getting into trouble was due to my reactions, having being teased over the colour of my skin. In the London school, I had found no problems; at this school, I was finding that I was now being teased more than ever before. Once a few knew that this upset me and I became angry, the teasing was done more for fun on their part rather than anything malicious. It was equal to that given to a fat child or any child who does not seem to fit in with the majority. When there were groups teasing me there was little I could do. The only chance of retaliation was when one of my tormentors became isolated from the group. The minor fight and arguments that then started was the main reason I was often in trouble.

Most of the teachers thought I should ignore such name-calling. For a short period this was possible. When it went on every day, my short temper tended to get the better of me. One of the favourite names to call me was based on a character from a comic that most of the boys had read in a story entitled 'Packi and His Elephant'. The regular tease was to shout out "Packi where's your elephant?" I regarded that as one of the less hateful comments.

SCHOOL PUNISHMENTS

At the age of nine most of my lessons were with our own class teacher, it gave me the most chances of attention over any poor behaviour, and was now seen by her for my wrongdoings. Punishment-wise I was more embarrassed to be hit in front of others; I was apt to show my tender feelings. Crying in front of my class was far worse in my mind than the original punishment. If my friends were able to be brave, they did not often show their true feelings. If I was a nuisance, I never really learnt to behave at this school. Each time I was questioned over my latest activity, I never seemed to be able to explain why I did so many things that they disapproved. The events just seemed to happen; it was never my intention to be disruptive in any way.

If our teacher decided that a punishment with her 18-inch ruler on our legs was not the correct method, you were asked to remain after the rest of the class had been dismissed. Most of my punishments were now after the lesson had finished. Alone with the teacher it allowed for a more involved telling off that would not have been possible during a lesson period. Questioned in this way, it might be possible to have a good enough reason for one's behaviour; this then allowed release without any punishment. A few in our class found that there was one stage worse than the ruler on the legs. With all the other female teachers in the school, if a punishment like the cane were necessary, they would send you to the Headmaster. Our teacher seemed to be the exception.

Our teacher could use the threat of punishment. Her ruler was always on the top of her desk; if we were coming close to it being used, she would often tap it lightly on the desk. If we had any sense we would then behave. The cane was never brought out to threaten us; she used the fear of those who had already received it, to announce to others that it was kept in her drawer and would be taken out when you were to be given it. This was a very good way of keeping the fear of such a punishment in our minds.

A few of our friends never did believe us when we told them about our teacher keeping a cane in her desk; they always thought it was only the Headmaster or a couple of the masters that ever gave you the cane. The few of us that had received the cane from our teacher were in hope that the non-believers would soon be shown it. In the normal way these friends never got as far as being hit with the ruler because of their constant good work.

In my mind, the cane that our teacher used did not really count as a cane. This was not the long bamboo cane that I had experienced in the Headmaster's office, or at the other schools I had attended. It was a shorter thinner smooth cane about the same length as her ruler and did not hurt as much as the normal cane. With this cane, there was a second advantage for me. As it was not the official junior school cane, as she referred to it as the 'infants' cane', there was never the need to enter it onto the punishment pages; only when the official junior school cane was given, did it have to be recorded. The Governor from the Home when he paid his visits to our school would not know of my deeds. I was just happy the cane was always given without an audience.

Our teacher had two methods of using the cane. If the punishment needed to be a little harsher than the ruler used on the legs then the cane was used on your legs. To be hit on the legs with the cane was painful; it seemed to sting for such a long time afterwards and the marks could last for several days. There was often the request by our teacher that we should pull down our socks; this exposed the flesh of our legs just below the knee, allowing more pain to be felt. In a way I was happy over this order; once your socks were pulled up after the punishment, there was no sign of having had the cane. If you had gone a stage further than the cane on your legs, it was then given on your hands. The cane could land anywhere from the centre of your palm to across your fingers; if just your fingers were struck then it did really hurt.

Once over, I was allowed to sit down where a little more about my poor behaviour was discussed. I would now find my teacher consoling me and explaining that it was not her intention to make me cry, it was that she had run out of options of how to curb my bad behaviour. With any other teacher that had ever punished me, there was always hatred in my mind after the event. The cane given by my teacher did hurt, but I was unable to feel dislike for her in any way. I was happier that none of my friends had been around to witness my punishment. Only once did I feel that I had been punished in a more severe way than normal on one of the days I was given the cane on my legs. That time it had really hurt; it might have been on a day when she was angry with others and had taken it out on me.

Our teacher was quite capable of making one cry with an extended telling off; there were few in our class that could take a telling off that lasted more than ten minutes without crumbling. When I met the rest of the class outside, on many occasions I allowed them to think it had been a telling off I had received. If I announced that I had been given the cane, the information might get back to the Houseparent, and I did not want a second punishment for getting into trouble at school. Three on each leg was the maximum I ever received.

STAFF

Each flat normally had two full-time staff looking after us. When I arrived, our flat was slightly different, having only seven of us and only the Sister full-time; the helper was often there only part-time. When Sister had any time off, the helper looked after us on her own. It became known to all that Sister would soon retire. A new lady now came in, first as the day relief for Sister, then as a trainee Houseparent. It was finally revealed shortly before Sister actually retired, this lady was going to be our new permanent Houseparent. The staffing level was also increased; we would have a second adult permanently to join us; the only point when it would drop to one adult would be when one of them had a day off.

Our numbers now increased to ten to match the other flats, by adding two young boys and a young girl. The four youngest now formed into a group. The eldest girl was on the point of leaving school and going to college. Her presence in the flat had been more to help Sister than to play with us. The other four were older than me, and had been in the Home far longer than I had. They formed into a second group of four; I just did not fit into either group easily. For most of the time I had to be placed in one of the groups – neither of which really wanted me, nor I them.

With the new Houseparent, we found our lives were much easier on chores; but to me there were still too many restrictions over my life. The Houseparent told me that if I wet the bed, I would be given the slipper. On going to bed, I was in fear of the punishment for bed-wetting. I soon learnt that it was not an idle threat; even on Christmas morning at the age of nine there was no amnesty for wetting my bed.

One matter we found different between Sister and the new Houseparent was in the way that they reacted if we were in trouble. We had all been used to what to expect if we were in Sister's bad books: first there would be a strong telling off then a selection of chores would be set. Once Sister was satisfied that you had learnt your lesson, the chores would come to an end. If Sister gave me the slipper I would be taken to the bedroom and punished and that was then the end of the matter.

With our new Houseparent there was a very different reaction. We had been quite used to Sister getting angry over very minor matters, but she never physically hit us out of anger. If you were close to the Houseparent, you could find that she hit out at you; often it was the back of her hand and wrist that would land on your head or shoulder. As children, most of us were quite light in build; the Houseparent was quite short and stocky. One of her hits could actually knock you down. If I were going to be punished, I would have rather have been hit with the slipper or the cane. To get her hand suddenly hitting you was upsetting. We soon learnt that if we had done wrong, it was best not to be close if she was losing her temper.

I was also given the slipper from the Houseparent. The first time other than for bed-wetting, was after I had failed to clean my play shoes before lunch. They were not very muddy and as I was going out in them after lunch, I had just put them in the shoe cupboard. If they had been very dirty and started to drop bits of mud onto the other clean shoes, I could see why the Houseparent would be cross. As there was just a little dirt, I could not see the point in cleaning them if I was going out as soon as lunch was over.

There was a telling off; that I did not go straight away and clean them was the reason that I should be punished. Unlike Sister, I was now taken forcibly in front of everyone to my bedroom. There might have been a chance if I had really apologised at that moment to get off, but within seconds it was too late; I was made to lie across the end of the bed after she demanded that I should give her one of my slippers. The hits came quite fast; four heavy blows soon ended the matter of not cleaning my shoes. I was in tears but not given any chance to recover. I was now led out of the room and back to where my shoes were. Now I was told clean them; I was not going out again that day.

I annoyed the Houseparent after this punishment by never wearing my play shoes again. Every time we were sent out to play, I wore either plimsolls or wellingtons. Slowly the shine on my play shoes vanished. The Houseparent did not ask me to clean them again. When my feet grew to the next size up, the play shoes were removed and never replaced.

The second time I managed to get the Houseparent cross enough to use the slipper on me was when one of the younger boys said that I had taken some of his sweets. I was innocent of this matter; he had been foolish enough to leave a half-open packet of sweets around; the first one passing had simply taken them.

I was finishing the last of my own sweets at the time. Had I spat it out, he would have easily seen it was not a type he had purchased. By the time the Houseparent was told of the loss of his sweets, I had finished my sweet so there was no way I could prove my innocence. Now accused of stealing his sweets and teasing him by eating them in front of him, meant I had to be punished. The journey to my bedroom was made.

NATIONAL CHILDREN'S HOME, THE GIFT HOUSE OF OLD BOYS AND GIRLS, HARPENDEN.

The Houseparent wanted to make the punishment hurt. I was angry at having to be punished over something that I had not done, so there was little co-operation over taking my trousers down and giving her one of my slippers. Only the threat that if I did not take down my trousers, she would remove both my trousers and underpants, got me to co-operate over the matter. At the age of almost ten, I would have been too embarrassed to be hit on my rear without anything on, even if there were no others to see. I was already in tears with anger, before the blow even hit. The three blows were as heavy as the previous time; more tears came quite easily. I was told to pull my shorts up, and asked did I now admit to stealing the sweets; my anger was still there so I refused to admit my guilt for something I had not done. Having stood up I was now bent back across my bed and a further three hits with the slipper were given after my trousers were taken down again. I was really in tears.

I was taken still crying to the boy who had lost his sweets, and told to say sorry. Having had the slipper, I was not in any mood to apologise to a younger child. Just inches away from him, my anger got the better of me: one slight shove from me and telling him I did not take his sweets ended my freedom. Removed at speed, it was possibly a surprise to all that I was not clouted all the way to my bedroom. The only comments from the Houseparent were that I should know not to steal. This time my trousers were not taken down; six hits came in quick succession. Pain-wise it now really hurt, having a dozen hits I thought was an impossible number for such a minor offence.

I had gone past the crying stage; the Houseparent ignored my screaming. I was not going to be returned to the others. As it was early afternoon, it was too early to send me to bed. My bed was now stripped of all its blankets and sheets. I was told to lie on my bed until I was thought of good enough behaviour to rejoin the others. Knowing how the mind of the Houseparent worked, I would have thought she would have told me to lie on my back, but I was allowed to lie on my front. As she left, I was told that she did not want to see me out of the room for any reason.

My crying slowly stopped. The pain however was still there to the full; it felt as if my rear was hot and cold at the same moment. Unlike with the cane there were no actual ridges that I could feel, it was an all-over throbbing pain. I must have stayed lying on my front for a long time. One of the older boys sneaked in and stood by the door – he was risking similar punishment just for his visit. I was told that the Houseparent was not in a mood any more, and that soon she would be in to see me. It was now known that I had not taken the sweets; one of the girls had put them safe to stop them getting eaten, and she had only just come back from playing outside, so did not know that the Houseparent had accused me of taking them. Within seconds, he departed. I should have been happy to hear that I was innocent, but it was too late, I had already been punished. Shortly the Houseparent came in. I was not in any mood for her, even if there was an apology, I kept my head buried in my pillow and faced the wall. Now I was told to get up from my bed. It was not really an apology; it was suggested that had I not pushed the boy, I would not have been in so much pain.

During tea I stood up to eat, the others took my standing up to show that I had really been hit. Although they did not know the number of times, they knew it had been quite high in number. After tea was finished I was on the list for washing up. To make up for the punishment I was let off, but going to watch the television was a little painful. When my normal bedtime came I was not hurried off but I was allowed to stay up as late as the older ones. Being punished that day did have a few benefits, as I was able to watch a couple of programmes that I would not normally see.

When we were sent off to bed, the older three begged to see what my rear was like. Their description was that it was blue and red. I was given a mirror to hold so I could see the reflection in the main mirror; it did not look that bad and the pain had generally gone now except if I touched the main area. Once in bed, I spent my night on my front or on my side. The following morning I was back to normal and had more or less forgiven the Houseparent. I was excused chapel that day; I hated to think what sitting on the hard wooden seat would have been like. For lunch, I seemed to be given slightly better portions of food.

I thought school on Monday was going to be normal, but when it came to leaving the flat to go off to school I was kept back until last, and then told that I could have the day off. I knew the Houseparent did not want me telling all my friends about the punishment. Now alone, we came to an agreement. If I did not tell my friends, I might find the odd reward came my way if I was good. I could now see some pleasure in life; telling my friends at school how I was punished was not really something I would have done. In the normal way, I would not even tell them over being hit by a teacher – telling on the staff at the Home was even less likely. For a little while, my life at the Home was easier, when the entire matter was forgotten and everything returned to normal.

When I was to be punished by the Houseparent in the evening, I would be taken to her sitting room, so as not to disturb the younger boy in my room who had already gone to bed. Often my own slipper was not requested; as her sitting room was next to the shoe cupboard it was easier for her to select one of the larger slippers from the shelves. If they were all in use, then one of the rubber galoshes that belonged to the older girls was chosen. With her room being fairly cramped, if I were to bend over there would not be enough room for her to get a good enough swing at me. The palms of my hands were the targets on these occasions.

On the days the Houseparent had time off, the helper was in sole charge. Some of the older boys were a little more mischievous, but we all knew that anything we did would be reported to the Houseparent on her return. It appeared that I was not to be given any leeway over my activities so a few of my actions resulted in the slipper. There was the choice offered to me by the helper, either I could accept the slipper now or wait for the decision by the Houseparent on her return.

The slipper from the helper was always quite light. There might have been the chance that the helper would have forgotten and not reported me. I chose punishment at that moment; it seemed an easy way out and was soon over. If I received the slipper for bed-wetting from the helper, it was in font of the other two before we went off to the bathroom;.this to me was a little embarrassing, but I was never in tears.

When the Houseparent took over from Sister the chores lessened slightly, but it was easy to see that a few other flats could be wonderful to live in. At one point when our flat was closed down for redecoration and minor alterations to the layout, we were divided up between several other flats for a week or so. I was placed in a flat where the others were my age or slightly younger.

The style of life was so different. Although there was no real misbehaviour, the flat seemed to run so smoothly. Chores were not things that were either ordered or required; if you did help out, it was through wanting to be helpful, rather than being told to do something. There were no punishments. Even when a boy of my age who normally lived there wet his bed, he did not receive the slipper in the morning.

Meals were strange as for almost every meal we were given a choice of what we would like to eat. The meals and general life it appeared were normal and not put on for guests. Eventually our flat was ready and we appeared from our various locations. If most of us had experienced slightly different ways of life, trying to hint that other ways of running a flat were possible, such matters were soon quashed and our more boring existence returned.

The Houseparent brought a few ideas that were more modern into the flat. The walls now had a little more decoration. When Sister had been in charge, there were a few framed pictures of angels and similar works of art. The Houseparent replaced these with framed pictures of children at play. Most of them were just simple sketches; it was thought that we should also play and act in a similar fashion. If the Houseparent had some humour, a naughty sketch showing a boy peeing was hung in the boys' bathroom. This was later moved into my bedroom and hung above my bed for a short while. I did not know if it was just a joke by the Houseparent or done to humiliate me; I took it as fun and did not get upset over the apparent insult. Other humour was also now part of the daily life. A small door plaque was fixed by the Houseparent on the inside of the lavatory door which read, 'Hey you, Who me? Now what, Please Wash Your Hands.' Such humour to Sister would not have been allowed.

Our green industrial soap was now replaced with ordinary domestic soap. Toilet paper changed to a soft style and toothpaste now came in tubes with a mint taste. It was nice to go back to flavoured toothpaste. Originally I had brought a tube of toothpaste to the Home on my arrival. With the other three wanting to use it as well, I needed to change to the solid blocks of toothpaste provided by the Home. My mother could have afforded buying the occasional tube of toothpaste for me but having to fund it for the other three as well was not possible.

Odd items on occasions could find their way into the flat. A modern designed pair of chairs was with us for a short while. Made entirely out of white polystyrene, they were certainly unusual, and very light in weight. The material was the same as found in certain types of packaging; if crumbled it could turn into thousands of small tiny balls. We were warned not to damage the chairs, but simple use over a few days by a group of children and odd slight damage did occur. It was not long before odd pieces of polystyrene were helped from the solid chair by idle hands. Within a short while, the two chairs left the flat and found their way to the incinerator with the rest of the burnable rubbish. One item of modern technology that was of useless design; in a way it was possibly a good idea that we did damage them and get them thrown out. A careless match and a serious fire could have started.

The Houseparent decided to have a rather vigorous sort out of the contents of the flat. For once, it was not the contents of the lockers, but a cabinet in the main hall. This unit held everything from tablecloths to cleaning material; it was not for us to go through, as most of the doors remained locked. If the Houseparent was bringing the flat more up to date, a number of items that had originally been kept by Sister were now going. To keep us occupied a couple of us had the task of removing what the Houseparent called rubbish, either to the area in the utility room where items ready for the incinerator were kept, or the longer journey to the dustbin. It was in our own interest to decide that the majority of the items the Houseparent was discarding could be burnt.

NEW ROOMS

With our bedroom divided up, the older two had a room on their own, the brother and his sister took over what had been the Relief Houseparents' room, and the boy a little younger than us came into our room. As there was only a slight difference in ages between the two of us, it was thought we should now take some responsibility for looking after the two younger boys. My room mate seemed to have the first choice over who he wanted to act as a big brother to, selecting the younger boy in the other room; he possibly guessed that as that boy shared the room with his sister, she would do a lot of the work.

Our main chore in the morning was helping them getting dressed and making their beds. At their ages of three and almost five, it was thought that they were too young to do this all on their own. Once we had washed and had dressed ourselves, we set about dressing the two younger boys. Both of them were at the nursery school so their clothing was not that difficult to sort out. The boy I looked after could more or less dress himself correctly, but for speed it was easier to physically dress him. It took little effort on his part if he was willing to sit still. There could be fun for me if he played up; I would lightly snap the leg elastic on the waterproof pants he wore under his trousers, until he co-operated with dressing. He had been told that when he joined the infants and it was known he could be trusted for longer periods, the pants would not have to be worn, except on long journeys when it might help save embarrassment.

Once our own beds were made, we set about helping the other two boys. On many mornings I needed to find him clean sheets, as often he had brought up odd bits of mucus due to his illness. The Houseparent apparently welcomed this; it was not really the best sight before breakfast.

The regular wet beds between them were much easier to face. As their sheets were taken to soak, we had them tell each other that they had made the best stain. Taken in this way, both were quite happy to think of it more as fun. I wished that I could face the event in such a way and not be punished by the Houseparent. Getting up in the middle of the night to visit the lavatory after she had gone to bed seemed the easy way to me of avoiding a telling off and the punishment. There were occasions when I did not manage to wake up in time; I was given the slipper when the others went off for their wash. I knew not to make a fuss over the punishment with my mother giving me the plimsoll for wet beds before I came to the Home. If the Houseparent mentioned to my mother that I was making a fuss, I would be in even worse trouble.

Other than bed-making and helping them dress, there were few chores other than to help with shoe cleaning where they might need a little bit of a hand. We encouraged them to go out in their wellingtons to avoid cleaning their play shoes. The Houseparent did not give us any praise if their shoes were clean; they were the ones praised if their clothes were smart.

Helping with chores was not normally something you volunteered to do; the Sister or Houseparent normally found enough of these without the need to ask for more. It was however worth offering to do odd chores for other Sisters and the staff at the Home as odd extra treats could come your way. If you were playing anywhere near the administration block you risked being called to take messages to the staff or to find out the location of a member of staff.

From time to time items were donated to the Home; these could be clothing, toys, books, or various other objects that might make our lives more fun. Comics and annuals were something that I was interested in. On a few occasions I was close enough to the offices to see what might be taken inside, but not close enough to be found if simple messages needed to be relayed to members of the staff.

The best assortment on one occasion was when a pile of comics that must have been in an attic for many years was given to the Home. These comics from more than ten years ago had stories that I knew I had not read. I was not the only boy around and such gifts were meant to be evenly shared out – however as the comics were more story type rather than picture types there was not much interest from the others, so I was allowed to take as many as I could carry. There was a need to limit the amount to return to the flat with as your locker would not be allowed to overflow.

THE WINDOW

One of the new members of our family was not in as good health as the rest of us. He suffered from a serious problem although not something that could be passed onto us; it meant that although being able to appear to be reasonably healthy, there were many restrictions as to his life.

A special diet always needed to be followed, and at all meals, two forms of revolting medicine had to be taken by him before any food could be eaten. We were never to share our sweets with him; the Houseparent did allow him some sweets but there was only a very limited choice he was allowed.

Before going to bed, there was a session of physiotherapy to bring up the congestion from his lungs but, for the most part, he fitted in quite well with the rest of us. This only affected me during the night. On many occasions, there were bouts of coughing. For some reason I tended to wake up, and within moments, he would be asleep again. For me it was different; once I was awake, getting back to sleep again was always difficult, and often at the moment I was starting to nod off the coughing would start again. The following days I would be generally irritable due to the lack of sleep, and even resorting to wax earplugs did little good. The Houseparent looked after the boy with great care and saw that we did not upset him or bully him for any reason.

Matters came to a head one day shortly before tea. Three of us had been given the instruction to put away our toys and tidy up the dayroom before tea started. Two of us started to tidy the things away. The boy had a jigsaw puzzle partly completed; this was in the lid of the box. It would have been quite easy to move the lid of the box to a flat surface rather than to put the puzzle completely away. This was suggested by the two of us, but he was adamant that the puzzle had to stay in the middle of the table. He would not get into trouble for leaving things out, and as we were the older ones, we would be at fault.

The other boy had a good idea; he was going to go out and pretend that he was telling the Houseparent of the refusal to put the puzzle away. Going out of the room and along the corridor he was out of sight. There was no intention of actually telling the Houseparent, it was simply that this method might get the puzzle put away. Spotted by the Houseparent, he was given the message to go and tell the boy to come for his medicine. On his return, it was with glee that he told the boy that the Houseparent wanted him, although not mentioning it was for his medicine. A flood of tears now started. I took this opportunity to put the box with its puzzle onto a higher flat surface. This upset the boy even more, and I was nowhere near when he grabbed the box and upset the puzzle totally. The tears now became a loud howl; the two of us decided that it was perhaps best if we were not on the scene.

A hasty retreat was now made to the bathroom, where a washing of our hands occupied the time whilst the Houseparent went to investigate why the boy had not come for his medicine and to see who was making that awful noise. A safer place would have been in the secure lavatory cubicle but this was already occupied, and the boy inside possibly thought it best to remain there if there was trouble around. The Houseparent pounced, my partner in crime vanished at this moment, and as I seemed to be the culprit, there was little point in him staying around to see if he was also guilty. There was a major telling off for my bullying activity. I was grabbed by the shoulders and shaken to show how I should feel to be bullied by someone else.

The Houseparent although not tall was well built, and this was no match for my light build. I was lifted slightly off my feet. My head then went back onto the lavatory door; a pane of frosted glass in the door might have been slightly less hard as it shattered than the wood or my head.

If I started to scream, it was due to the lumps of glass that were embedded in the back of my head. It was possibly a surprise for the boy inside the cubicle to find that my head had broken the glass. Like my many nose bleeds I now seemed to drip blood onto every available surface. I was wrestled to the bath and the cold tap was turned on at full force to wash away the blood and to clean my cuts. It was not that she was trying to drown me; it was that the force of the water was so strong it just felt like she was. At the same point my head was held under the flowing tap, I was struggling to get free. My screams brought all to see what the commotion was, but all were soon sent away. Now dragged to the bedroom, I was put to bed with a towel wrapped around my head. Left alone the Houseparent went to sort tea out for the rest of the family group.

The nursing Sister was sent for; soon my cut was examined and there appeared to be no glass remaining. The force of the water had made a good job of cleaning out my cut. I should visit her tomorrow and a further look would be made as to how my cut was healing.

Left alone I was angrier at missing tea than I was about the cut to my head. Shortly after this, both the nursing Sister and the Governor came to see me. It seemed I would survive. Once they left, the Houseparent said that I would be brought some tea and I was allowed to visit the lavatory at this point. In my mind I felt well enough to get up to eat, but I was confined to my room for the rest of the day. The only point that I saw the others was when they came to bed; it appeared I was to be kept quiet. Once left alone, they told me there had been a massive row before the Governor arrived, between our Houseparent and the Nursing Sister over my injury.

The following morning apart from some blood on my pillow, I felt fine. I might want to get even with the boy at some point, but that could wait. Once breakfast was over, instead of chores I was sent over to see the nursing Sister. My cut had healed nicely; her only thought, once some antiseptic ointment was in place, was that I should try not to put my comb through that area for a while. In a couple of days, I should be back just to make sure everything was fine. On returning to the flat expecting to get ready to go off to school, the Houseparent told me that I could have the day off school, and to go and change into my play clothes.

I was given the choice of either finding something to do quietly in the dayroom or to go outside. I opted to go outside, and I was asked to return by noon for some lunch. As things went I was quite happy with the day off from school, and apart from my head itching a little where there was a little clotted blood, I felt fine. Wandering round the Home when there were no other children was the best thing about the place. Other than a small amount of noise coming from the nursery school there was nothing else that informed you it was a Children's Home; it was just like having a large park to yourself.

Eventually around noon, I returned to the flat for lunch. Once over I was again given the choice of inside or out and I opted for outdoors again. I was happy, but things returned to normal later in the afternoon when the others returned from school. The Houseparent commented I had not been seen since lunch and wondered if I had been up to any mischief. Tea and chores over, I was free again until bedtime. The others had asked about my head, but as I seemed to be fine, nothing more was really said.

The rest of the day was spent outside. It was only when I was returning to the flat, I was met by one of the boys who said I was to go over and see the Governor. Not really having done anything wrong over the past few weeks, I did not appear afraid when I rang the bell and went into the office in his house.

Within moments, it was easy to see that things were not fine. I was told that if I did anything like that again I would be severely punished. It was over in seconds.

I did not have time to realise if it was two or three strokes. Unlike his small stick that he carried in the grounds, I was punished now with the long cane. I only felt the first stroke, but from that point on it was simply pain.

It could have been worse had I been given it on my hand; the Governor had possibly noticed the sticking plaster I had over my left palm. This had been a souvenir from school over falling over in the playground. My thought was if I had been given the cane on my hand, would it have hurt more or would the sticking plaster have lessened the pain.

I wondered if the Houseparent had asked the Governor to give me the cane, or if the Governor had decided I needed to be punished. With the Houseparent not here, I did not know why I should be given the cane. I had not bullied the boy. I was told to return to my flat. That I was crying was in my mind the worst part; there was only a short distance between our flat and the Governor's house.

I hid in some bushes and wiped away my tears. I was shaking; at school when I was given the cane I was prepared for the ritual of the telling off and then the punishment. This time it had been so sudden. The punishment was unfair; I had not bullied the boy, and it was not really my fault that the window was broken.

It took some time before I felt the courage to go into the flat. The others were not around; the older three were at the scout meeting and the younger two boys had already gone off to bed. Only the helper was there, and not knowing about the previous day's activities in full and as there now was no sign of my tears, I was sent off to have my bath.

The warm bath was painful. I had no way of knowing what the bruises looked like and I would have to wait until the others returned to find out. Soon in my pyjamas, I was given supper and then sent off to bed. In a way I was happy about this – I did not really want to talk about receiving the cane. The older boy returned later. If I admitted at this point about the cane, he would only want to see my bruises and if caught out of bed, there would only be further punishment. I did not see the Houseparent at all that night; it was the helper that came to see we were in bed.

The following morning with the normal rush at getting ready for school and breakfast, there was no opportunity to find out if I was still bruised. During breakfast, I expected all to be informed over my visit to the Governor and the punishment I had received, but nothing was said. Only when I was just about to leave, was I taken quietly to one side by the Houseparent and asked if I was feeling all right to go to school; it was mentioned that it might be best if the matter was now forgotten about. At school if I admitted to friends over the punishment I had been given, the teachers would soon find out, then they would be on the look out for other things I might be doing wrong. Finally, the school day finished and life returned to normal.

It was only later that I found out more about the reason for my punishment. Unknown to me the Houseparent had come up with an excuse and had told the Governor that 'I had performed' on her. How or what I had actually done to the Houseparent was not something I had been accused of when I visited the Governor. All that he said to me was 'that if I did anything like that again I would be severely punished'. I simply thought that he was accusing me of bullying the boy; he never explained the full reason he was going to cane me. The Governor apparently had accepted her word over the matter, and had not asked any of the others about the event.

If I had actually been accused of this event, I would have asked how was I allowed enough time to undo my trousers to do such an act. The Houseparent had grabbed me almost the moment I had been found by her. It might have been quite possible that my trousers were soaked at the time my head went through the window. I don't think I had an accident in my pants but it could have happened; my thoughts and what I remembered were more on the pain from the glass splinters in my head than if I was wetting myself with fear.

When I had been dragged to the bath and the cold tap turned on to its full extent, there was a lot of water splashed about, so if the Houseparent had needed any evidence of me soaking her, it was easy to find. On being taken to bed there did not seem to be a telling off other than for bullying the boy. If I had actually done such an act to her deliberately, everyone in the flat would have been told about it. If my punishment had been warranted over such a matter, why did she tell me the day after that the whole matter should be forgotten about. The Governor had even contacted my uncle that day, to report my activities. I wonder if the suggestion of giving me the cane was made then.

CHANGE OF FLAT

As well as the increase in the number of children in our flat, there was also an increase in animal numbers. There was a dog for the Houseparent, and guinea pigs and a rabbit for the younger children. At first, the younger children found their pets wonderful playthings; the actual cleaning out of the cages was not such a nice task for them.

My Saturday chore was now cleaning out the rabbit; I did not mind this. It was always surprising how much mess one rabbit could make. During the week, he was fed and watered, but on a Saturday a whole morning could be spent first cleaning out the cage, then removing all the used straw and other material, then cleaning down the entire patio. It was difficult to call me in to do other chores until I had completely finished my tasks. If there were puddles on the floor in the flat, the dog took all the blame.

The other major change to the flat was that we all moved downstairs when I was getting close to eleven years of age; the staff and almost everything in the flat came with us. A slightly different layout of the flat gave us one extra bedroom. I now shared a room with the boy who was slightly older, the two eldest and the two youngest boys having two rooms, and the youngest girls not now having to share with her younger brother. One benefit to me was that there was no more coughing from the younger boy to put up with at night.

Keeping things simple over the move was achieved by unscrewing the flat numbers and swapping them over. All mail still went to the correct address when it was worked out where each flat really was.

MY TOYS

Once toys went into your locker they were normally safe; other children were not meant to take toys from your locker. With three older boys, this rule would have been useless had I liked the types of toys that the average boy requested. Puzzle toys were one of my favourite possessions: everything from wooden puzzles in the shape of various objects, plastic squares that had several interlocking pieces, and nail puzzles that consisted of a selection of bent nails that were to be unlocked in a series of unusual moves. Several of these had to be kept out of the older boys' hands as the only way they could solve the problem was to use force, and once this had been applied the puzzle was ruined.

The other three thought I was a little odd; my main possessions were annuals, books, puzzles, pens, paper and other toys that they decided more resembled items you would find at school. None of the other boys showed any interest in a ballpoint pen I received as a present. Instead of the normal blue ink, this had twelve different colours inside. To select a colour all you needed to do was pull down a small lever on the side of the pen. The whole rainbow of colours was represented. The pen had never been an expensive type; some of the ink shades did not work very well, and the large diameter of the pen made it rather difficult to draw with, but it was fun to use.

The Sisters or Houseparents occasionally confiscated toys and other possessions. There might be a number of reasons why such an act was thought necessary. For boys it would often be due to us having something we should not have. Matches, cigarettes and knives would be taken off us if ever found. Those that were sensible did not bring such things into the flat.

Certain toys could also risk removal if it were thought we were playing with them in a way that would injure either others or ourselves. If we had toys that did not belong to us, they might be removed until the rightful owner could be found. At times, if we were badly behaved, taking away our favourite toy, might be a way of improving our behaviour. If a toy were taken away, it might be returned that day or a day or so later; it was rare for us to be permanently deprived of a toy.

Very occasionally for health reasons it might be necessary to confiscate a toy. The older Sisters might have upset a few younger children, when they recounted past times when one of their children had gone to the isolation ward with a favourite teddy bear or the like. On their return to the flat when they were better, they could not understand why the toy did not return with them.

In an effort to prevent a disease spreading to other children, such items were burnt when the child left the hospital. If we had any thought of finding such treasures at the incinerator by the orchard, our hopes we dashed when the Sister told us that the nursing Sister had her own little incinerator at the hospital for such items. By the mid 1960s, there were few serious diseases that required such drastic action.

Toys might remain in the possession of a Sister after a child had left the Home; sometimes a child leaving the Home was not able to take all their possessions away with them. If they returned for any reason, then having something that was theirs might make returning to the Home a little easier. How long such toys should be kept was up to the Sister – such items would be put in a box and generally forgotten about.

THE OUTSIDER

One problem I had was to have other children around me, having spent most of my time on my own other than during school time. My reaction to having to fit in with the group was not that successful. If I was teased or wound up in some way, I had great difficulty keeping control; it might end in a fight, tantrum or tears. With not knowing how long I was going to be in the Home and the lack of freedom I was used to, it took very little to upset me. I would have been far happier to be in the boarding school; although I might have been punished more often, life had seemed far more enjoyable. By now, I would have been in the middle or upper form and could really have had fun.

VISITS

I was the most fortunate in our group over the matter of visits. If things went smoothly then I could expect a visit every three weeks or so. If I had gone out of my way to be disruptive and upset the running of the family group at the Home, I could have easily expected that visits to be less frequent. As my mother had to spend a large amount of time looking after my grandmother, on certain occasions an expected visit might be delayed. It was disappointing but it soon could be made up. Others in the flat had either few or no visits. How they managed to keep happy with almost no contact was something that I could not understand.

I often managed to get longer periods away from the Home during the summer holidays. This was the period when I was happy; for most of the time I was out of the house. The confines of the Home made me take full advantage of my freedom. For my mother there was one extra bonus – for the full weeks I was away from the Home, the two pounds fee did not have to be paid to them. My food, pocket money and clothing that I needed during my holidays could soon use up the money my mother saved.

Visits from my mother took two forms. If there was enough time and my grandmother was in a reasonably stable condition then I would be collected on either a Friday evening or Saturday morning and taken to London; my return to the Home would be early Sunday evening. If my grandmother was not very well and needed quiet, I would simply get a visit from my mother mid-morning on a Saturday; I would have a day out with her instead of going back to London. These normally started out by visiting a small café near the school annexe. The treat was to have a rum-flavoured cake topped with a dollop of cream, and a cup of real coffee. Then it was a trip by bus to a nearby town. Money was not that plentiful, but during the trip out there was enough for lunch, and possibly tea and if I had been good, a small toy. If we did not go on a trip, we might visit one of my aunts and uncles. I would be spending my entire day in the same town as the Home, and could actually see my school from their window. I was never allowed to visit on my own during my stay at the Home. Getting away from the Home was all that mattered. I was slightly disappointed at not being taken back to London for the weekend but a day away from the Home and its stifling life was something I was quite happy with.

Visits to London were the treats that I really lived for. I tried to be good in front of my mother in an attempt or hope that she might decide that I could stay in London and not have to return to the Home. Sunday afternoons when it was time to get ready to return were always the worst. I tried to keep a brave face on it, but the thought of the boring and frustrating time ahead of me until the next visit did get me down. If I had played up at this point, I could guess that a decision might be made that perhaps visits back to London were not such a good idea and that it might be best if my stay at the Home became like the others'.

To the staff my trips to London enabled me to spend more time with my mother. In reality during my weekends and holidays in London, little time could be spent with my mother. My grandparents needed full-time attention, and other than the journey to and from the Home, my mother never really had the time off. I could stay indoors and keep quiet, but that would have been as dull as life at the Home. It was the chance of life in the normal world during the visits to London that helped me with my life. If I had been confined to the Home and did not get any visits or time away from the Home, there was a good chance I would have become a real problem.

Weekends in London although not pre-planned, were always mapped out in my mind with a range if things I could do depending on the weather and if the adults had any plans. If I had returned to London on the Friday night then Saturday morning at the earliest opportunity I could be free as soon as breakfast was over. Saturday morning cinema was my main activity. It might have been odd but although there was a cinema in the town where the Home was, our lives seemed to be organised so that it was only on very rare occasions that it was ever visited, and then only as a family group at Christmas. With our number, we could have always organised a sell-out on a Saturday morning, which most of us would have been willing to spend our pocket money on.

Only managing to get to London at odd weekends, I was certainly at a disadvantage when it came to the serials, but as there was an introduction at the start, it was possible to make up for the missing episodes. Joining the queue to get into the cinema was a little odd. I seemed to revert to being one of the local London kids. A child on their own would soon be picked on. However I found it quite easy to find other boys around my own age, and although I might not have seen them before, gaining temporary membership in their gang for the morning was fun. In the Saturday morning cinema, there were two distinct groups; there were the cinema staff and any older children that had gained the coveted free admission to be monitors against the rest of us.

Sundays were mine until about four o'clock. This was the point when I had to have returned home; miss this deadline and all the following Sundays in London would have been miserable. Cinemas opened late on Sunday afternoons so that was normally out. Swimming first thing in the morning and a visit to an outdoor market, were often how my freedom was spent that day.

Life in London was so different. During my activities, the Home became only a vague memory; it was so odd to experience all this freedom of the sights and interest, then to have two or more weekends when almost every moment of your time was organised in a way that allowed you no freedom. I could have quite happily gone for a long walk in the area surrounding the Home on my own without causing any problems at all. Confined inside the Home was so frustrating, when it was possible at other moments to have such freedom. The late afternoon of a Sunday could come round so suddenly. The return by train seemed to pass in no time, then it was into the Home and life was back to normal.

Once alone in London, there were always interesting things to do. On visiting playgrounds and the like, I found it quite easy to merge in with the local boys of my own age. We did get up to some mischief, but nothing serious was ever attempted. London in the mid 1960s for boys was similar in appearance to the London that boys of our age found at the end of the war. Large areas had been cleared for redevelopment. Although often fenced off to keep the likes of us away, there were few fences that could keep a determined boy out. Weekends were often the best for such exploration; there was seldom any work going on at the building sites so we had relative freedom of what we wanted to do.

New buildings that were being constructed were seldom of much interest to me; old abandoned buildings that were days away from being demolished were far more fun. With care, we could play as we liked. We might keep a few bonfires going, but we never decided to set fire to any of the buildings simply because there was so much fun to be had whilst they still stood upright.

Salvage companies had often arrived before us. Some of the buildings could have been dangerous; that they had removed all the floorboards was simply a challenge. The ability to hop from one joist to another above a large drop to the floor below was fun.

The houses had often been in occupation until quite recently. Families moved out and often left all manner of junk behind. Some of the local boys were good at collecting anything that looked to be of any value and would then take it down to the local markets; the rest of us regarded odd items of cracked and unwanted china as playthings. Dropping china and glass on the floor on purpose was strange – often it never broke and we had to put more physical force into actually smashing them.

The adults also scavenged lead and copper pipes; some of the houses we explored had water running from the walls. The best finds were in houses where there was flooding in the basements and cellars. If some floorboards had already been removed, then light helped us in our search for treasure and adventure. If it was total darkness then assortments of battery-powered torches and lit candles were used. It was simply down to luck that we never found a cellar into which gas had escaped.

Stepping onto the floors of cellars even if you wore your wellingtons was always a bit of a risk; you simply did not know the depth of the water in the building. At first we might test the depth of water with a stick. After a time this would get boring; you would then take a chance. Old play clothes were the best type of clothing for such activities, although most of us would normally have liked to wear long trousers or jeans; there was a definite advantage in shorts when the water was up to your knees. By the time most of us returned to our homes there was little evidence to where we had been. Ordinary play in playgrounds and the like seemed to satisfy most parents as to acquisition of dirt.

Only at one point did I nearly meet with a serious accident. We had clambered across a row of garages that adjoined a group of houses that had just become abandoned. In our rush to get at this new site, we were in a little bit of a hurry; cutting a corner of the final garage, I went across an asbestos roof. Like someone sinking into a frozen pond that was giving way, I was slowly disappearing. With luck I managed to get to the side without going completely in. The drop would have been about ten feet; although I might not have suffered any major injury, getting me out would have proved a challenge to the boys I was with.

One item we did take that was not really abandoned was lengths of rope. Hung from trees and high buildings all manner of play activities could be thought up. Possibly the adults soon claimed them back, but to us that was fair; all we did was hunt the next one down.

Commercial buildings proved equally interesting. The Underground station at Swiss Cottage had stood for many years; owing to redevelopment, a newer updated station had been built a short distance away underground. The old station building above ground still functioned, with a small group of shops surrounding the building; it slowly seemed to fade away until finally the metal panelling to keep the public out went up. Part of the building was soon demolished, however the vast carcass seemed to stay untouched. We never regarded ourselves as the public; the old shops were the first to explore. All the stock had gone but there were plenty of odd finds available; clean cardboard and paper to draw on was my main acquisition. We did have fun in the shop that repaired and sold umbrellas. Several damaged and uncompleted umbrellas made marvellous swords; no injuries were achieved even though our play had been quite violent.

The floors above the station were a mess: stacks of old newspapers, books and other rubbish were all over the place. If we helped clear up the place it was to throw all this stuff onto the stairwells and then slide down the pile. With the amount of paper and cardboard, we found it was quite a soft landing. A group of lavatories to us were asking to be smashed up. The water had been turned off and anything of remote value had already been removed. Smashing such heavy objects up was actually exhausting. Our final act was to smash a couple of the remaining plate glass windows in the arcade that had survived the demolition by the workers on the site. These were not the largest windows, but when eventually we did manage to get a brick through, the sound in this desolate arcade was deafening. Departing quickly was a wise move.

If I had a whole day to myself, the Zoo in Regent's Park was one place I could visit. The cost to get in would take most of my pocket money, but if I had sandwiches and a drink my duffle bag, the day could go without further expense other than the bus fare home. Often I made a first quick tour round the Zoo. There were notices as to the times animals were fed, and returning at the correct time often brought much more interesting sights, rather than the normal points in the day when most animals seemed to be more or less asleep.

The vultures were the best of the birds to watch. On one visit when the keeper was feeding them, I was the only one watching this activity. Perhaps the keeper was a little worried that I might be upset at the sight of the food going into the cage, and asked if I wanted to go and find my parents. I was quite happy to watch the birds come down and squabble over the food.

The advantage of visiting the Zoo on my own was that I did get to visit parts that family groups did not see. In the Lion House, I was allowed to go and visit the rear of the building; wearing an old raincoat and wellingtons, no harm could come to my clothes. This part of the Zoo was not as clean or as fresh as the front of the cages, but as long as I was quiet and did not make any sudden movements, I was quite safe. The big cats were far more active in this area.

Coin-operated machines were always of interest to me. If I was in London and had a little pocket money, any machine was a good bet as to where it would soon go. Everything from an automated snack bar, where to obtain food or drink you needed to put money in a slot, vending machines that dispensed cartons of orange squash or milk, and a cinema where hot dogs came from a vending machine.

One machine that was always a regular interest to me was the automatic photo booth. Adults might have thought the odd half-crown that I used up to get four or five pictures of myself, might have been a waste of my pocket or birthday money. I can now see this was money well spent. Over the period I was in the Home and had used these machines when I was in London, I probably had over a hundred pictures of myself. Many were discarded over the following months, but the few that survived can show a small boy having some fun. Without these images, all that would be available from my time in care would be a single photo from the Growth Study Test and one photo holding a chimp from my holiday stay in London during Christmas.

On some occasions, I did put my suit on if I was going out on my own. A slightly longer bus ride than visiting the park took me into the centre of London. The shops I could visit if I was smartly dressed were far more than if had I gone dressed in my play clothes.

I often had money to spend in the period after Christmas and my birthday. Once I had reached nine, it was thought I was old enough to decide what I spent it on; if I wasted it then that would be my own fault. There was little need to tell me not to buy toys that might be dangerous; guns and other fighting items were things I would not be spending my money on. As I already possessed a spirit-fired steam engine on a plinth, it might be felt that there was little else that I could buy that would be more dangerous.

Another toy I had in London was a chemistry set complete with test tubes, a burner and a small assortment of chemicals. In the instructions somewhere was possibly the wording that adult supervision was recommended for certain age groups. As my mother had little free time, I was allowed to work through the experiment book on my own. Once this was completed, I set about my own inventions. The most dangerous one was heating half a test tube of oil until it vaporised and then setting light to the gas. Certain household chemicals when mixed and burnt could have other interesting results.

Even when funds were limited, it was interesting to go round the large department stores on my own. Without my mother, I was able to go to the sections of the store I was interested in and take more time, rather than the quick glimpse that I might have in the normal way. It was not only the toy sections that I visited. As I was smartly dressed, the clothing section for boys was something I quite easily matched for quality of appearance in a few of the top stores. Some of the clothing for boys in the stores was what I could only wish for, but to most of my friends the clothing would be regarded as soppy; even if I did have such things, I would never be able to wear them in front of them.

My mother only had a limited amount of time to be away from the house. If I needed clothes or the like during the holidays, spending time with me going shopping was always a problem. With me not spending much time with my mother, it was often noticed that I had grown an inch or so since she had last checked my height. It was now thought that, within reason, I was old enough to buy clothes for myself. Before I left the house there was always the instruction of what I was to buy, and as if to reinforce the instruction it was noted on a piece of paper, which I should show to a member of staff. If I purchased something not on the list or chose something unsuitable then my next pocket money would be used to purchase the correct item. I knew that this would happen if I did ever try something silly.

As I was on my own, it was up to me where I looked for clothing. Some of the more expensive shops did at times have clothes at reasonable prices. Although my mother set a limit for the purchase and did not give me any more money than was necessary, I was to obtain a receipt and return any change to her. If I had been a girl, then fashion might have played a major part over my choices. To me it was just purchasing items that were more traditional and dull in colour. Something that was modern and brightly coloured was not my idea of clothing I wanted to be seen in.

I was well behaved and did not cause any trouble. Had any friends been near, there would have been bound to be some problems. A couple of the stores had food halls; many of the items on offer would not have been of any interest to most children of my age, but on occasions small samples were on offer to passing customers. Never really a glutton, I could not resist many of the offerings. If I surprised the adults, it was that the delicacies that they produced were actually to my liking.

The other interesting form of play was visiting playgrounds. The standard types that had slides and other play equipment were seldom bothered with on my visits to London. I preferred adventure playgrounds. These could spring up on various undeveloped building sites for short periods and were the most interesting to me. Often there was some adult involvement in the running of the playgrounds. This was mainly to stop total anarchy but, within reason, we were given a free hand to what we did and constructed in a playground. To many adults these playgrounds were nothing more than glorified rubbish dumps. Wood and sheets of corrugated iron were used to construct things that seemed to have little merit on design. For most of us, that we were allowed to construct play equipment and items totally to our own designs was the main object. Students and adults in the holidays often did help us over some of the major items. A rope swing on a pulley might be twenty feet in the air and travel for thirty yards. This needed some expert help if it was to remain safe for any length of time, but in the main we were left alone, and anyone misbehaving was told to go away.

There were a few minor injuries; these were mostly splinters and minor cuts owing to the salvaged materials we were using for our construction, but no serious injuries were really sustained. To the adults this form of play possibly was slightly safer than allowing us free rein over the local redevelopment sites. Our material that we used in the adventure sites often came from buildings that were soon to be demolished. Some of it was scrounged by us and other items were brought into the playground in more controlled amounts. The adventure playground in St. Johns Wood was slightly fortunate as an additional source of unusual material; a small film studio almost directly opposite did seem to give us on occasions all manner of odd items to make use of.

London was a smokeless zone; it was hoped to control the numbers of bonfires that were in use. On most days, a small bonfire was kept going with all the offcuts of wood and cardboard that we did not have a use for, and as long as we did not allow the fires to be out of control or to make large amounts of smoke, the adults used to allow this form of play. If only the Home could have allowed these freedoms for us to make an adventure playground, life would not have been so boring.

My ability to become injured whilst at play in London was equal to that at the Home. Often on my eventual return, there would be the odd grazes and cuts to be cleaned up. Injuries in London though seemed less painful as the injury had long since passed when I eventually arrived indoors.

The most serious happened when I had been playing on a few abandoned cars with some local boys in an area that was ready for redevelopment. We were aware of the broken glass and did try to avoid cutting ourselves. It was at the front of an intact car that I injured myself. At some point I slipped and my hand went into one of the headlights on a car. I must have done it with quite some force as the lamp shattered. Until this point, we had always found it a difficult challenge to lob stones at headlights until they smashed, but this time it broke quite easily. The pain was not that bad. It was the lump of glass that was sticking out of my hand when I removed it from the lamp that was the more revolting sight. Without any real pain I pulled the splinter of glass out; the spurt of blood that followed the glass was possibly my best effort yet. The boys I was with suggested that I ought to go home. During my walk home, I took a closer look at my cut; if I pushed the triangular flap of skin back into position the blood did stop, but it then hurt. I walked the mile home, leaving a small trail of blood on the ground. Once home I was soon cleaned and bandaged up.

If I wanted to explore, the Underground gave me the most freedom. With this form of railway transport, there were only two points where adults might inspect your ticket. This was at the very start of your journey and at the very end when you left the station. Unlike an ordinary railway, all the lines interconnect, so it was not only possible to get from one end of the line to another but to swap over onto different lines and travel in various directions. In reality, you were only permitted to travel the distance of the train ride that you had paid for. If I was bending the rules slightly in that I was actually travelling to the destination I had paid for, it was just that I took a rather indirect route. A day could be spent travelling wide across London and into the more remote country areas.

I soon learnt that it was best to stick to the more populated areas for this type of travel. Some of the more remote stations only got occasional trains. If you got off at one of these stations, it was often a long wait between trains. A double platform, and it was quite easy to return in the opposite direction. If it was a station with two separate platforms, it was necessary to go through a ticket inspection. All I was able to do was to wait for a train to take me a little further up the line, making sure I never arrived at the final station where ticket inspection was inevitable. At certain days of my exploration, I did buy a Rover ticket; this allowed me unlimited travel on buses and the Underground. I could stop and start my journeys at any point.

As I was always on my own when I went on these longer journeys, adults never questioned me over what my intentions were; it was when I was with friends that we seemed to be watched carefully by the adults. I tried to travel to as many parts of the network as possible. It was quite an easy feat for the more built-up areas, but in the almost country areas the delay in the returning trains and buses wasted too much of the time that the ticket was valid for.

MANY HAPPY RETURNS

There was a new event for me at the age ten: a birthday party. Until now, constant relocations really prevented any gatherings of friends. The Houseparent had decided that I could have a birthday party in the flat, and invite a friend from school who was not at the Home. There had not before been the possibility of a birthday party at the Home, as my visits to London had coincided with my birthdays. This year I was going to have a party, but it would be a few days after my birthday, when I returned from my holidays in London.

It was an easy choice of who would come as my guest. If my friend was a little apprehensive of accepting the invitation, it was due to the odd tales that he had been told about the Home, though most of these were exaggerated. Reassurance that he would be free to leave at the end of the party gained the acceptance. After all, we all left the Home to go to local schools, and he would have been able to gain his freedom the following morning.

Many friends from school would have liked to enter the grounds to see what the Home was really like, but apart from an open day when everything was made to look attractive, they never saw the boring everyday routine.

The day came, and as normal I was quite excited. As a special treat my mother had been allowed to attend. This was possible as my party was on the same day that I returned from London. The Houseparent seemed to find an extra pair of hands very useful as the helper's day off and my party coincided.

Birthday parties were generally more relaxed times, and with a wide range of ages in the flat, activities and games had to be organised so that no one group seemed to be left out. I was always at a difficult age, neither one of the older ones, nor one of the younger ones.

The Houseparent had worked out how the party was to run, at what point food would come out, when games were played, and at what time the party was to end. It was a full and hectic event, and with the need to keep an eye on the younger members of the group and see that they went to bed at a regular time, perhaps the party finished earlier than had it been designed for my age group or older. All had fun; even my school friend seemed to find the rather well–organised style of life interesting.

A memorable souvenir of the event was to receive from my guest a quality fountain pen as a present, far better than the ballpoint pens provided by the school or the fountain pens that could be afforded with ordinary pocket money. Any hope from the adults that my writing would improve with the use of a better pen was short lived; my style of writing remained the slightly shaky scrawl that was to be found in most of my workbooks.

SUMMER HOLIDAYS 1967

My summer holidays in London had been interrupted by returning to the Home so I could go on a group holiday with the others. The older boys went off to scout camp so really it was not the entire family group. It was thought that a holiday by the seaside would be something I would not want to miss. Whilst for all the others a trip to the seaside was a new experience, for me, although it could be fun, it was nothing new; I had spent two years by the sea before coming to the Home.

Having to return from London was perhaps not that much fun. If the holiday was to start badly the journey was by road. Car and coach travel have never been my favourite method of travel due to travel sickness. We travelled up in a car and a small van; most of the journey for me was in the van peering out of the small back window trying not to feel sick.

Holland on Sea was our destination. By late afternoon we had arrived at the small bungalow on the top of the cliffs where we were going to stay. We were told not to wander off. There was a short trip down to the beach for a quick look around and then it was back to the bungalow to sort out everything.

Along with the Houseparent, a married couple were going to help look after us during the holiday. At this point, I was allowed to eat and generally became happier with the holiday. The sleeping arrangements for us children were on thin waste–cotton filled mattresses, placed on the floor in various parts of the bungalow. The adults had proper beds. I was going to share the room of the married couple; it was thought I would be the quietest of the group and not want to spend the night chattering. After a light supper we all went off to bed; it appeared the sooner we were asleep, the sooner the next day would start. I was quite happy sleeping in a room on my own; at some later point the married couple must have gone to bed, but I was not woken.

The following morning I did wake up quite early. It was not really dawn, but just starting to show the first stages of daylight. The curtain was partly open together with a window that was slightly ajar. My mattress had been placed under this window. It was not really raining outside, but a slight drizzle was allowing the odd drop of rain in from the open gap. I thought about closing the window, but as it was something that I had not really seen as to how it worked, I decided that I might make a noise and wake the couple up.

My other thought was on visiting the lavatory. I was not desperate to go but had I been in my own bedroom, I could have left the room without waking anyone up. With my mattress being positioned at the furthest point from the door and not knowing the layout of the room, I decided to wait until it was lighter so I could see my way out. Soon I was asleep again. When I woke up again it was still not fully light, there was the feeling of drops of rain hitting my head, but I also knew my bed was wet. The trouble I would be in for wetting the bed would be something I would find out later. I went back to sleep until it was time to get up.

I could have not have chosen a worse time to wet the bed. Unlike the Home, our mattresses here did not have a rubber sheet on top to give protection from accidents. That I had managed to soak the mattress through to the other side seemed to be a major wrongdoing. This was not the best way to start the holiday.

There was no time to punish me. I was soon in the bathroom with the bath running at full flow. In the Home, the hot water supply varied from day to day, one large boiler feeding twelve flats on one side of the grounds; it could be temperamental over its supply and on many occasions if too much hot water was used by all the flats, the temperature dropped considerably. Here the hot water came from a tank that had been heating up during the night. The bathwater was hot, although cold water was running into the bath at the same time. When I was ordered into the bath, it was far hotter than usual. Within moments I was in tears owing to its temperature, with the bath being quite full there was no room to add any extra cold water. I was told off for acting like a baby. Eventually I was allowed out of the bath, and whilst I dried myself off, the Houseparent went off to get my clothes.

During breakfast my accident was revealed to all; as I was one of the eldest here it was done to shame me. We were all reminded that before going to bed, we should make sure we visited the lavatory. If there were any more bed-wetting, part of our holiday money would be used to purchase rubber sheets for those that needed them. If only I had not been made to come on this holiday, life would have been much more fun.

Another disappointment for me was later that morning. We were all bought ice creams; this was something we rarely had at the Home. The excitement did not last for me. How I bumped into one of the girls I did not know; it was a total accident, her ice cream fell onto the grass and was ruined. The worst part was that we had only just received them and had managed about two licks each. Instead of accepting my word that it was an accident, my ice cream was removed from my hand and given to the girl – life was not fair.

The Houseparent took me to an empty room. Even as this was a holiday, I was not going to be allowed to disrupt it for others. The slipper for wetting the bed was now given to me; the hits with the slipper were soon over. At least I was not receiving any extra hits for the ice cream event, but it was enough for me to hate this holiday.

Whilst the others were indoors playing games, I was now sent outside to sit by the side of the building to think about whether I wanted to improve my behaviour. Keeping out of the others' way whilst I got over my tears was a good idea. It would have only taken one of them to tease me, for me to lose my temper.

That night my mattress was moved into the hall. Even with it staying out of doors for the day it had not dried out. After lying in my bed for a short while, I could feel the dampness of the mattress. With the warm weather, it was not too uncomfortable, but during the night, I could not help wetting the bed again.

Having already been told I had ruined the mattress after the first night, I knew that I could not do any more damage, so I was not worried over a second accident. I could expect that when we were back at the Home, some of my pocket money would be stopped to pay for a replacement mattress. On getting up, I was given the slipper, and told once I had finished my bath, to put the mattress and my sheets outside; it was thought pointless giving me any clean sheets.

The threat by the Houseparent of using our holiday fund to purchase rubber sheets did not happen after one of the younger boys wet his bed on the second night. For the rest of the holiday his soaked mattress was placed at the end of the hall next to mine as a punishment. Both of us wet our beds each night due to their continual dampness; each morning we dragged our mattresses outside to dry off slightly.

In an odd way, the Houseparent was kind to me over my bed-wetting. Normally if I was given the slipper I would be in tears. Here, although the punishment of the slipper was still given, it was very light, not hard enough to make me cry, but loud enough to let all the others know I was punished over my actions. All seemed to take enjoyment during the holiday of peering around the corners in the bungalow and watch the Houseparent slipper me.

At odd times the holiday was fun. When taken down to the beach there were several activities. We were told off for prodding a seal that had died quite some time ago and had turned to a hard lump of skin. A couple of donkey rides were organised for the youngest members of the group; ponies were available for anyone too large to fit on a donkey. I was the only one to take up this offer.

Nearly all my holiday pocket money went on this activity during our stay. I was a bit of a nuisance at times, when group activities or food was organised; I was at the opposite end of the beach on a pony. The owner of the ponies gave me longer rides as there was not a parent around waiting for the ride to end. It appeared if one child was already on a pony, it was a good way of drawing other children in. I was not in any hurry to get back to the rest of the group.

During the holiday, some of our holiday fund was pooled together to buy a kite. The big black pirate kite would have been a wonderful toy to have in the grounds of the Home with its vast space. Where our holiday bungalow was, there was not enough room to run to allow the kit to be airborne easily. Eventually the kite was up in the air. Strong winds made it unmanageable, and within a short while it had tangled itself around some wires that ran high across from some wooden poles. Possibly it was luck that the string snapped as soon as the kite became tangled. It was doubtful if the wires were for telephones to the holiday bungalows. Our flat could have had one less returning depending what the voltage in the wires had been.

On the next visit my mother paid to the Home, the Houseparent wasted no time in reporting my bed-wetting and all my other faults during the holiday. Any hope of my mother thinking I was old enough to go without a rubber sheet on my bed in London now vanished forever, even though I had not had any problems during my visits home.

CUBS

This type of group activity had never really been to my liking even from the start of my arrival at eight. To me there seemed little point in organised games in the hut, or demonstrations of how to tie knots. Once you had perfected the granny knot and the hangman's knot, the need for others seemed slight in my mind.

The way badges were awarded was frustrating; most of the Sisters and Helpers seemed to provide the documentation to the Sister who ran the cub pack, for almost every badge possible. The tests you had to do for general housework and similar activities we seemed to do as normal events of the day. The Sister who would have filled in the necessary forms for me seemed to think otherwise. Whilst all my friends seemed to gain arms full of badges, other than the regular cub badges my jumper remained badge free. Eventually because of my age, I became a Seconder. Even with a new Houseparent, no badges came my way.

Discipline in our pack was quite strict; the Sister in charge would turn a blind eye when any Sixer decided to sort out a younger member. If you were a failure in some competition and had let down your Six, it was an expected matter to be hit in the form of a caning with the wooden beads. These were strung on a long shoelace and were always in the possession of each Sixer. When hit on your bare legs it did hurt. All I could look forward to was becoming a Sixer at some point and preserving the tradition.

It was not a case of not trying to like cubs. In my first year, I had even been given a copy of the Wolf Cub Jubilee book; possibly the most interesting part was a diary section in the centre of the book. This was started at length in January, but slowly diminished in cub content as the year went on. The text in the book was informative and some of the activities I did try out. There were slight objections to my attempts at lino printing; the main drawback was the thin style of lino offcut I managed to acquire rather than the messy ink that one needed to print with.

Restrictions when I showed the content of the book to adults were placed on bow and arrows, life-saving, making an oversize catapult, a raft (there was no water anyway). I also failed with the pop-gun and a whistle by not having the correct type of tree to supply the wood, and ink from a toadstool to write with was something I was not going to be allowed to try.

The main event of Cub Jubilee Year was to help build a racing car in the shape of a rocket. One of the adults helped us during its manufacture. With only limited resources, our effort was passable but did not have any of the luxury parts that we saw in the other challenges when the day came.

An odd item of the 7th Harpenden cub pack was our uniforms. When you joined the cubs, you would usually have a new uniform. For our pack, we started with a uniform that had seen a previous cub, with any badges that had been awarded removed. You started cubs with a rather worn jumper. We needed neater looking clothing for odd events, so the older and taller members were issued with some scouting items. It was not the current issue and appeared to have come from packs outside the area. Once our local cub badges were affixed we did look smart in our buff shirts but totally different from every other cub pack.

Whilst our uniforms during the competition fared well our rocket did not. During an early run, it failed on a downward slope and we could only watch from that point on.

I was nearing the age to join the scouts, however shortly before this I should have been promoted to a Sixer together with a friend of equal status, but we were passed over and two other members took charge of our Sixes. At this point, I wanted to have no more to do with cubs. My first requests to leave were to the Sister in charge of our pack, and when this failed it was the Houseparent that I asked to leave cubs. From that point on, all the adults questioned me as to why I wanted to leave. To me it seemed an easy thing: I would no longer attend.

Resigning from cubs was not allowed. It was similar to a television programme, where a man who had resigned from his work, was kept captive in a village. He attempted to escape but was always brought back. For us it was the same, run away from the Home you and would just be returned.

It was not that I was allowed to finish cubs instantly. For several more weeks, I was made to attend, even if I showed no real enthusiasm over any of the activities. Finally, the adults decided that my presence was no longer required and I dropped that evening activity.

DULLNESS OF LIFE

The Home was set in forty acres of grounds; to the adults this should be enough for any child. For us there were other views. There were plenty of areas to play ball and similar games; there were plenty of areas if we were interested in chasing games, two large woods, while not large enough to get lost in, some of the younger children if left alone, could become frightened.

There was also a play area with various items of outdoor play equipment to challenge all age groups. Most of the items had traditional methods of use; we soon invented other ways of using the equipment. The slide was to be climbed up on the smooth metal surface. Once at the top you climbed over the edge and slid down the supporting poles. It was wise never to be the first down the slide; often a pool of pee was at the lower end where the slide levelled out. This was intended for the girls; it was the only time we agreed with the saying 'girls first'.

However once you were in the Home and these were all soon conquered, ones mind soon was set on matters that if you were caught at, there would be trouble. The orchard was out of bounds. For most of the year, if there were any apples on the trees they were not ripe enough to eat. When they did become ready to eat, the nearest trees turned out to be cookers. It was only at the furthest location were there any dessert apples, but the risk of going that far often was simply too great. If spotted by the groundsmen you would be chased away. If the Governor caught you then it would be worse.

The incinerator was another magnet for toys. Playing with fire was too much of a risk according to the adults, but if we were left alone most of us were sensible enough not to get hurt. It was only the daft few who wanted to practise fire walking in the hot embers and ruining what they were wearing that could bring regular adult attention to the area that spoilt it for the rest of us. Going into buildings we were not meant to be in was another pastime. To most of us, an unlocked door was an invitation to enter.

The railway line that ran at the far side of the Home was the main London line. Although there was only a low fence separating us from the line, all knew it was stupid to be on that part of the railway. For most of us, it was the small little-used line nearby that became our haunt. With few trains, once you were out of sight of the Home you were safe.

One dangerous part was the very high bridge carrying the railway over a main road. The dare was to go to the edge of the parapet and look over. If any of us had fallen, there was the certainty that you would not be returning to your flat. There was one thought that possibly stopped us from doing any foolish acts, it was down to a small cemetery in the grounds of the Home; we knew where we would end up.

Dropping small stones from the top of the bridge whilst trying to hit the top of vehicles was a very stupid pastime, but to us there seemed to be no harm in our pea-sized bits of gravel. If it had been explained, that such a small item when dropped from a great height could have devastating results if it hit a windscreen, we might have resisted that form of play. It was down to our bad timing that when the stone had dropped the required distance, our target had long since passed beneath the bridge.

The woods and far grass field solved my boredom; it was somewhere to pass time before we had to go in. If the Home had possessed a supervised library or quiet building where things could have been made, then many hours of my time could have been spent without getting into trouble.

Some of the younger children might have been a little afraid of going into the woods alone; even the large grass fields could be upsetting to them at times. The long grass was a haven for rabbits. In an ideal world, they would have soon made a run for it when we approached. Because of the overpopulation in rabbits a few years earlier, a disease had been introduced to keep their numbers in order. Often whilst at play we would come across a dead rabbit. On occasions it might be one that had died some time ago and was slowly rotting away. To a few older boys, a dead rabbit was a plaything. All were wise enough not to actually handle one of these; however, a long stick, a little thought, and a dead rabbit could be made to fly.

From time to time, various activities were organised. The results might be a rather waste of time but it could solve boredom. Basket weaving was not normally an activity to interest boys, but the thin cane rather than raffia did have a use; the offcuts, when in pieces a few inches long could be smoked. With a general shortage of cigarettes, boys could experiment with many substitutes. It was not really for the smoking aspect, but as it involved fire then I was interested. Eventually the adults found out what was happening, the ends of each long length of cane were now painted, and when you came to an end of a section, you had to ask for any excess to be cut off. This was then removed and taken from us, and our objects took on a speckled appearance where the start ends of the canes were more visible. The basket making seemed to end a little later when most of the members did not return for future meetings.

Hot summer days were possibly the most boring; even the keen footballers found little interest in kicking a ball about and quiet organised games of cricket were never bothered with. Huddled in small groups, most of our time was spent planning our next deeds. If anyone had a magnifying glass then the long dry grass was an ideal place to lurk. We never managed to set fire to large areas, but several scorched patches were occasionally found. Burning initials onto the soles of one's shoes or trying to imitate versions of animal tracks as found on the soles of some of our shoes when they were new, was a short-lived craze. This pastime ended when members of the group returned indoors and were found by the Sisters, with various artistic images burnt into the flat sides of their wellingtons. For once, I had the sense not to allow my clothing to be damaged in such a way.

At times, we appeared not to be at fault. The cricket pavilion just sort of caught fire. It was exciting to watch the fire brigade come and put it out. It was easy for the children to be the main cause, but apparently we were all innocent or everyone had a very good alibi. Days after the fire, the remains of the pavilion became a plaything, with an unlimited supply of charcoal to draw on the concrete area. Those of us not interested in cricket or football, thought that perhaps we now made better use of the building. If anyone had wanted to have fun setting fire to the remains of the pavilion, they would not really have done any harm. I quite liked the smell of damp burnt wood. Our use of the charcoal ended when a member of the staff decided that our drawing on the ground was naughty, and that we should receive the slipper over the matter.

BULLIES

Bullies came in two groups. There were the ones that thought it was fun to make a smaller or younger child's life a misery, and the other sort that might be helping someone else even up a score. If you had older friends or means of rewarding a bully it was quite easy to get an enemy sorted out. Often your foe would never know it was you who caused their misery.

Telling an adult about such actions was never any good; later on when the wrongdoer had been punished the accuser would be dealt with. I had the advantage of being a fast runner. Often labelled a coward I could often outrun my pursuer and let easier targets be found. If you did tell on someone and the staff found them innocent, you would be punished instead, and would later receive a thumping from the boy who had been found innocent.

Firework night could allow bullies to have fun under the cover of darkness. A large bonfire and firework display was arranged in the grounds each year. For several weeks we scrounged all form of burnable material for the bonfire. If the groundsman helped, it was by diverting the rubbish that would normally have gone to the incinerator, to our pile.

The adults thought we should not possess any fireworks. The older boys managed to obtain bangers from friends at school, and then would sell them at a slight profit to younger boys, allowing more fireworks to be purchased. During daylight hours, we experimented with the bangers by taking them apart and piling the contents up, before having the courage to light the loose gunpowder without getting singed; or accepting the dare to hold a banger in your gloved hand whilst someone lit it.

On the actual night we started off in the family groups, but soon after the bonfire was lit, the older boys started to drift away from their own group. Their fun would be with the remaining fireworks; letting them off behind unsuspecting younger children was their idea of fun, and in the darkness they could not be identified.

The only injury I experienced was not my fault. An older boy had a firework that was a rather feeble Roman candle you could hold in your hand; this showered a fairly meek spurt of sparks out of the end; rather one of the more elaborate type that had to be put in the ground. Totally bored with his few seconds of fun, it was decided to see if the firework could provide more enjoyment for him. The end was not hot, only warm to the touch. Stuffing it inside the leg of my wellington was a minor prank. Had the firework been completely finished it would have only caused slight discomfort. In its inverted position, one final burst of sparks was the result.

One of the other Sisters came to my rescue. It was not long before I was in the hospital at the Home, with all the others who had been injured that night. The main injuries seemed to be burns from sparklers. The Nursing Sister with many years experience was always ready and waiting for the stream of minor injuries that visited her.

My injury seemed to tie for worst of the night with a boy who had been hit with a piece of burning wood. As he needed more urgent attention, once my charred sock had been peeled off my leg and the inside of my wellington, I was sat on a chair with my foot in a large bucket of cold water. Within a short time I was given full attention by the Nursing Sister; it was at this moment that Sister arrived. There was more pain from her telling off than from the Nursing Sister putting a dressing over my burn. Not wanting to get anyone in trouble, it was easier for me to admit that I had been foolish with fireworks rather than someone had caused the accident. The only punishment was that next year I would be staying indoors, and not going to the firework party. Once in the flat, it was bed before the others arrive back. The following day it was returning to the Nursing Sister for a fresh dressing. Not making a fuss over the matter seemed to end the event.

BLAME

One game everyone played was to try to get someone else blamed when things went wrong. If you were seen to be good then life was easy; get blamed for problems and life at the Home could be awful.

One of the helpers tried to get us interested in modelling with clay. If we achieved a reasonable item, she knew someone who would be able to fire the work to preserve it. It was similar to school only there, the teacher in charge deemed few items suitable. To see an afternoon's hard work rejected and thrown in the bin on regular occasions was a little disheartening. The efforts we achieved at the Home were worth firing for posterity. They were put safe in the utility room to dry out before transporting to the kiln when dry.

The following morning I was set upon by both the Houseparent and the Helper. Our work that had been put safe to dry out now had some new additions. Many of our items had been mugs or plates. Nearly all of them had comments engraved into the soft clay such as 'poor work', 'must try harder', 'failure' and similar comments. One item however had the words 'Good achievement' neatly engraved onto its flat surface.

My offering was the only item to get praise; to me it was clear that someone was trying to get the blame put on me. The adults could not see this; the work of the words had to have been done by me. I tried to argue that it was not me, but I was the one in line for punishment. If only the adults had realised that the engraving could not have been mine, the lettering was too neat, and a word like 'achievement' was one that although I might know, I would have never have attempted to spell. As a punishment, I was given four hits with the slipper. The items we had made were thrown away; the clay sessions never restarted.

I was told that if there were any more problems of mischief at night, I would get the slipper again. Leaving my room at night after the Houseparent had gone to bed now became a risky business. If there were any problems caused by the others during the night, I was going to be in trouble and receive four hits with the slipper for any misdeeds that she found, or to accept two hits for a wet bed.

As one of the youngest, it was quite easy for the others to put the blame on me for any bad behaviour. Two older ones blaming a younger one, it was easy to see which the Sister or Houseparent would believe.

As some point, some of the family group were acting out a scene from a film we had all been taken to, where an umbrella was used to make a person fly through the air. We did have enough common sense not to leap off our balcony using the younger girl's umbrella in the hope it would allow us to fly. On the ground, the older boys had attempted to see if simply jumping up in the air would allow a moment of flight. The umbrella went inside out; during an attempt to put it back into shape it fell apart. The decision to give it to me ended their responsibility with it. The umbrella's owner had seen it go inside out and was now upset. It was not long before the adults found out about the latest problem, as I was the last one having hold of it, I must have been the one to damage it.

If the girl had said it was the older ones that did the damage, I would have been believed when I said that I was not the one to break it. On questioning the older ones about who was responsible, all denied causing the breakage. As usual, I was in trouble. Once the hits from the slipper were over, I was informed that I would have to pay for a replacement. Pocket money for the next few weeks was reduced until the price of a new one was made up. A few things like this set me against almost every member of the family group.

One matter that could cause me to become angry was when I was told that I was wrong and I thought I was right and often could even prove it. On returning from a visit to London, my mother might bring a few odd little items for the younger members of the family. They were never anything major, but just a small token gift.

On one occasion around Christmas, she brought a couple of novelty gift tubes. Slightly bigger than a cracker, when a metal ring was pulled at the bottom of the tube, several small toys were fired out of the other end. There was a clear warning not to look at the top as you fired the tube. To make sure everything went without any problem, my mother set the tube off in front of the younger ones, and allowed them to hunt for the odd little gifts and paper bits that were showered across the room. The tubes had come in packs of two so my mother handed the other tube to the Houseparent, as she might like to set it off when the entire family were around.

The tube was put safe by the Houseparent and forgotten about during the first few days of Christmas. When it was brought out, it was mentioned by the Houseparent that she had something else for us. At this moment, I did not get into a rage. What did set me off was when the Houseparent peeled away the paper covering the top and tipped the small selection of little toys onto the table. I spoke up saying that she was meant to have pulled the little ring at the base of the tube, to shower the gifts into the air. I now received a telling off for trying to tell an adult how to open something.

I sulked with rage until we left the table; the tube was left on the table and I retrieved it. Pointing it away from my face, I pulled the little ring. The tube now fired, and although, the toys were now gone, a small stream of paper objects came out. If I had waited until the Houseparent had completely left, everything would have been fine. Now I was told off for playing with the tube and sent to my room for a short while for my disobedience. This was another part of Christmas at the Home that I disliked.

FOOD

My views on the food at the Home did get me into trouble at one point. Normally on the days Sister was on duty, we knew exactly what was on offer. With Sister's years of experience, she knew what we liked and disliked and to balance a meal so that at least there was something that was liked by each of us. My comment to a friend as we walked back to the Home, was that tonight was a day when the relief was in charge of the meals, and on those nights the meals were not very good. A friend from the Home would have known not to let the comment go any further; he did not live at the Home but his mother worked part-time there. Within a couple of days, the Houseparent cornered me. It appeared that my comments had been mentioned to his mother, who in turn had passed them on to her. Now I was questioned as to what I did not like about the meals. I was more used to savoury tastes and the like. The meals here were designed for the average sweet-toothed child, and possibly were not for the likes of me. For my tea, if there had been cheese on toast, Welsh rarebit or more savoury items, I would have been far happier with that style of meal rather than something more elaborate. For the rest of the day it appeared I was not in favour and was set extra chores.

None of us was allowed any food fads. Sister had a simple rule: if it was on your plate, you ate it. If she knew that there were certain items you did not like, then the portion size of the item was reduced, but it was very rare that an item was left off your plate simply because you did not like it

My main hate was parsnips; for some reason the taste really revolted me. During Sunday lunch, this hated vegetable often appeared at the best meal of the week. The only way I could find of eating this item was to cover it in salt and eat it with an item that took part of the taste away.

After the Houseparent took over from Sister, our meals changed slightly. There was a little more freedom of what was not eaten. That good food was going to waste was not so much of an ordeal. On occasions, the Houseparent demanded that something was finished. It could turn into a battle of wills.

With Sister, the offending item would be taken away to reappear at the following meal; once eaten the normal meal could continue. This was only bothered with if the uneaten item could remain fresh enough. Extra chores would be found for you over any item that could not be saved.

The Houseparent seemed to find that sitting at the table after the meal and looking at the item, often had the desired result. If you wanted to go out to play or watch television, then finishing the meal under her watchful eye was possible. It was mainly the younger ones who suffered this punishment. If you were on washing up, watching someone face a pile of cold cabbage, seemed to make your chore last even longer. If we did try to help in the odd moments when the Houseparent was distracted, it was to remove part of the pile from the plate. Had we thrown it in the bin, the crime would have been found out; mixing it in with some dirty washing-up water made it look as if it had come off several plates.

On the days we were not able to help, we often finished our chore before the offending plate was cleared. For the person sat at the table, making excuses that they had to visit the lavatory never worked. The only real solution after making this request was to be either sick or allow a puddle to form under the chair. Then the item did not have to be finished but the mess that was made had to be cleared up. If the washing up was still in progress, those were involved in that task were the ones to clear up the mess.

Most of the time our food was perfectly fine for growing children. All our meals were well balanced; compared with our friends at school, we were probably better fed than they were. On the housekeeping side there was a budget to keep to, so it was not possible to follow all the requests of a child for the latest item that arrived on the food front.

The only food that really was poor was bread. Often during the warm summer, the sliced wrapped loaves could soon turn mouldy. When the Home had baked its own bread there had never been a problem. Often at the weekend, the modern style sliced bread could be found to have mould growing almost as fast as you looked at it, but once toasted it was fine. One thing I had already learnt was that any food having a minor amount of mould is fine to eat; if it's too mouldy and walking faster than you, then possibly it's too far gone.

One change was that there were far more sweet items served at meals than I was used to. The best pudding in my mind was trifle. If it was a day old and had been kept in the larder, the fruit had a slight tang to the taste, and this was when I enjoyed it best. Most of the others did not seem to share my taste over the fermenting fruit.

I was greedy only on one occasion; it was having an extra portion of a pink milk pudding. It was on Saturday lunchtime shortly before we were all taken on a shopping trip into town. Although I had not felt unwell when we set out, the walk so soon after lunch upset my stomach. It was just luck that when I was sick it was on the pavement; had it been inside a shop, there would have been a good chance that I never was allowed to eat another pudding.

Some of the food that did come our way was quite luxurious by our standards. The Home had an arrangement with one of the famous named supermarkets in town. On a Saturday afternoon, the van from the Home went down and collected any food that had reached the date marked on the packet. Once back at the Home the Sisters were allowed to make their selection from the wide assortment of items that would not appear in their normal food allocation. If I developed two favourites, it was for cheese and onion crisps plus sugar-coated jelly babies.

Several savoury items occasionally appeared in the selection, often disliked by the majority of the household; it was a nice treat when either Sister or the Houseparent brought back something where I became almost the only recipient other than the adults. Sometimes it was simply the name on the product that put the others off; if they had tried the cheesecake they might have found that it was not really like cheese as they knew it.

There was once an item I was pleased to see at the Home – real coffee. This was with us for only a very short period; the Houseparent had acquired a couple of tins of ground coffee. Other than the Houseparent, I was the only one who liked the real coffee to drink. On a few days that I was thought to have been good, I was allowed a cup. A few simple luxuries like this and my life could have been wonderful.

MEDICAL RESEARCH

Our regular visits for the Growth Study Tests every few months were welcomed by most of us. An entire morning off school was something of a treat. The tests took about two hours. There were not that many of us in the group, but as we were all seen individually, although there were several staff involved, much of the time was waiting to be seen. The tests took place in one part of the

main hall; this part of the hall was kept locked, other than on the days of the medical tests, because of the specialised medical equipment used only for our measurement tests. Ordinary children might have been a little scared of having to strip down to their underwear and have parts of their bodies measured in size and density; we took it as fun. The growth studies became a major source of reference on child development.

As well as our measurements, photographs of our body stature and growth were taken from our front, back and side. These were done naked, and as there were no girls present, we did not find any reluctance at having such photographs taken.

If a few of us were embarrassed at times, it was when the staff might have touched certain parts of our body during the tests. When it came to standing up for the photographs, on occasions a few of us experienced erections. With the others occupied with their own part of the test, it was generally only the staff that witnessed our embarrassment. At our young age, we did not understand why things like this should happen. If this had been in front of the Sisters or a Houseparent we could have expected some form of punishment; the medical staff took little notice of us.

The only other activity was to be given several X-rays that took in various parts of the body. For safety reasons, instead of wearing our ordinary underpants during the X-rays we were provided with a special pair of thick plastic pants to put on; these apparently provided protection to our gonads from the X-rays. A trick that was played by various boys was at the very end of the x-ray session; leaving the plastic pants slightly damp was a joke for the next boy who came along to find when he put them on.

On most occasions when our tests were over, it was necessary to return to school for the rest of the day. On odd times it did become possible to get the entire day off if it was felt that you might miss your school lunch, or those that were taken to school by coach found that there was no transport available. We had a souvenir to show our friends that were not on the tests – odd ballpoint pen marks that were applied to our arms and other areas, that provided accurate reference points for measurements. If we were well behaved a souvenir photo came our way on a few occasions, but taken when we were fully dressed.

MY TEMPER

It took only a few minor events to occur before I lost my temper. The Houseparent had the solution to my problem of needing to release my excess energy, by giving me the instruction to go and find an isolated spot in the grounds and to shout my head off. For a few occasions I tried this idea, but to me it did little good. When sent out on this exercise, I was not in a mood any more, so did not really have any excess energy to use up.

I was not the studious type; however one of my main possessions were my comics and annuals. If I could be left alone then there were no problems. Interrupt me with minor chores, instructions to join in games with the others and matters that served no real purpose, then I did seem to cause a nuisance at some later point. At school, I was given the instructions by the teachers that if I was indoors and someone was upsetting me, instead of getting angry I should quietly leave the room and go for a walk along the corridor, and by the time I had completed the circuit of the corridor I should be calm enough to return to my work.

FALL OUT – OCTOBER 1967

It was difficult to point to one moment when things at the Home started to go wrong. It was that several things started happening at once, that seemed to give the adults the impression I was not happy at the Home and I was falling out with every member of staff. In truth, I had never been happy at the Home. In my mind if I did anything to solve the problem, it would be my mother that it would affect and upset the most.

The main railway line with the fast trains I had thought of as an easy way of ending my stay at the Home; and also the high bridge that the main A5 road ran beneath was an alternative solution. I would not really have been scared of ending my life; the reasons for not going through with the action, were that it would upset my mother and it might hurt on impact. If there had been no possibility of returning to my mother, I do not think I would have been able to tolerate the Home until it was time for me to leave senior school. The test I had been to in London had given the adults the idea that I was not happy living at the Home, but I don't think I had really let on as to my thoughts, if my stay was to be for many years to come.

GROWING UP

If a few things about growing up had been explained to me, life at the Home could have been easier. I was odd: if Sister had still been in charge, having brought up a large number of boys over the years, she might have understood the problem that seemed to occur for me now I was almost eleven and in my last year of junior school. The Houseparent had not needed to deal with many teenage boys. If I had been sent over to the nurse, or possibly able to talk to the Governor or his deputy, things might have been explained to me over the matter of growing up.

For education and my activities with others I was thought of as younger than my actual age; however my I.Q. and physical development might be classed as older. At the age of almost eleven, I was taller than most of my own age group, and even my looks had changed over the last couple of years. At school, the

music teacher had taken me out of singing lessons because my voice might be starting to break. Had adults explained a few more of the events that coincided with this event, life would have been much easier.

At night, I was having trouble sleeping, even though there were now only two of us in the room. Whilst the other boy seemed to sleep all through the night, bad dreams and minor disturbances kept me from the sleep I needed. I was waking up in the middle of the night with the feeling that I needed to go for a pee and that the front of my pyjamas was slightly damp. The major telling off that I received when my pyjama trousers and lower sheet was found in the laundry basket by the Houseparent made me hate living here. If I had worn thick cotton pyjamas it might have not been noticed; now that I wore light blue or light green nylon pyjamas the stain was easy to see.

When it became a regular event, I was in trouble every morning and given the slipper for this disgusting act. It was not a case of wetting the bed, but if it had been explained what 'wet dreams' or 'nocturnal emissions' were, and what was going on during this growing-up period, I might have understood. Being marched to the bathroom for a morning bath after the hits with the slipper and having to strip my bed whilst everyone else went for their wash did cause embarrassment. To them the only reason I would be sent to have a bath would be due to wetting my bed; even the younger pair although not teasing me to my face could make fun of me.

Finally, the Houseparent lost patience with me. She could have made it worse, but I was spared any witnesses when she told me that my night-time problems must end. There followed a couple of extra hits with the slipper above the normal two hits. I was informed that I was to wear a pair of underpants beneath my pyjamas. These were not going to be boys' underpants but thick girls' knickers. Over these knickers I was to wear a pair of waterproof rubber pants. When I could show that I was not going to cause any more problems, I could go back to being treated like an ordinary boy. There was the threat from the Houseparent if I did not wear the rubber pants, that on the mornings that either my pyjamas or lower sheet were found to be damp, I would be given four hits with the slipper.

I was unhappy over the matter. It took the helper to eventually calm me down and explain what was happening during this growing-up stage. It seemed that I might be affected several months before others of my own age.

The following nights I hid myself away when it came for getting ready for bed. An age gap in years meant that the three older boys had much later bedtimes as they were all at senior school, and with the two younger boys having early bedtimes our paths did not cross and I could be on my own.

I kept the matter a secret for some time, but eventually one of the older boys found out what I was wearing beneath my pyjamas. Before he could start teasing me, the helper threatened that it would be quite easy to give him similar items to wear.

I did not protest at wearing them to bed. In a way, I was quite happy if it stopped the telling off and slipper from the Houseparent. Now in the middle of the night I was waking up after an unusual dream. They were not bad dreams, but simply different and I could now understand what was happening to me. I would then go off to the lavatory to have a pee and return to bed, then sleep until it was time to get up. As the knickers were damp in the morning, the waterproof pants had kept my pyjamas and lower sheet from needing to be changed.

I was less restless at night now and did not really mind having a quick bath first thing. That I was not going to be given the slipper or teased by having to take the lower sheet off my bed on getting up, meant that I did not mind this punishment. Everything would have been generally fine had I been left alone. During Christmas, the Houseparent decided to show me up in front of most of the others one evening. With the holidays, our bed times had become a little more relaxed, and instead of getting sent off to bed according to our ages, the Houseparent tended to pack us all off to bed at a slightly later time.

My embarrassment was caused when she sent a couple of us to get into our pyjamas then to return to watch the television for a little longer. In the normal way if it was later in the evening younger ones would be going straight to bed once they had finished their wash or bath.

The comment by the Houseparent to me as I was leaving with the youngest in the group was that I should remember to put on my waterproof pants. Only one older boy until now had known of this matter and had used his better judgment to keep quiet to save getting into trouble. Now that the two younger boys knew, the others soon found out. I was fair game for teasing when the adults were not around. Whilst there was little I could do if the older ones teased me, having two younger boys make fun of me was annoying. I had originally imagined that waterproof pants were only made to fit young children, but that the Home had them readily available in my size must mean that others of my age wore them.

DRESSING UP

A comment was made that I did not seem to join in imaginary games. It was that I did not really see the point of games like Cowboys and Indians, or to go out and play with the older boys and their toy guns in an imaginary game of war. At the start of December all of us tried to be on our best behaviour in the run up to Christmas; this was to try to persuade the adults that the presents we really wanted came our way.

I was sent out to the Administration Block with the instruction to get myself some dressing-up clothes; I might be going to a party where there was a dressing-up competition. One of the Sisters was in charge of a small assortment of dressing-up clothes that normally came out of store shortly before Christmas to enable anyone who was going to a fancy dress party to have something interesting to put on. Keeping them in one location meant that all had a fair share.

During the Christmas season we quite often attended parties and fun events, so this instruction I did not think of as odd. If there was a reason that none of the others were coming over at the same moment, it was due to me returning to London the next day for a weekend away from the Home.

I was confronted with a range of cowboy outfits, spaceman costumes, Red Indian headdresses and several other items that I did not really think stood any chance of winning any sort of prize. Finally, I was talked into a pirate costume. The main items were an eye patch and a blue and white striped shirt. I changed the idea of trousers that a pirate might have worn to a pair of riding breeches, but this was finding that there was a pair of long black leather riding boots, possibly as near as I could get to the type of boots a pirate might have worn. The pair of riding boots had actually made my day. Before coming to the Home I had owned a pair of long riding boots, but lost them due to my mother putting them on the bonfire before we moved back to London.

The boots I had chosen looked brand new; the Sister remarked that several girls had tried them on before me, but found they were either too tall or too narrow in the leg. With my skinny appearance, the fit was correct. The Sister thought I should return to my flat, fully dressed up, so that my Houseparent could see me. Leaving the building I had to take a rather long and hidden route back; I did not want to let any of my friends see me in a pirate costume.

The Houseparent seemed to accept my choice although other than the eye patch there was nothing really that could be classed as dressing up. If Sister had been in charge there now would have been the order to go and put everything away until it was needed; instead it was suggested that I could keep dressed like that until bedtime. If I complained that I did not like dressing up, the chance was that future Christmas presents might be at risk, so I played along, and stayed dressed up during tea and stayed like that until bedtime.

Friday was a bit of an odd day. Most went off to school as normal, but a few of the classes at our school were being given an extra day off owing to decorators needing to get to a few rooms before the Christmas holiday. The girl in our flat who went to the same school as I did was going to go off as normal. For once, I was not the one going off in a bad mood; she had to go with a group of the older ones instead of me.

One disappointment was that I would have to wait until the end of the day for my mother to collect me. If only it had been known earlier about the extra day's holiday, I would not have to waste a whole day here. Once everyone had left for school, the flat seemed so empty. As the Houseparent knew I would not be going to school today, my school clothes had been put into the laundry basket the previous day, just in case I forgot and now went out to play in school shorts. I had made sure that the long trousers I had acquired were easy to find, and even though the weather was mild, I did not want to wear my play shorts outside.

Possibly the trousers looked a little odd due to my height; they were a good fit around the waist, but rather short in the legs. I was now told that if I was going to wear the long trousers I must wear the boots; she did not want me looking badly dressed in front of others. If I remained clean during the day, I could wear my costume home for the weekend. It was a challenge I won; long trousers during the winter were great to go to London in.

The choice of a pirate costume in a way was a good idea; the school had organised a Christmas play for which a few of our class had the more interesting parts, rather than just being one of the choir or other unknown part. Putting myself in front of others was not really how I wanted to be in the Christmas play; I really wanted to help move the scenery. Our class was given a short part in a play to act out the rhyme 'Tinker, Tailor'. I managed to get a part in the middle of the verse as the Rich Man, so as not to be either at the start of the line or the end.

Parents and staff helped organise all sorts of costumes for those that had parts in the play. If I asked the Houseparent to help, I could bet something would be chosen that would let the others make fun of me. I played down my part when it came to the allocation of costumes. A fancy shirt was all that was provided for me. I completed my outfit with the riding boots and breeches. The time I spent having to dress up ready to go on stage was down to a few seconds.

Once on stage, my part was soon over and I was free for the rest of the play, until the whole cast were required to make a final appearance. If I had hoped to lurk somewhere in the back of the group, I was pushed to the front for the simple reason that I would be able to sit in the front of the group and not get anything I was wearing caught up in any of the stage equipment. I felt daft sitting amongst a group of infants, together with a girl of my own age who was also lacking any form of bulky dress. For the second presentation of our play the following evening I made sure that I was not anywhere near the front when the final group was formed on the stage. The infants sat on their own; I was not the only one with the idea of hiding away. Once school had finished, I was allowed to return to London for part of the Christmas holidays.

CHRISTMAS 1967

I was unhappy at Christmas in having to return to the Home for the week or so of Christmas festivities. The adults thought all of us should be at the Home during Christmas. I would have been far happier in London; there may have been less going on indoors in the London flat, but with all the cinemas and other activities that were possible, I would have preferred my solitary life. My only worry during the few days before Christmas whilst I had been on holiday in London was simply down to the plans that my mother was making for leaving London.

Once back at the Home, although I did not really intend to go out of my way to be annoying, there was friction at various points. I was almost eleven; to the adults as I was still at junior school this firmly put me in the younger group; the older five in our flat seemed to have so many extra privileges.

At one point, I think I annoyed the Houseparent. I was sent to my room; I guessed that at any moment, she would follow and I was due for the slipper. I waited ages; I could bet it was done to make me more afraid of what was to come. At first I had stood by my bed ready for her to come in. To speed things up I had already loosened the belt on my trousers ready to take them down if the demand came. If I was daft, I could have left the room and gone to see where she was, but in reality, I was not in any hurry to be reduced to tears. With our bedrooms having no personal possessions other than clothes there was little to keep me amused; I simply waited. Finally, the helper came in and announced it was time for lunch. It appeared, as this was Christmas, the Houseparent had not wanted me to upset the rest of the flat; if I had been punished and was in a mood, I could have easily upset the others.

For a short while, I did try to take part in events in the flat, but it was not how I wanted to spend Christmas. I had to admit that I liked the organised trip to the pantomime; we were taken from the Home near to where I lived in London. Outside the theatre was a bus stop with a route that stopped at the end of our road. If only I had been allowed to catch the bus to my home instead of having to return with the others to the Home it would have made my Christmas.

The Christmas party a coach-load of us attended was also fun, but knowing my problems with coach travel, I did not really tuck into all the food on offer as I knew exactly what would happen on the return journey. There was the chance to win a prize in the fancy dress competition, and if the elastic on my eye patch had held together I might have stood a chance, but quite early on it looked as if it was mostly girls in the running for most of the prizes.

At Christmas, some of the rules over our behaviour were a little relaxed. I announced that I wanted to wear the pirate costume during the entire holiday. The moment I had chosen to make this request was at the very point that anyone that had borrowed costumes from the store was returning them. Dressing up and looking conspicuous was never something I normally did, and if the staff guessed I was spoiling for a fight over a minor matter like this none came. The Houseparent agreed that it would be fine for me to dress up for the entire Christmas holiday as I might enjoy it more.

With the eye patch broken and now lost and the striped shirt spending more days in the laundry basket waiting to be washed, it was decided that as it was colourful it would need to be washed as a separate item, like most of the coloured shirts that were worn for games at school. As we were now on our holidays there was very little of our clothing that needed special treatment so my striped shirt was not going to get any immediate attention.

If the others thought I was silly wearing riding breeches and boots for the full festive period I did not mind. As I was regarded as one of the younger ones, I was not going to wear shorts if I could help it. That I was actually taller than one of the boys who was a little older than myself did not seem to matter. I could understand that for junior school the uniform was short trousers, but in the Home we still had to wear them when we went into town, or for church and the like. When we were out together as we seemed about the same age, I looked rather stupid being taller and still in short trousers, while he was wearing long trousers.

The Home having rather religious beliefs, I expected to be ordered to dress in my best shorts for the various services, but the Houseparent went out of her way to see that the riding breeches were clean and neatly pressed. I played along with her and spent ages putting a good shine on the boots. It did get me out of other chores as I seemed to her to be fully occupied.

The Christmas service was extra special. All those who could sing were in the choir, and even small groups that were not good enough for the main choir had practised extra pieces, and were huddled in various parts of the chapel for their turn to come. If the adults felt I should join in, it was by giving me the instruction to help with the collection and the giving out of song sheets. In my mind, it was better than having to sit in the pews for the entire service.

Once Christmas was over, I managed to return to London for the final week or so of the holidays. The Houseparent decided that I might as well keep the pirate outfit; as the eye patch was now missing, it did not seem worth returning it to the Sister in charge of the clothing store. I was happy to be allowed to wear it back to London again. With Christmas and birthday money to spend, I could do so much. The weather might not have been fine but in London, there were plenty of places to shelter that were interesting. One major activity was to be taken to a theatre in the centre of London to see a play, whose main memorable line was 'I don't care'. Then it was returning to the Home, to find out more about what plans there were for me.

JANUARY 1968

During the first week of term after the Christmas holidays, it was announced by the staff that I would leave my junior school and go to my new senior school. The rules that they seemed to have set, dictated that I was to be aged eleven before I could leave junior school. With my birthday early into the New Year, everything slotted into place.

On my final day the deputy head teacher had asked me to come to his room at the end of the day. This was perhaps the only day I actually did not mind visiting him. He was a teacher we knew who gave out sweets. Having family in the retail sweet trade, he was known to have a small supply of sweets in his cupboard. If you were in his class on your birthday, he would allow you to choose a few sweets or a large box of chocolates. We all knew these were dummy boxes of chocolates that were completely empty inside. A few of the girls did choose such a gift, but no boy was ever seen holding a large box with a pretty illustration and ribbons.

On the previous occasion of making a visit to his room, it had been with a friend due to some trouble we had been in. He was teaching one of the top forms. The Headmaster was away that day, so standing outside his office for the lunchtime break owing to our behaviour had not been possible. Our crime it appeared did not warrant the cane, however the slipper given at full force on our rears did really hurt, almost as much as when I had been caned by him. If we could have left his room immediately after the punishment, everything would have been all right, but being ordered to stand up and endure a further telling-off in front of his class whilst we were in tears was awful.

This visit at the end of the day was a pleasure. As well as giving out sweets on your birthday, on the final day of school all in his class would be given sweets, and it appeared I deserved this as I was leaving. Some of the teachers might have said it was worth giving me sweets to get me to leave.

Last Junior School photo

Once his class had left the room, after a short delay I was taken into the back room and allowed to choose a small selection. This slight delay meant that when I did leave the school playground everyone else had vanished. Within a short time I was back at the Home, a few of the sweets remained, but it was best not to tell the Houseparent the actual number I had eaten on my walk back.

There was a row now because I was a few minutes late. On my last day of school, it might have been expected that a few things might have delayed me, but to the Houseparent this was not allowed. Even if this was my last day I was expected to arrive back on time. I did not really sulk during tea, but my last day of junior school should have ended on a happier note.

SENIOR SCHOOL

I was happy with my new school, although it meant leaving the flat before the others as I had to travel a further distance. By the second day I had made a friend that came from close to the Home so I was not alone when I went into school, and although we were not in the same year and our ages were two years apart, we became good friends early on.

Back at the flat, there had been a week or so of the older boys simply trying to wind me up. Now I was at a different senior school from them, I was the enemy. I was an easy target with a new and different school uniform.

I was teased about the style of my new uniform; this was a plain dark blazer, and was far smarter than they wore. The item they were able to tease me over, was that for first and second-year pupils at the school I was at, short trousers were the norm. To them senior school pupils would wear long trousers.

Some of my new friends had told me that in the following school year there was going to be a change to the school uniform; the first and second-year pupils would have long trousers set as part of their standard uniform. I wondered if I could persuade the Houseparent to let me change to long trousers before that time to stop the older ones in the flat from teasing me.

On the occasions that they succeeded in winding me up, my temper got the better of me. The only time I was happy was when I left the grounds and headed off to my new school. At the end of the afternoon, it was coming back through the gates, and knowing that until the following morning, it would be a battle for me to keep out of trouble from the others in the flat. I could delay my arrival back into the flat by completing my homework at school; at the end of the day one form room was available for any pupils that wanted to do their homework at school. To the staff at school it was a way they knew it would be completed and for a few, possibly a more quiet place to do it in.

LEAVING FEBRUARY 1968

Things were starting to change; I knew that my mother and grandmother were soon going to be leaving the London flat and moving to Wiltshire, where an aunt and uncle now lived. The flat in London had only been twenty-five miles away and quite easy to visit. If they were moving to Wiltshire, it would be almost impossible to come and see me, and the visits to my mother would not really be possible due to the distance.

At some point, it was mentioned that as soon as my mother had settled in I would be able to join her. They thought by the start of the summer holidays, it might be possible for me to leave and return to her. I had the idea that if I was not able to return straight away to my mother, then their original idea that I might be moved to a different Home could easily come about. If my mother moved to Wiltshire with my aunt and uncle, to the adults it would make little difference if I were moved to a Home further away.

Returning to the Home was not something I had relished. I had tried to live in the group and appear to be part of it. However you grouped the various members, it normally meant that I did not fit in. Life at the Home on my return seemed to be easier. I did try to fit in, but the slightest thing that did not go right and I seemed to be the one that was blamed and punished.

One way of keeping me happy was to allow me to visit a friend who lived outside the Home. Once tea was over, I was allowed my freedom. A set time was given for my return and it was down to me to obey this time or risk this privilege being removed.

Fortunately my mother suggested that I might be able to return to her earlier than originally planned. There were a few days of minor chaos around half term that ensued when it was confirmed by the Houseparent that I was leaving.

The packing up of my possessions in the flat took some time. The contents of my locker were reduced considerably with a frantic selection of swapping to get toys, books and the like that would actually fit in my case together with my clothes. The Houseparent saw that I had a full selection of new best clothes and an assortment of respectable play clothes. Of my own possessions, there was a slight problem over bicycles. The one that had replaced the bicycle that I had brought to the Home was not in current working order as it was partly in bits and under repair. My original bicycle was now really too small for me and was in the possession of one of the younger boys. Even if my bicycle had been in working order, when my uncle came in the car to collect me, the larger size of my current bicycle would have been impossible to get into the car.

The final point came, all farewells were said and that was simply the end. I sat in the car with the hope that I would not have to return. I should have been happy; it was not that I was sad to be leaving the Home, but almost three years of my life had been spent here. There was the feeling that although I disliked the place, my future was not that certain, and there was the thought that if the ideas my mother had did not go as planned, I would be returning here. If there had been an absolute guarantee that I would never have to return, I would have showed my true feelings as to how I felt about the Home.

FREEDOM

For almost three years, leaving the Home had seemed impossible. My uncle had collected me shortly before lunch. After a quick lunch at my aunt and uncle's flat, we set off for London. Soon we were in London; and all my possessions were back in my bedroom. This had originally been my grandfather's room, but now it was mine. To be able to sleep in my own room without anyone chattering in the night would be wonderful. In the Home only the oldest girl had a bedroom on her own, something I would have loved.

As well as a good assortment of clothes, I left the NCH with a large world atlas. This was similar in design to the type sold by Reader's Digest but with different covers and a logo of the NCH embossed on the front. Although I was very pleased with this gift, I removed the logo and lettering. I did not want reminders of my stay each time I opened the atlas or if any friends were to see it. The other gift from the NCH was a Bible with my name embossed in gold lettering.

One matter I did not really understand about my leaving; my mother questioned me several times about why the Home had requested her to take me back. I thought I was returning to her as we were going to move to the country. I had not been told at the Home during the last couple of months that I had done anything wrong at the Home, and that I was to be expelled.

What should have been a very happy event of returning to my mother in London before we left for Wiltshire, was overshadowed with the thought that I must have done something wrong, but I just could not think of any reason for the Home to demand that I should leave.

National Childrens' Home Harpenden circa 1920

Above   *Girls in the sewing room*
Below   *The printing school*
Right top   *The printing school*
Right centre   *Girls in the laundry*
Right bottom   *Boys baking the bread*

NATIONAL CHILDREN'S HOME, PRINTING WORKS, HARPENDEN.

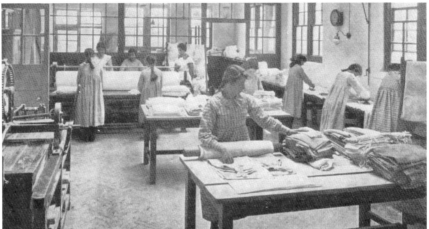

THEIR HISTORY OF ME
or 44783 as I am also known.

These are the records of an eight-year-old boy called Philip, who was put into care in the mid 1960s, at the Highfield Branch of The National Children's Home, Harpenden, Herts.

They explain the reason why the child was placed into the care of the NCH. The history of the child whilst in care, is shown in various letters and other documents that were kept during his stay at Highfield.

It must be remembered that when these documents were written in the mid 1960s there never was the intention for them to be seen by anyone other than the staff looking after the child during his stay. Some of the text and original written notes have been combined to avoid unnecessary repetition.

MY NCH HISTORY

My mother was going to return to London to look after her sick parents. There would not be room in the flat for me. A solution was needed.

1. 27.01.65 Letter to Uncle from Governor NCH Harpenden, asking for an appointment regarding Philip.

2. 01.02.65 Note from NCH regarding a visit to the Uncle.

3. 02.02.65. Letter to Uncle from Child Care Officer.
I am writing to ask if I can see you and your sister-in-law on Tuesday morning February 9th, regarding your admission enquiry.

4. 03.02.65 Letter to the NCH at Harpenden from the Uncle.
Thank you for your letter. It will be quite convenient for you to see me on Feb 9th, but as my sister-in-law (the mother) is working in the Isle of Wight, it will be rather difficult for her to be here, if that is all right with you may I suggest 11.30 as a suitable time. If there is anything else you wish to know in the meantime, my wife is at home until 1pm each day, and will be pleased to help in any way she can.

5. 10.02.65 Note from Governor of Harpenden.
I had a long talk with the uncle and aunt of the boy. The uncle mentioned that he needed to be disciplined as he could be rather badly behaved.
Visited The Uncle 09.02.65. The mother is due in London in a week's time, with her son Philip. She will telephone or write, and I will write full report after seeing them. At present she is living on Isle of Wight. Philip is 8 years old and is half Indian.

MY ANSWER.

The visit by the Governor and the Child Care Officer to my aunt and uncle seemed to seal my fate. It appears to have been mentioned by him that I needed to be disciplined. I was not really a wild boy, but I was most happy on my own or with just a couple of friends; large group activities were never to my liking.

If the comment that I needed discipline had not been mentioned, I might not have been allocated to the flat, that to nearly every child in the Home was one of the least appealing flats in the Home owing to the Sister's strict but fair regime. The Sister in charge was not unkind in any way, but having possibly the most experience in years over every other member of the staff in looking after boys, her method of upbringing would be the nearest I would get to a father figure for discipline. To give me a title of 'half Indian' is not really correct as my father came from Ceylon.

6. 23.02.65 Letter to Child Care Officer from The Mother.

With reference to a letter from my Sister. I have now returned to London, & would be pleased to have an appointment at any time suitable to you.

7. 24.02.65 Letter to The Mother from Child Care Officer.

Thank you for your letter telling me you are now in London. Is it possible to see you during the day on Tuesday, the 2nd March?

8. 26.02.65. Letter to The Child Care Officer from The Mother.

Thank you for your letter, I would be very pleased to see you on Tuesday March 2nd; the afternoon would be most suitable, although I shall be at home all day, as I now have my mother home from hospital & she needs rather a lot of attention in the mornings.

9. 02.03.65. NCH FORM Particulars of child for whom admission is sought.
Name of child. *PHILIP JOHN (Boy).*
D.O.B. *1957*
Place of Birth. *Paddington Hospital.*
Baptized. *No*
Religious Denomination. *C of E.*
Present Address *London NW2.*
With whom. *Mother.*
Name of Father *Linton Jansen, Nationality Singhalese (Burger). Country of Origin Ceylon. Occupation Trainee in hotel management.* Health *Good. Religion Burger R/C.*
Name of Mother *Dorothy Moira Howard.* Nationality *English.* D.O.B. *09.10.21.* Country of Origin *England.* Address *London NW2. Occupation Ex-housekeeper.* Health *Good.* Religion *C of E.*
Wages *Four Pounds,* Total weekly income *Four Pounds*
Grandparents *Father 88. Retired Accountant. Mother 68 Retired.*
Aunts and Uncles

Harpenden: (Main contact with NCH) Sister & Brother-in-Law. No Children.
Harpenden: Sister & Brother-in-Law. Daughter (age 24).
Harpenden: Brother & Sister-in-Law. Son (age 6),
Daughter (age 8).
London: Brother. No Children.
Information: regarding the health, character, habits and mentality of the child.
Very lively. Lack of concentration.
Reason for application.
Mother is having to look after her mother who has had a stroke & father 88 years. Lack of accommodation, and supervision for Philip.
Who takes responsibility for receiving the child if he should prove unsuitable for continued residence in the Home - *Mother.*
What weekly payment is offered towards the child's maintenance? - *Two Pounds per week plus clothes.*

MY ANSWER.
The reference to my father as a Burger:
Descendents of Dutch settlers who arrived in Ceylon during the Dutch occupation in the 17th and 18th Century. They were encouraged to inter-marry with the Singhalese. On the whole they have kept their European habits, and generally speak English, though many also speak Singhalese.

10. 02.03.65 Report of Child Care Officer.
The mother's sister in Harpenden had originally approached the Governor at Highfield to ask his advice about her nephew Philip. The mother was at the time working as a housekeeper on the Isle of Wight, but I was able to see her this week as she has now come up to London to look after her parents.
The mother is 43 years of age, and has so far been able to look after Philip herself during these past years. Just before Christmas, however, her mother had a stroke and has been in hospital up until now. The mother is the only one who is in a position to come and look after their parents.
The grandmother is still slightly paralysed by the stroke and has difficulty in speaking; the grandfather who is 88 years has also to be looked after fairly well as he suffers from bronchitis. The mother has a pleasant flat on the second floor, just off the main Edgware road.
The mother's difficulty now is trying to look after Philip at the same time who is a very lively energetic 8-year-old boy.
According to his uncle from Harpenden, he is in great need of discipline.
The mother has already told Philip that there is a likelihood he might be going to 'boarding-school' and he seemed quite cheerful at this prospect of being with other children.
It was very difficult however, to carry on a conversation with Philip as he seemed to suffer from an intense lack of concentration.
He seemed a very likeable little boy, and is only lightly coloured. The mother only knew his father a Singhalese, for a very short period, and has since lost all contact with him.

The mother is planning to look after her parents indefinitely, but thinks that as soon as her help and support is no longer required she will then be able to find another job as a housekeeper and will have Philip back, but at this stage she thinks he will be slightly more disciplined and that she should then be able to cope with him as well as a job. Her family is now giving her four pounds per week and she is willing to contribute two pounds per week for Philip's maintenance as well as buying all his clothes.

I would like to recommend this application and that if possible Philip could go to Harpenden so that his mother could visit fairly easily as well as all the other relatives who are living in the area. I don't think the mother would ever lose touch with the boy and she would gladly visit once every three weeks.

Possibly when Philip is 11 yrs and changing schools the possibility of him being returned to his mother could then be considered.

Governor of Harpenden Notes – After visit by Mother to Highfield.

It was originally suggested by the uncle that the boy needed to be disciplined. When the mother was questioned over this matter, she thought it was perhaps a good idea as that at times he could be a bit of a handful.

We spoke about the various sanctions that were available; the mother was in agreement that for any minor events, if the Sister in charge of Philip punished him with the slipper, there would be no objection from her. If there were any cases of bad behaviour then she was quite in agreement that he could be punished more severely.

MY ANSWER.

Describing me as a very lively energetic 8-year-old was perhaps the most accurate words ever spoken. I was on the go from the point I woke up until when I went to bed. If I was perhaps a loner it was due to my mother simply not having as much time due to work, as she would have liked to spend with me, so I was used to playing on my own.

A classification of me as an 8-year-old boy today would be that it was quite easy to add the words hyperactive and several of the more modern labels that children who do not seem to fit into the adults standard categories receive.

My mother was asked about the matter of punishments I might receive if I did anything wrong during my stay in the Home. When I was small my mother had given me a few light smacks; these were normally enough to bring me back into order.

At the age of five my grandmother had once caned me. This did get me to be well behaved, and if my mother had used this form of punishment on me at the time, I knew I would have followed every command she made.

From the age of six my mother had normally given me early bedtimes or decided that treats could be suspended, as at my first school the Headmistress was against physical punishments. Had I not gone to that boarding school I might have found my mother could have been a little firmer with me.

When I reached seven, the event at the last infant school where I was given the cane, had shown her that I could be kept in order. My mother decided that at the age of seven I was old enough to receive the plimsoll from her over minor matters, which that year were just over a dozen different times for various matters of bad temper, damage to property and wetting the bed. There was the cane for any serious problem. This, my mother had only needed to give me twice. All my punishments from my mother had been quite light in nature; it was done to try to keep me under some kind of control.

The Home seemed to have accepted the suggestion from my uncle that I needed to be disciplined; this in my mind was a little unfair as we had so rarely been together. My mother had probably written to her sister telling her of my latest wrongdoing; this was how my uncle came to the idea that I needed to be kept under control. My mother agreed that the Sister in charge of me should use the slipper on me if I became troublesome; if there was anything worse in my behaviour then it was easy to see that the Governor of the Home could intervene.

The item in my file *"Possibly when Philip is 11 yrs and changing schools the possibility of him being returned to his mother could then be considered.* Was it decided before my arrival at Highfield that I was going to be with them for three years, whatever my family outcome was? If my grandmother and grandfather had died at an age before I was 11-12 years, would I have stayed in the Home, or would my mother have taken me straight out? It might be taken, that the next three to four years in the Home would be used to calm be down, whatever the situation of my grandparents was.

I did find out that my mother's last employer did want her back, but the invitation did not include me. If my grandparents had died early, would my mother have been able to find a housekeeping job that would have taken both of us?

Early on, if it had been explained to me that around the age of eleven there would be a good chance of leaving the Home, then possibly my life would have been a lot easier and the number of problems I caused would have been far less.

11. 17.03.65 Letter to Child Care Officer from the Headmistress.

The mother came to see me when she was due to leave to go to London and mentioned that she would be making this application. It seemed to us here that Philip badly needs real care and affection and stability of home life. The mother was never prepared to give any information about her own private life, but Philip obviously needs the interests and concern of a father.

He was backward in most subjects although he was now beginning to make real progress with his reading. His work was generally messy and untidy. He is highly strung and his behaviour with other children tended to be aggressive and unfriendly.

I found it necessary to punish Philip with the cane on one occasion; he found authority very easy to accept once boundaries were set. However, he got on well with all the staff and we all felt that given stability and a proper routine, Philip would make good progress academically and emotionally. Clearly, the residential school he temporally attended was not suitable for him.

If the flat he and his mother are living in impose severe restrictions on the boy, and if the aged and sick grandparents make living in the small flat difficult and emotionally strained for him, then I feel strongly that a move would be best for Philip.

SCHOOL REPORT from the Headmistress, requested by the NCH.
Attitude: *Fair,* Effort: *Fair,* Attainment: *Weak,* English: *Weak,* Arithmetic: *Weak,* Social Studies: *Weak,* Handwork: *Weak,* Physical Training: *Fair.*

MY ANSWER.
The letter and the report from the previous Head Teacher on the Isle of Wight did not really give me a very favourable account. I did not manage any marks in the other grades on the report of Excellent, Good or even Average; but was marked as either Fair or Weak.

It was at this school that I found that if you did wrong, punishments would hurt.

12. 19.03.65 Letter to Mother from Child Care Officer.
At its meeting this week, our committee agreed to accept your son Philip subject to the completion of the usual documents.

The medical Certificate should be completed by a doctor, the School Report by the child's school teacher and the general Agreement should be signed over a 6d stamp as indicated. When you return these documents, please let us have Philip's Birth Certificate.

We will let you know as soon as we have a vacancy.

13. 27.03.65. General Agreement Form signed by the Mother.
I declare that the said child enters the National Children's Home and Orphanage. I hereby agree that the Principal of the Home is duly authorised shall have the custody care and control.

I shall not remove the child from the Home without giving at least one calendar month's notice in writing (unless the Principal shall consent otherwise in writing) pay to the Home any monies then owing by me to the Home in respect of the said child. That if required by notice of the Principal to do so I will at my own expense remove the said child from the Home within one calendar month after the date of such a notice. That if I shall commit any breach of the forgoing provisions I will forthwith pay to the Home the amount expended in the upbringing of the said child as an ascertained debt calculated at the rate of Three Pounds for each week of the period during which the said child shall have been in residence at any branch of the Home, subject to the deduction from the amount so calculated of any sums paid by me to the Home in respect of the said child.

I further agree without reference to me to give instructions for the sanction of carrying out any surgical or dental operations in the said child including vaccinations or immunization of the said child.

MY ANSWER.

The clauses in the documents allowed the NCH to return me to my mother at very short notice; it also had a penalty condition if my mother wanted my return. The money to keep me might by modern standards not seem very much. At this period there were no benefits the state provided. I was an only child, there was no child benefit for the first child, and my mother was a single parent and there were no benefits on that score either. My mother was not really working in paid employment while looking after her parents, however as she was not unemployed, there were no unemployment payments.

The rent for the London flat came from my grandparents' pension, although the family was never on the poverty line. Rent, heat and food took the vast majority of any available funds.

Had there been some benefits, and help to look after my grandparents, the need for me to be sent to the Home may never have been needed.

Two sets of aunts and uncles now paid two pounds each to my mother to look after my grandparents. Half of this was now paid to the Children's Home to look after me.

My mother had two pounds a week to add to the budget of the household to provide for her share of the food and heat. If there were to be treats like visits to me and for presents and the like, it had to come out of this amount.

14. 20.03.65 Letter to the Previous Head Teacher from the Child Care Officer.

Thank you very much indeed for your letter which has been most helpful. Philip is going to be admitted to one of our branches at Harpenden, Herts. and a copy of your letter is being passed on to the Governor.

15. 26.03.65 Medical Certificate from a Doctor to the NCH
Name Philip.
Age 8.
Present health. Good.
Sight, hearing and speech. Normal.
What diseases has the child suffered. Measles.
General observations. In good health, lively & healthy boy.

MY ANSWER.

The report from the doctor shows that I had no problems; to her my speech was normal. It was not a case of just being seen for a few moments. The doctor lived next door to us. If I had been unusual in any way, there would have been some comment over my speech and behaviour that she had often seen for my first five years of life.

16. 29.03.65 Admission Particulars Form
Philip John Age 8 Illegitimate, mother 43 ex-housekeeper, putative father trainee in hotel management whereabouts unknown. Singhalese.

Religion of child C of E
Payment Two Pounds per week by mother.
MY ANSWER
Putative = acknowledged, assumed, reputed.

17. 29.03.65. Letter to NCH from Mother.
Please find enclosed Medical Certificate, General Agreement, School Report and Birth Certificate.
I am sure Philip will be happier living in one of your Homes with other children, than being cooped up in this London flat with two elderly invalids.
Thank you for your very kind attention.

MY ANSWER
Want to bet on me going to be happier in the Home! And I thought I was going to a boarding school.

18. 12.04.65. Letter to Governor of Harpenden NCH from Rev. Gordon. E. Barritt. NCH London.
This boy has been accepted by the Committee to come into our care. The enquiry originally came via yourself as relatives live in Harpenden.
Philip's mother lives in NW2, with aged and infirm parents. We would like him to come to Harpenden to enable regular visits from his mother and relatives to be made.
Could you please let me know the date you are likely to be able to receive Philip.
Note. Added 21.04.65. To Sister in Charge Flat 1: Governor of Harpenden would like this little boy to come into your family. Would any day be convenient for him to come?

19. 22.04.65 Letter to Rev. Gordon. E. Barritt. NCH London from Governor NCH Harpenden.
Thank you for your letter of 12th April. We can take this little boy straightaway.

20. 30.04.65 Letter to Mother from Rev. Gordon. E. Barritt. NCH London.
I am writing to let you know that we now have a vacancy at our Harpenden branch and could accept your son, Philip at any time.
It is understood that when Philip comes into our care you will be able to make a contribution of Two Pounds per week.
Will you please see that Philip's medical card is handed to the Governor. Enclosed is a copy of our Notes to Relatives and a Clothing List, which is to be regarded as a suggestion only and not a condition of the child's admittance.

MY ANSWER.
The letter all the adults in the family had been waiting for. There was now room to take me.

21. 06.05.65 Letter to Headmaster Manland Junior School from Governor of Harpenden NCH.

Thank you for agreeing to take Philip.

For your information, Philip has come into our care because his mother is having to look after her parents, the grandmother has just had a stroke, and the grandfather is 88.

22. Admission card

Philip Date of Admission 06.05.65

23. 14.05.65 Letter to Mother from Governor of Harpenden NCH.

I am pleased to say Philip seems to be settling down quite happily with us.

We hope you will be able to visit him regularly, and that his relations in the district will also keep in touch. I suggest you see Philip every three weeks. We ask parents to visit on a Saturday. We would like you to take Philip out when you come as this makes a little outing for him, and gives you a chance to have him on your own. It is quite all right for you to have him for the whole day if you wish. I should like you to write to me at the office whenever you wish to have him, and we will always reply within a day or two letting you know if the suggested date is convenient.

I suggest you make your first visit on Saturday 22nd May, as the Sister in Charge will be away on holiday the following week, and I expect you would like to see her. When you write I should be glad if you could mention the time you hope to arrive.

We shall be pleased for Philip to come home to you for occasional weekends, and for part of school holidays, and, as the case of visiting, I should be glad if you would make arrangements through the office.

MY ANSWER.

I had been at the Home for one week and seemed to be settling down according to reports from the Sister in Charge. I tried to be good, having had a life where other than at school I have only been surrounded by adults, I am now with other children of all ages twenty-four hours a day.

I have been informed that my stay will be for the period while my grandparents are ill. Therefore, I have no real idea of how long I will be staying here. All the other children in the flat I have been placed with have been here since they were very young. It is easy to understand their views that they will be staying at this Home until they leave school, and to take on similar ideas that this was probably going to be my future as well.

My life seemed so different, having been used to long periods of peace and quiet. Unless I found some deserted spot outside in the grounds, there was always someone around. Even when going to bed, I had to sleep in a room with three other boys. As they were older, there was simply the knowledge that both through age and time spent here, I was going to be last in the queue for everything.

The suggestion from the Governor that my mother could see me every three weeks was merely a suggestion, however my mother took this as a final decision as to how often I could have visits.

From that point on unless there were other matters arising, my mother visited me every third week. Sometimes I would go to London for the weekend and on other occasions I was simply taken out on the Saturday.

The Home requested that parents only visit on a Saturday. There might have been difficulties for some parents who worked six days a week. For many, Sunday would have been a much better day to visit, but as the Home was strongly Methodist, any such fun on this day would be against all the rules.

These amounts of visits seemed also to be acceptable to the Sister in Charge. It appeared that there was the hint given that any more visits than this might upset others in the family group who were less fortunate over visits.

With my mother wanting to visit me every third Saturday, it gave my relatives living close by little opportunity for contact with me. One set of aunts and uncles it appeared would have welcomed the odd visit. If the Sister had not wanted to see me getting visits at the Home, then I would have been quite capable of walking to my relatives' home; it was actually in the direction of the walk I made to school each day. However, to Sister, our spare time was fully occupied with events at the Home; no visits to aunts and uncles were ever made on my own.

24. 16.05.65 Letter to Governor of Harpenden NCH from Mother.

Thank you very much for your letter. I am so pleased I know Philip is settling down happily at Highfield.

I shall be delighted to come on Saturday 22nd to take Philip out for the day. The train arrives at Harpenden at 9.45 am, so I should be at Highfield about 10 o'clock, I am looking forward very much to coming. Do I call at the main office first, or do I go straight to see the Sister? Thank you for your very kind attention.

MY ANSWER

This was my first visit from my mother; I was taken into the town for the day. There was the hope in my mind that my mother might take me back to London at the end of the day out. Late in the afternoon, I was returned to the Home. I now knew that I was here for the duration. Quite a large amount of time was spent by my mother asking Sister if I had been any trouble to her. It appeared that Sister did not have any complaints to make.

25. 19.05.65 Letter to Mother from Rev. Gordon. E. Barritt. NCH London.

Now that Philip is in our care at Harpenden, we hope he will settle quite happily.

We understand you are willing to contribute a total of two pounds per week towards his maintenance and we enclose herewith our usual Payment Agreement Form for you to sign and return as soon as possible.

We note from our Accounts Department that you have already made one payment of four pounds for which a receipt has already been sent.

26. 19.05.65 Payment form Signed by The Mother

I agree to pay the sum of two pounds per week to National Children's Home and Orphanage in regular Weekly instalments of two pounds, the first to be made on the 13th May 1965, and shall continue as long as the said Philip is in the care of the National Children's Home and Orphanage.

27. 06.07.65 Letter to Governor of Harpenden NCH from Mother.

Would it be possible to have Philip home this weekend from Saturday 10.15 am until Sunday evening, 10th and 11th July.

I'm sorry it's such short notice, but my Mother is in hospital and does not appear to be returning home during the next few days. I thought it would make a good opportunity for me to have Philip while I'm free of my nursing duties.

If it's too late for a postal reply, may I ring up about 6pm on Friday, perhaps you would be kind enough to leave a message to say if he can come.

Last time Philip came home we all noticed a vast improvement in him. He seemed so much more sensible and obedient.

I am very grateful for all you and the Sister in Charge are doing for us.

MY ANSWER.

There was the comment of a vast improvement in my behaviour; for my mother to make this comment it showed I had changed. Although there had been only one physical punishment from the Sister in Charge, simply making me conform to their way of life was punishment in itself.

Within a few weeks of coming into the Home, I soon found from the others that it was easier to make it look as if one was obeying every command that was given. Slowly I could feel I was getting more and more frustrated at the petty rules that seemed to have been made at some point, yet never changed even if circumstances dictated.

If I did not show to be making real friends with the others in the group, it was down to being the youngest boy. With the others having later bedtimes, often starting to play games in the evening was soon interrupted with me getting sent off to bed by the Sister.

I would have loved to be allowed to go out of the grounds on my own, but other than to and from school you were not allowed out of the Home without an adult. For pleasure, it was to be allowed out into the grounds on my own and not organised into any game or group activity.

For the visit to my mother if there was any difference, it was that I wanted to try and not to be noticed in any way if possible. During my first time with my mother, there was the hope if I did seem to be quiet and almost invisible, there might be the chance I would not have to return to the Home.

28. 05.08.65 Report from Child Care Officer.

The mother was limping when she came to the door and had a very painful and swollen leg. She has Philip home for a week's holiday from the Branch and arranged it this week because she thought that her mother would still be in hospital and that she would be able to take Philip out.

However, her mother was discharged last weekend and cannot be left for more than an hour at a time as she has now had three strokes and seems likely to have another. Philip has had to go out on his own and the mother is disappointed not to be able to join him.

The mother seems to be a very conscientious lady who has given up a good deal to care for her parents. The rest of the family are all working and, though they visit her, can never stay very long. The mother is, therefore, very tied to the house. She visits Philip every third weekend and sometimes has him home. She thinks he is happy at Harpenden and that it is good for him, though of course she herself misses him very much. She is looking forward to the time when she can have him living with her again but there is no knowing how long the present situation will continue.

On my return to the office I made several fruitless telephone calls to the Woman's Voluntary Service etc., to see if anyone could relieve the mother of her duties for a few hours. What she really needs is a week's holiday to spend with Philip and give her a break from her very demanding parents.

MY ANSWER.

My mother had a very bad leg for many years; the heavy work of lifting both her parents did not help matters. In the normal way, my mother would have been considered unfit for work. As no other relatives were willing to help out, my mother was left to look after both her parents every day and night.

My mother thought I was happy at Highfield; when she visited everything was happy in the household. If she had really known how I felt living at the Home and how near I was to giving up, she might have found some way of taking me back. All it would have taken was for her to be firmer with the rest of her brothers and sisters over the matter of their parents and both of us might have had a more enjoyable life. My mother looking after her parents was originally going to be only a temporary solution but within months it became permanent.

If life was so odd for me, it was when I was at Harpenden I was not allowed to set foot outside the grounds except for going to and from school, yet once in London I have total freedom in a built-up area with heavy traffic. At eight years old, I had enough road sense to survive, if only the Home could have realised that if they allowed me to go for walks outside the grounds. I would not come to any harm.

29. 06.08.65 Letter to the Mother from the Child Care Officer.

I was glad to be able to meet you today. I feel that you really need to have an occasional break from your duties and am wondering if there is anyone who could relieve you for an hour or two. I have rung the W.V.S. at Hampstead but it seems they are unlikely to be able to help you. I have also been given the address of the Voluntary Services in Willesden. Maybe someone could sit in for a couple of hours while you go out. I should also bear in mind the possibility of having your mother in a Convalescent or Nursing Home for a week or two to give you a break. No doubt your family could help with this financially, as you are doing them a service. Hoping that your leg will soon be better

30. 04.08.65 Letter to Governor of Harpenden NCH from Mother.
Thank you for your letter, I give my consent for Philip to be vaccinated against smallpox, and immunised against diphtheria and whooping cough.

MY ANSWER.
Vaccinated against everything. Until coming to the Home, visits to the doctors had been a rare event. Other than catching measles as a very young child, general childhood illnesses had not affected me. With little contact with other children until the age of six it had not exposed me to the regular selection that other children seem to get. Even when I did start school, I remained healthy, although I did catch several colds. Possibly the protective London grime and living in a household where my grandfather could smoke forty strong unfiltered cigarettes a day and with two other members of the family not far behind, had given me protection against all ills.

Other children happily took time off school with mumps and chicken pox but for me a cold was something I could snuffle through lessons with. At the age of six, there was the prospect of having my adenoids out; my speech it appeared was not having any improvement even with elocution lessons. The hospital appointment came for the week we were leaving, so no more was done about the matter.

At the Home, it appeared it was best to have us all inoculated against the major diseases. Vaccination against Smallpox in the normal way would only be given to a child if they were planning to go on holiday to a problem country, although for the majority here, a holiday by the seaside was the nearest they were going to get to tropical and distant lands. As a precaution, we were vaccinated against major diseases. Compared with other injections with long needles that did sting, the actual Smallpox vaccination and the after effects went without any complications or discomfort for me.

31. 17.08.65 Report of Child Care Officer.
I called on the mother to find out whether she has had any success in finding someone to stay with her parents so that she could spend some time with Philip. She is hoping that her sister will come for a day one weekend soon so that she and Philip can go out. She also said that she thinks she could have found somewhere for her parents to go away for a holiday, but they did not want to go, and she was unwilling to put undue pressure on them. However, if the situation is the same next year she will make more effort to have a break; this will probably need planning well in advance, but the Old People's Welfare will probably be willing to help.

The mother looked much fitter than when I last saw her and her leg is nearly better.

31a. November 1965. Half-Yearly Report by Sister in Charge.
8 years 10 months.
General Condition: Good.

Height: 4ft. 5in.
Weight 4st. 8lbs.
A nervy, highly-strung child, and yet he does not lack confidence.
He is a little old man in some ways, and yet babyish in others.
He is now much more able with other children.
He is less aggressive and cries less due to frustration.
He has settled very well.
Interests and Hobbies.
Cubs, and will be joining the Club.
Very active but will settle down with pencils and paper.

MY ANSWER

The Sister has given her verdict on my behaviour after being in her care for six months. I was not used to such large groups of children around me all the time. If I was highly strung it was simply that I was afraid that if I did anything wrong, I would be physically punished.

My main fear at night was not of my surroundings or matters like thunder and lightning, it was the single fear of wetting the bed. I forced myself to wake up during the night to visit the lavatory to prevent it happening.

32. 00.01.66 Report of Child Care Officer.

The mother was enjoying having Philip home for the Christmas holidays and was looking much fitter than when I saw her in the summer. She is still very much tied to the house as her mother has frequent attacks of illness and she cannot leave her alone for long. Although the rest of the family promised to give her a lot of help, they always seem to be busy and she does not get much support.

The mother said she feels that she needs a break from caring for her parents and I suggested that the rest of the family should be able to pay for someone to look after them for a week while they go away in the summer. She agreed this might be a good idea, and I hope she will follow it up.

Philip came in later and was obviously enjoying his holiday. He is very excitable and talkative and not a bit shy, although I had not seen him before. He has to go out on his own most of the time when he is at home, but he is very resourceful and seems to know his way around.

He talked happily about Harpenden and of the other children in the family and appears well adjusted to life there. His mother visits him regularly every third week and takes him home, and helps make him feel secure.

The mother said she misses him very much and would love to have him home all the time, but under the present circumstances, feels that there is far too much strain on the relations within the family, although for a week at a time it is very satisfactory to have Philip at home. Of course the mother has no idea how long she will be required to look after her parents.

Philip seems bright and intelligent, although his mother said he lacks concentration and feels this is probably why he does not do very well at school. This confirms the original school report that we received. It would be interesting to know whether Philip has become more settled since his stay at Harpenden and how he behaves towards the other children in the family.

MY ANSWER.

A different Child Care Officer visiting me for the first time chose the best moment to visit. With one day after my ninth birthday and being able to spend it at my home in London, I had really everything that I could want. I might have been a little excitable, with new toys to play with on my own and extra money; these were matters I could get excited about. The comment of not being a bit shy was quite true. Having been surrounded by adults all my life, I could not see any reason to act in any other manner.

With my mother at home looking after my grandparents, if I wanted to do anything, it was up to me to organise it. Within reason I had the freedom to explore locally, a radius from home of about three miles being my real limit. Any further than this and I would not have normally had the funds for transport.

The view that I was well adjusted to life at Harpenden according to the Child Care Officer showed that, given the circumstances, life at the Home was not giving me any real problems.

The adults looked at my school reports and other reports and see that I have a lack of concentration. It was not that I appeared stupid or the like, my attention soon moved onto the next matter before the first had been finished. In their minds, I was starting to settle into a family group. To me if I was like a few of the others and had to spend my entire life at the Home, my reaction to being in the group would have been different. There was a need on my part to try and show I wanted to be part of a family group, but this was simply to get permission to be allowed out for the odd weekends with my mother.

33. 10.01.66 Report of Child Care Officer.
Discussion with Sister in Charge at Harpenden 05.01.66

The Sister in Charge feels that Philip has settled down well at Harpenden. She agrees that he is highly strung and very often talks so fast that his speech is almost unintelligible. His manners have improved a lot since he has been in care, and he has become more controllable.

It would appear that while his mother was working as a housekeeper she had little opportunity to bring Philip up properly, and probably encouraged him to keep quiet for the sake of the household she was living in. The mother said she notices an improvement in his behaviour now.

Philip's aunts and uncles have visited him from time to time and brought him Christmas and birthday presents and sometimes offer to buy clothes.

The Sister in Charge had no complaint to make about Philip's behaviour or his relationship with other members of the family group. She feels that the mother misses her son a good deal and would very much like to have him with her. The mother has said that she is worried about the difficulty she may experience in finding a job when she is free to look for one, on account of her age. She feels at the moment that she is giving all her life to her parents, and perhaps not sufficient attention to Philip and his long-term needs.

MY ANSWER.

The Sister in Charge had no complaints about my behaviour; I knew well enough how to behave in front of a lady who commanded the same respect as my grandmother expected when I was younger. If I was highly strung it was possibly that as I was always active. If anything did upset me, then I was active enough to show any feelings in rage or the like. Leaving me to be on my own with or without other adults around was all that I really wanted.

The comment that my mother did not have the time to bring me up properly sounds unfair, but she was simply doing the best she could. From the age of six, my mother started work at about six in the morning and was often still at work into the evening, with the odd short break in the afternoon, mostly at a time when I would be at school. The other need was for her to keep me quiet, as we lived in the homes of her employer; I was given little opportunity to act as an ordinary child. If I became a little wild at times, it was down to frustration. The only main way of keeping me quiet was to send me to my room; this made me even more frustrated. If I was hit with the plimsoll it often had me falling into order for a short while.

If at the weekend, I appeared to be very active and easy to upset, it might have been due to the excess of sugar I was eating. Food now had far more sweet items available at all meals than I had been used to. On a Saturday afternoon, I tended to spend my entire pocket money on sweets and then eat them all before tea. If I did not, it was the fear that the older boys and others in the Home would take the sweets off me. Without the older ones, the sweets could have lasted me a week.

The odd visits from my aunts and uncles were always very short, and might last an hour or so. Most of these were on days when my mother was to visit and due to my grandmother's health, was not able to that day. A large amount of their time was spent talking to Sister. Other than showing them around the flat and the grounds, little else could be done when they visited.

34. 18.01.66 Letter to Rev. Gordon. E. Barritt. London NCH from Governor of Harpenden NCH.

The Sister has given me the following report on Philip.

Philip has settled in the family very well, and is learning to play with the other children in a more normal way.

When he first came his idea of friendship was nearly strangling an older child or tripping him over. This did not meet with approval and he ended up crying after they retaliated. He is not such a cry baby now. He is learning courtesy 'please' and 'thank you' seemed unknown to him, and he is learning to live with other people, especially children, and to mix.

He is highly strung and nervous, and this shows in his speech and actions. He may have some night-time problems as he now started to wet his bed on odd nights. He is an old-fashioned child, and yet at times sounds like a grandparent, though this is gradually disappearing.

He is happy at school, but very backward possibly due to the number of changes he has had, rather than to lack of intelligence, but this will take time to prove. He is quite an easy child, and I am sure the time spent with his mother is a great help. He makes no fuss when he returns.

MY ANSWER.

The official report of the branch shows I was starting to mix more with other children. With the wide range of ages and as there were both boys and girls, the chances of being able to find someone who had the same ideas of how to spend time were fairly remote.

In other flats, there were friends who had similar interests to my own, but Sister had the firm rule that friends were not allowed into the flat, nor were you permitted to visit any other flat. Many of the other Sisters allowed friends to come and go as they pleased as long as it did not cause any disruption, but it did not include us.

It was quite easy for an older member of the group to make you cry. Sister was not present for every minute of the day. This gave plenty of opportunity for four older members of the family to pick their moment if they decided to have some fun. It need not always be physical; words could be equally harmful and threats about what could be done to me were enough to make me cry.

The comment that I had only recently learnt 'Please and Thank you' was not entirely true. Having been brought up surrounded from a very early age by adults, these words were very ingrained in my vocabulary. However, when I did choose to utter them, they would be given directly to the adult concerned; there was rarely the need to voice it very loudly. Should I have failed to use such words then there would have been many complaints.

At the Home this was now different. With the general noise and activity going on continuously, it appeared it was almost mandatory to yell it out loud so the whole group could hear. If the Sister had been with me alone when there was the need for me to utter such words they would have easily been noticed.

It is true that I did have night problems. My main fear at night was that I might wet the bed; to prevent such an event I made an evening visit to the lavatory. Sister thought I should not need to visit the lavatory soon after going to bed. My need was due to having a large drink of milk last thing at night, which I was not used to. If I got caught out of bed, I was blamed for not going before going to bed. Sister did not want to see me out of bed early in the evening, and sent me back to bed without being allowed to visit the lavatory.

If I was an old-fashioned child, it was for the simple matter that until the age of six, I did not play with or meet other children; my main contact during the day was with my grandmother or grandfather; their views on how I should act made the most impact on me.

Happy at school? Yes it gave me an opportunity to return to the real world, with the freedom of ordinary people and children to mix with rather than the almost stifling regime of life at the Home.

The number of changes in schools had a bearing on my schoolwork. I was now in my seventh school within three years, settling down, learning all the new rules, names of pupils and teachers. Often coming into the middle of a set of work that I might have already completed or had never started, always meant that I needed a little while to settle into the new location.

35. 16.03.66. Letter to Rev. Gordon. E. Barritt. London NCH from Governor of Harpenden NCH.
I have heard from Philip's mother that she will be able to have Philip for practically the whole of the school summer holidays this year. The dates are Friday 29th July to Sunday 4th September. I expect you will wish to arrange for the Child Care Officer to visit her during this period.

36. 18.04.66 Report of Child Care Officer.
I called hoping to see Philip, who is at home for three weeks of his Easter holiday, but he had just gone out.
The mother must have been busy as she did not ask me in, though we had a fairly long chat. She said that her parents are getting more and more helpless, and are extremely dependent on her.
Philip has apparently enjoyed being at home, despite the fact that his presence has caused some friction, and his mother said that although she is glad to have him for the holidays, she is quite sure she could not manage him any for a longer period. She says he sometimes expresses some reluctance to return to the Branch but she feels sure he is happy at Harpenden, despite this. He is still a very excitable child and finds it difficult to concentrate and his mother worries about this and feels he will not make any progress at school, although he is intelligent.
The mother is hoping to have Philip home again in the summer. She has not made any plans for going away. Other members of the family are going to Spain for their holidays, but she does not seem to resent this, saying that they only have two weeks a year and need a change.

37. MAY 1966 Half-Yearly Branch Report by Sister in Charge. Age 9 years 4 months
General Condition: Good.
Height 4ft 6in.
Weight 4st 10lbs
Illness in last six months: Gastroenteritis (Gastric Flu). There are a few occurrences of bed-wetting; this is due to his refusal to visit the lavatory before going to bed.
Philip is much calmer than he was, not quite so highly strung.
He goes home very frequently, but returns quite happily.

MY ANSWER.
Now I had been at the Home for a year, I had possibly worked out how best to avoid trouble, but the simple confines of the Home meant that as almost every

normal activity was either boring or not allowed, active minds found only mischief to pass the time.

In one year I gained about two inches, my height put me on equal terms to several of the older boys, but my weight gain over a year was around five pounds. This meant I was well under 5 stone; I still had a rather skinny appearance.

Generally, we were all fairly healthy. With minor coughs and colds, Sister packed everyone off to school; only at the weekends and holidays would it be suggested that you stay indoors. If at any point you did become too ill to go to school then it was bed all day.

The gastric flu in March did make me feel really ill. For the first couple of days, I was in bed at the flat. There was nothing I was able to keep down. The slightest movement, even when I was lying in bed made me feel the worst I had ever felt. When I attempted to get out of bed, I was completely disorientated. The walls, floor and ceiling seemed to be coming up to meet me; the only way I could ever make it to the lavatory, was to physically crawl along the floor. This was fine during the school day, but when the others returned home, my life was made even more miserable. Had Sister told them it was something they would catch if they were close to me, I might have been left alone; as the four of us shared the same bedroom, it appeared it was not that catching.

Eventually Sister decided that I was ill enough to go over to the small hospital in the grounds. I was at least happy for the peace and quiet, although I still felt rotten. For three days, all I could manage was some liquid glucose. The hospital had two small wards. I was the only one in my ward, so it was nice and quiet. After three days, I was starting to get better. One evening my uncle came to see how I was, but even then, I was not well enough even to say hello.

I spent a further four days in hospital before being sent back to the flat. If proof were needed that I was better, it was that I could quite happily munch my way through a large bag of jelly babies. Normally the fine sugar coating seemed to put me off by the feel, but these jelly babies had a fine caster sugar coating and strong flavour. The short stay in hospital possibly was one of the reasons why my report mentions that I was calmer and not so highly-strung. A week of starvation was just an easy way of making me slow down and be quiet.

The matter about my bed-wetting was not really true; it was not a case of me refusing to visit the lavatory before I go to bed. Visiting the lavatory before going to bed was something I actually did. My bed-wetting was down to the Sister refusing to let me use the lavatory if I needed to pay a visit within a few hours of going to bed. If I was sent back, without being allowed to visit the lavatory the result was that I did wet my bed.

If it was mentioned that I returned to the Home quite happily, it might not have really found the truth. The train journey late on Sunday afternoon returning to the Home was never any fun. Whilst the ride into London seemed to take forever, the twenty or so miles by train on the return journey seemed to rush by. There was little point in telling anyone how I really felt. Had the others in the flat known how I felt on having to return, my life could have been made even more miserable.

I don't think the staff at the Home or my mother ever realised that I was unhappy. After I had been at the Home a few months, I had been told that my stay was not going to be for very long. Now I had been here for over a year, I was starting to feel that I was never going to be able to leave.

When I did get time to myself in the grounds at the Home, I was happy to find peace and solitude but at the same time, it allowed me to have the thought that I did not really want to stay at this Home any longer. Running away would not do any good; you would be sent back and have to face whatever punishments were correct for such an act.

At the age of nine, I was starting to contemplate other more drastic measures, but there was the hope that perhaps the following month or the month after, I would be able to leave the Home and return to live with my mother. The other matter was who would get the contents of my locker.

38. 24.06.66 Note to Sister Ann (Hospital) from Governor of Harpenden.

I have had a phone call from the Medical Officer for Highfield. Philip has an air-gun pellet just under the skin just above the inside of his left knee; this was revealed in a recent X-ray.

MY ANSWER.

As part of medical research, a few of us were measured, weighed, photographed and X-rayed at regular intervals. This was not done for use by the Home, but simply the Home was the ideal location, where it was thought that the subjects would readily be on hand enabling a study over several years. There were no injections or the like, simply endless measurements of all parts of our bodies. As the tests always took part on a school day, it was an ideal reason for missing a morning of school.

An injury that I had received a few months earlier, when I thought I had been hit with a stone from a catapult, now revealed itself in one of the regular X-rays. That I had an air gun pellet in my knee meant that action would have to be taken to remove it.

39. 11.08.66 Report of Child Care Officer.

I called to see Philip while he was on holiday with his mother for the whole of the summer holiday. His mother was enjoying having him but was finding it a strain, as it was difficult to fit Philip in with the old people in the family.

Her mother and father are both practically bedridden now and her mother has had another spell in hospital since last Easter.

The mother looked quite well and seemed to be coping. Next week her brother will be on holiday and has agreed to stay at home on one day so that she can take Philip out for the day.

Apparently, her brother takes very little interest in Philip and never offers to take him out himself.

Philip seemed bright and happy and as usual had been going out a lot on his own to the park and he has joined the local library.

He has made one or two friends locally and met Lenton who is in his family at Harpenden, and has been to the park with him.

I should think Philip is still quite a restless and excitable child and his speech is very unusual, somewhat indistinct and perhaps he has an accent, but I am not sure where he gets it from.

When I arrived he was not dressed and apparently, his mother had been trying to persuade him to dress himself for a long time, however, after I arrived, he was dressed within minutes. I would imagine his mother finds it very difficult to be very firm with him.

The mother seems to be pleased with his progress and I told her that I had recently seen the Sister in Charge who said he was settling down very well and that she had not any particular problems with him, and said that the mother still visits him very regularly. The mother said that when she takes him back to Harpenden, she would like to see his school report, as she is interested in his school progress.

MY ANSWER.

London. The freedom from the Home for a length of time was all I could wish for. As my mother needed to stay indoors, most of the time I was free to explore London. Activities like bus rides, the cinema, and swimming were all things that I missed whilst at the Home. Many of my friends who had been at the Home for years had never had those pleasures, so did not know what they have missed. Even without money to spend, walking around the outdoor markets was a pleasure.

On my own there were few problems that I could get into. However, during the holidays I met up with one of the boys from the flat, who also lived in London. Our weekend visits often did not coincide, so meeting up was not that often. However, with my taste for freedom and my friend's ability to egg me on, perhaps it might be best if I was left to go out alone. However, having a regular friend available was not something to miss out on.

If I was not dressed when the Child Care Officer arrived, it would simply have been reluctance to dress in the clothes that my mother had selected. My intention throughout the summer was to go out to play. If I did meet up with any other boys of my own age locally, then play clothes were essential for any form of enjoyment. My mother however thought I should be always smartly dressed. During my stay in London, I was limited over the choice of clothes.

At the Home, I was one of the few boys who had a suit. The only reason for being given this was that it fitted me. The others in the flat were not jealous as the suit came with two pairs of short trousers. They had no interest in the suit from that moment on. On trips to and from the Home, I wore this suit and looked smart. Unless someone knew me, no one would have guessed that I came from a Children's Home.

My mother had decided that as I had smart clothes then it was best to wear them. Where I wanted to play and the boys I might want to play with, had I appeared in a suit, the survival for the suit or me would have been very slim. An old school raincoat even if it was summer, and similar play clothes, and almost any situation could be tackled with new friends and a London location. Although I would not have refused to put the best clothes on, a little delay often resulted in me getting my way over what clothes to wear on most occasions.

If I had started to calm down at the Home, it was that the system was slowly starting to grind me down. Only the freedom of visits home to London gave me something to look forward to. Once in London, I was able to go at the pace I wanted to.

School reports were taken to the Sister at the Home; often my mother did not visit during the period the school report was at the Home. The summer holidays meant that it would be available until our return to school in September. We took the reports sealed in their envelopes. Our friends who did not live at the Home often opened their reports just to see the awful comments all the teachers had written about them. For those of us from the Home, looking at our reports was not something we ever managed. Only after the Sister had read them, did we get to learn which of us had achieved the worst selection of comments. At the following meals, various complaints would be made about what had been noted in our reports.

40. 07.11.66 Report of Child Care Officer.
There is now a new Houseparent in the flat. Miss Rosemary Foale is looking after Philip since the original Sister in Charge has retired. She has told me that his mother continues to visit regularly and to have Philip home for weekends.

Philip, apparently is rather a strange child, and it has taken him a long time to settle into the family. This is because the other children have been there much longer than he has and partly because age-group-wise, he tends to be the odd man out.

He is still inclined to be aggressive towards other children and this may be because he is teased by them. He is inclined to bully younger children, but is slowly ceasing to do this.

MY ANSWER.
The whole flat had recently been through a major upheaval; this affected the others far more than it had me. The Sister in Charge who had looked after some of the family for most of their lives had now reached retirement; she was now severing almost all links with the family group. Now the lady who we had known as a helper and relief was taking over from Sister. My knowledge of Sister had only been for a year and a half. Having lived surrounded by other adults all my life that had come and gone. That Sister was leaving meant a bit of an unknown change, but not really a major event to me. For the others, this event was decisive and very upsetting.

The Houseparent who now took over has had some experience of children, but compared to Sister's many years of actual practice, we now experienced the newer textbook style of childcare. This we found out was a completely different way of life for us. Our flat now has two groups of four, giving either younger ones or older ones. I did not fit in; at the age of almost ten, I was neither an older one nor a younger one, but I had to be placed in one of the groups for most activities. For chores and the like, I was grouped with the older ones; for bedtimes and activities then it was the younger group as I was still at junior school. The Houseparent now told me that if I wet the bed, I would be given the slipper.

If I was a strange child as the new Houseparent thought, it was something I could live with. I simply did not want to give up and fall into the dull lives that most of those around me accepted.

I was aggressive to younger children but this was down to my short temper; I would prefer to be left alone, but as our paths had to cross, so often problems did occur. The older ones were not involved with the young group as much as myself.

When the older boys in the flat teased me, I always got angry; they just did not understand how upsetting it was. If I was different from the others in the flat, this was due to the long summer holidays I was away from the Home. During this summer break, the Sister took less control of the flat and allowed the new Houseparent to make more of the decisions ready for running the flat full time.

41. November 1966. Half-Yearly Report by Houseparent.
Age 9yrs 10months
General condition: Good
Height: 4ft7in.
Weight 5st 0lbs.
Philip is inclined to be jealous and vocally aggressive, particularly with younger members of the group.

His relationship with all, including the staff, is very loose at present. There is a need to keep control of his behaviour.

He is slightly impertinent, yet, given the opportunity, he can be helpful and enjoys showing the younger children how to do things.

MY ANSWER.
With almost two years at the Home, there were limits to the amount of teasing and other problems I could take before I started to cause trouble. To be treated as one of the younger ones now I was coming up to ten, made me start to act like one of the younger group, rather than that of the older ones, whereas in reality, if allowed to follow my own resources, I could easily have been placed in the older group.

Living with adults all my life, possibly gave me a slightly different attitude than for most. I could be polite and respectful when I wanted to, but if treated as a young child then I could rebel. If I was given respect then I was quite capable of acting in a far more grown-up manner.

The Houseparent had given me the slipper for matters other than wetting the bed. The second time she gave me it, I had twelve hits with the slipper on my rear; it was given as two sessions of six hits. I would not have received the second six hits had I not pushed the boy who said I had stolen his sweets. In the end, the Houseparent found out that I was innocent of stealing the sweets. It was too late then; I had already been punished. This was one of the reasons I was not settled in the flat.

42. 07.12.66 Letter to NCH Harpenden from Luton & Dunstable Hospital.

If you will please arrange for this lad to come along to the Accident Services here at 10am on Thursday 15th December, we will be pleased to remove the air gun pellet from his left knee. As he will be given a general anaesthetic, it is important that he has nothing to eat or drink after midnight the previous day.

It would be helpful if you could complete and return the enclosed slip; I am enclosing the Consent Form for signature.

MY ANSWER.

Finally the decision was made to take the pellet out of my leg. If there was one benefit, outdoor games could be missed for the rest of the term.

43. 29.12.66 Report of Child Care Officer.

On 29.12.66 I learnt from his mother that Philip would be going home the following day for a week's holiday. I was sorry to have missed him.

The mother is still nursing both her parents, who are almost entirely bedridden. She has a very trying time and constantly wonders if there is a way of leaving someone else to care for her parents.

However, at the moment there appears to be no alternative and, of course, she does not know how long their situation will continue. Her mother is twenty years younger than her father, who is ninety. The mother is pleased with Philip's progress. She enjoys having him for weekends and is looking forward to having him for his holidays.

On 02.01.67 I visited Harpenden Branch and spoke to the Houseparent, who told me that there had been a considerable improvement in Philip recently.

He is much less aggressive towards the younger children and is also more popular with his peer group, joining in their games and activities. Philip has become more interested in school and seems to enjoy it now. He is also more affectionate.

On 05.01.67 I visited Philip at his home. He chatted happily about all he has been doing and the many presents he has received for his birthday and at Christmas.

He still talks very fast and has a rather excitable manner. He seemed to be enjoying his holiday very much.

On 26.01.67 I called at Harpenden branch and saw Philip on his return from school.

When I spoke to Philip, he seemed happy and had plenty of news, which he related in a rather excited and disjointed way.

Earlier I had visited his school and managed to have a word with both the Headmaster and the class teacher. It appears that he is showing some improvement in his schoolwork. The Headmaster has not needed to deal with Philip since the start of the school year in September, over any matters of bad behaviour.

The class teacher reported to me that there have been several occasions where she has found it has been necessary to punish him, but once reprimanded he settles down to work. He appears to be slowly settling down to school life and that when firmly controlled can show improvement in the lesson period.

At the end of our meeting I spoke to the Governor of Highfield, who confirms that with the previous reports of Philip's behaviour at school, keeping him firmly in line was suggested at the end of the last school year. Philip appears now to understand what is required of him during the school period and is settling into the routine more easily.

The uncooperative attitude Philip had to visiting the lavatory before going to bed has seen vast improvement. There are now only minor instances of bed-wetting during the past few months. After agreement with the mother, the new Houseparent has brought in a strict regime, and Philip realises that, he will be punished for any bed-wetting.

MY ANSWER.

I seemed to have made improvement. That year at school things were better; the teacher in our class dealt with anything I did wrong; I was seldom sent to the Headmaster. Her punishments were about the same as the Headmaster, as she would give the cane on your legs or hands, but they were easier to get over with once given. Now that I was not punished in front of the rest of the class made me less worried over the events. As I am almost ten, a few older privileges are starting to come my way.

The Christmas and New Year periods over the last two years had been new to me. Until recently Christmas activities had never been anything very special. Living with my mother, with her work over Christmas, our festivities were never anything major. It was possibly around the age of six, through events of the time, that I had realised that in reality there was no Father Christmas.

In London, any Christmas activity had really been for the adults to enjoy as their holiday. I was meant to keep quiet. At the Home Christmas was new and enjoyable, but I would have preferred the quiet life with just my mother. Parties, trips to the pantomime and other group activities, possibly did get me a little excitable. With my Birthday coming so soon after Christmas treats and presents, everything seemed to roll into one event.

If I seemed to be more affectionate it was possible that I had not been involved in many scrapes or battles with the others in the household. The need to be good up to Christmas might also have helped my chances of longer visits to London over the holiday period.

Now the Houseparent is in charge. If I wet the bed, I receive two hits with the slipper when I get up in the morning.

44. 30.03.67 Report of Child Care Officer.
Visit to Philip at his Home. Philip appeared to be enjoying his holidays, but his mother seemed rather concerned that, as usual, he never concentrates on anything for very long. Although he tackles things with great enthusiasm, he soon loses interest in them.

The mother looks very tired and is finding her parents a great strain. She had a day off on Good Friday and very much enjoyed taking Philip to Worthing for the day. As I had little opportunity to talk to his mother, I will call again soon.

I noticed that Philip has a great difficulty in writing and as he is now ten this is rather worrying. He appears bright and alert, but he cannot concentrate, he does not seem to progress.

I wonder whether there is anything worrying Philip and also how much information his mother has given him about his father. Once, when I tried to broach the subject, the mother was very defensive and I wonder whether her anxiety is transmitted to Philip.

In the original recommendation which we received from his Headmistress, it was suggested that Philip might benefit from some male influence. Unfortunately, his mother's brother does not take any interest in Philip and I believe his other uncles visit him very rarely.

On visiting Harpenden Branch the Houseparent mentioned to me that Philip never plays games at school and she hopes to go there soon to discuss this.

MY ANSWER.
If I always seemed to rush at things, it was simply down to the belief that there was never enough time to follow through every idea that I had in my mind. If other matters came to mind, then I could leave off and come back to it later.

For schoolwork, there was always the thought that there was not enough time to finish the work. For most lessons, failure to finish meant you might be asked to stay on for a few extra minutes to finish. With the requirement to be back at the Home on time, this often meant final lessons of the day would be rushed to avoid being kept in even for a few extra minutes to finish the work.

I could have proved my ability to write neatly if given the chance; in the art lessons a few were given the chance to do calligraphy. This was a lesson I could have begged for; the few chosen were those who had the neatest books.

If my written work was poor, it was down to the use of a ballpoint pen; given the occasional opportunity with pen and ink alone, I was able to work well. If the teachers had told me to take my time over my written work and that if I did not finish it did not matter, then I would have been able to attain a much higher standard of work. However, put me in a classroom environment and add the other factors of friends causing a nuisance around me and even an ink pen would prove fruitless.

Group games were never interesting to me and football was my main hate. It was not that I disliked physical activities. Possibly one of the best lessons at school was P.E. but only if the climbing apparatus was brought fully into use.

45. 27.04.67 Letter to Rev. Gordon. E. Barritt. NCH London from Governor of Harpenden NCH.

We should be grateful if you could arrange for Philip to be tested by the Tutor in Charge during the next few months. As mentioned in recent reports he has great difficulty in writing, and doesn't seem to be making progress. It would be helpful to know how intelligent he is.

46. 01.05.67 Note from NCH.

Please see letter from Governor of Harpenden NCH with the suggestion, that the Tutor in Charge should test Philip. Could this be arranged please?

47. 09.05.67 Letter to the Tutor in Charge from Governor of Harpenden NCH.

Thank you for your letter of 5th May. It will be quite convenient for you to come and see Philip and the Houseparent on Monday 28th May. I will inform his school and ask for a report from there.

Note: Unable to keep appointment – unwell – another date being arranged.

48. 23.05.67 Letter to Rev. Gordon. E. Barritt. NCH London from Governor of Harpenden NCH.

We were glad to have the report on the visit to Philip's mother. The Houseparent has visited Philip's school and seen his teacher. She stated that Philip was aggressive, but was reasonably easy to control in class.

She told the Houseparent that his work could be better if he could concentrate more, and she had noticed that he responded well to praise, and always improved and worked better afterwards.

The Tutor in Charge was due to see Philip yesterday, but had to postpone her visit on account of illness. She will no doubt be arranging another date with us shortly.

49. May 1967. Half Yearly Branch Report by Houseparent.

Age 10 years 4 months
General condition: Good
Height: 4ft 8in.
Weight: 5st 5lbs.
Sight: Eye Clinic. To have eye exercises.
Air gun pellet removed from Left Knee.

Philip has been more aggressive and belligerent and I learn from Susan's teacher that he has been bullying her at school. His own class teacher has dealt with him over this matter. He is apparently much worse when I am not around.

He seems to put up a barrier and does not believe he has done anything wrong, even if it can be proved. His relationship with some of the members of the family is improving.

When he is helpful or kind, and is praised for this, he glows and is a different lad for a while. He is desperate for more adult attention and will go to great lengths to get it.

Interests: Cubs, Electricity, Lego bricks and (boxes for hiding sweets only).

MY ANSWER.

An eye test revealed that there might be a slight problem with my sight, which in some way might have been one of the reasons for my clumsiness. Until this moment, any eye test I took part in had revealed that I had good sight in both eyes. The ability on my part to read the small print on the eye chart with one eye at a time, proved that I did not need glasses to correct any short sight. What however was never checked was my ability to read the same small letters with both eyes open at the same time. When I was given this test, it showed that I could find things a bit of a blur. At all distances, I appeared to be affected. The diagnosis was that I suffered from slight double vision.

More time off lessons attending the local eye clinic, and free time spent reading very small print, with a device placed in front of my vision seemed slowly to correct this problem. Although to get out of the dull chore of reading small print when I could be out at play, I told the adults that things were getting better, when in reality there was only slight improvement.

My fast pace was the reason for being labelled a bully. Whilst at the Annexe of the school, two of us could set our own pace for the return journey. When the Annexe was closed down and we had to rejoin the main school, such pleasures vanished. There were no chances now of gaining any extra minutes of freedom; there were many taking the same route to the Home. As I was still at the juniors, I now had the task of escorting one of the younger girls to and from school. Although only a year younger than me, it was thought that she needed to be escorted both to and from school. Known as a daydreamer, attention to her safety now was the main issue.

Until this point, older children from the flat who attended the senior school had this privilege. Allowance of extra time due to the school hours not totally coinciding had been made. Now at the same school, I was given the task, although any extra time for my benefit was not provided. I have to admit my walking pace was fast; my mother seemed to encourage this from an early age, through being busy.

Dawdling and daydreaming were not things I had ever indulged in. My idea was to get to school at the first possible moment. Playing and other activities before the bell rang for the start of the school day was perhaps the best moment of the school day. If friends had new possessions or had swaps to make, miss this early opportunity, and you could be jealous for evermore.

The slow pace of the girl started the day badly for me. Although I never really dragged her along the road, when crossing the road, I was a little more vocal and slightly physical.

My class teacher punished me after Susan's teacher made the complaint that I was bullying her. I was given the cane at going home time. As there was no time after I had been given the cane to get over the punishment, I was still in tears when I walked with Susan back to the Home. Three hits on each hand had really made me cry. From that point on I was not accused of bullying Susan any more. I don't think it was her intention to get me caned.

If I was desperate for adult attention, it was down to being fed up with most children's games and wanted something more adult to do or learn about. If I did get praise, then I was happy.

If I had any interest, it was on building and making things. Group board games were more or less unknown to me, although often receiving such items as presents there was seldom anyone to play with. Even in the Home, board games were not that much fun down to the wide age range. If you played with younger ones the rules were too complicated, if you played with older ones and appeared to be winning, they would change the rules to benefit themselves. Constructing objects and learning how things worked could be one of my pastimes. Never having acquired more than the most basic Meccano set, if I built things, Lego seemed to be the most desirable item through either presents or swaps. With electricity I was not allowed to try out experiments with the mains voltages – batteries in various stages of capacity had to meet my needs. One of my toys was a Morse code set. If there had been any interest from the older boys, I would have loved the chance to learn the system, but to all the others it was too much like a lesson and they showed no interest.

If there had been one extra event that had set me at odds with the Houseparent, it was when she had shaken me over my behaviour, resulting in the back of my head going through a glass window due to her force. Then the Governor of the Home caned me. These were the main reasons why I was not very happy at the Home.

50. 09.05.67 Report of Child Care Officer.

When I called on the mother I learnt that her father had died just over a week ago at the age of 90, which may possibly alter her position considerably. For one thing she is far less busy than she was, although her mother needs quite a lot of attention.

Secondly she has learnt that the flat that was let to her father by the firm he used to work for and that it is quite possible that she and her brother and mother will now have to move.

In this case one of her sisters may care for her mother and she may go back to housekeeping.

She is obviously not yet in a position to make any decisions about the future, but said she will let me know the outcome of her interview with the landlord.

The mother said she was always glad of the opportunity to talk about Philip and she told me about his various activities whilst on holiday. He was at home the weekend his grandfather died but Lenton's mother very kindly looked after him during the day for most of that weekend.

Philip apparently had a rather unfortunate experience when he went to meet Lenton at the swimming baths. The story seems rather confused but apparently he missed Lenton at the end of swimming and started to make his own way home. Some other boys were alleged to have beaten him up and then taken his towel away. He was sick. He came home minus his swimming gear and said that a man had given him a lift home. I said that I thought that Philip was probably too young to go so far alone in London.

We discussed the fact that Philip is so highly strung and seems unable to concentrate on anything at all for very long. He has always been like this. His mother does not think there is anything specially worrying Philip.

She says he always seems happy and as far as she knows has no problems on his mind, although I am wondering if something like this was preventing him from concentrating. The mother feels Philip is making reasonably good progress, although, she too, often feels that he could do better at school.

If anybody from the Branch goes to Philip's school it would be interesting to hear what his teacher thinks of him.

MY ANSWER.

A point in my life when things started to change was when my grandfather died. The event although a sad occasion, did not really affect me that much, but did start the ball rolling for changes in my future life.

In my mind, he was old, had almost never any patience for me, and wanted silence when there was no real requirement. With poor hearing, he had the television either too loud or the sound mistuned, and there were several other matters where our two lives never quite seemed to be easy when in close contact with each other.

There were worries each day for me. Was I going to be punished in the Home, would I be able to return to my mother, were the older ones going to pick on me? At school, it was the teasing over the colour of my skin, and if it was not name calling, it was the physical bullying that I had to put up with each day. The only way I found of solving the problem was to fight back; this resulted in punishments and more trouble. Once at home on visits to my mother, all these problems vanished, and I was happy.

Had I explained the full details of the day I had visited the swimming pool, the adults would have made an easy decision that perhaps my trips to my mother should cease. As my mother needed to look after my grandmother whilst I was in London, she could not spend any time looking after me. I went off on my own and was quite happy. If the adults had known the full truth of the day's events, allowing me out on my own from that point, would not have been a good idea in their minds.

Accepting the lift back after the visit to the swimming pool, from a man who was helping to find my way home, I thought was an innocent matter. During the journey in his car, I did have one slight worry as we headed out of London and up the M1 – we were heading in the direction of the Home. My only thoughts during the car journey were did he know I lived in a Home, and was taking me back. We stopped for a short time in a quiet country lane. While I thought the events that took place when he stopped the car to be a little odd, there was nothing frightening. Later he took me back to London, and dropped me at the end of my road. I quickly returned home; I knew if I mentioned the afternoon events to my mother, there would be trouble.

51. 02.06.67. Letter to Governor of Harpenden NCH from Mrs. Hiam. NCH London

We were very interested to receive the comments of Philip's school and it will be helpful later to see the result of The Tutor in Charge interview with Philip.

Report from Headmaster at Manland Primary School to Governor NCH Harpenden.

Philip is now in the third year of primary school. His teacher reports there have been several occasions when his behaviour has disrupted the smooth flow of lessons due to his aggressive approach to others. I think at times he will allow himself to be led astray. He appears to be bright, but he is not forthcoming in speaking about matters in front of others during lessons. This may have something to do with his location at Highfield, but I do not think that there are any real problems over this issue.

At certain times he is very capable of good work, but there seems to be a constant rush to get everything finished as fast as possible. During his previous year, extra written work was set as punishment for poor behaviour, although he completed the work without any problem, no real improvement in his actions was noticed. This year his class teacher has praised him for work that is above average in quality, there can be seen a vast improvement in both his schoolwork and actions for a short while. She has also punished Philip with the cane on several occasions when his performance does not come up to the required standard, he does not appear to show any resentment afterwards over this method of punishment.

In the nine months since the start of this school year, we are starting to see a slight improvement. He has reacted well to this style of help and appears to be happier in school. If this method is persevered with, we expect to see a general improvement in his work by the time he is due to leave in a years' time.

MY ANSWER.

Praise. The school was trying the Carrot & Stick approach on me. Several instances of praise were now given by my class teacher when my work was good.

My current teacher was also used for the stick part as well. Instead of my classroom punishments in front of all my friends, where a ruler was painfully applied to my legs, or where the teacher would send me to the Headmaster for punishment, I now received individual attention out of the gaze of other children, where a more formal telling off is given followed by a few light strokes from her cane on my legs or hands.

The teacher then had time to console my feelings, announcing that it was not her intention to make me cry; it seemed to be the only method of trying to control my behaviour. I found it was working and that as long as my friends did not see me at the time of my punishment, I was quite happy to try to give better results. It just appeared that after I received praise, punishment soon follows.

52. 28.06.67 Report of Child Care Officer.

Since her father's death, the mother's landlord has now told her that he would like her to be out of the flat in six month's time.

This will give her until November to find alternative accommodation.

She has been discussing plans for her future with her sister and brother in law, who are considering buying a small shop and post office near the south coast. If they decide to do this, they would take the parent with them. The mother could also go and help in the shop and Philip could also join them.

As yet, no definite plans have been made, but the mother would be very happy to have Philip with her again.

Philip has told her that he is enjoying school at the moment and his mother would be reluctant to move him from his present school. However, I suggested that if a move coincided with his going to secondary school there would be less upheaval.

I only had a rather brief conversation with the mother, as she did not invite me in. This was probably because she has a very painful back and leg at the moment and no doubt she wanted to avoid climbing the stairs more often than is necessary.

However I agreed to call again next time Philip is home. I understand that he is going for two weeks from July 22nd. He will then return to Harpenden to go on the group family holiday, and go back to his mother again at the end of the family holiday.

Philip has been home for the weekend recently and his mother continues to be pleased with the improvement in him. She is waiting to hear whether a holiday in an old people's home will be arranged for her mother. If so, she will be able to take Philip away for part of his holiday.

MY ANSWER.

Perhaps it was trying to keep my mother happy, that I outwardly showed that I liked both the Home and school. If I had let on that in reality I was unhappy at the Home, an earlier decision might have been made to take me out of the Home. By showing I was happy, the only thoughts the adults had was that I might get upset if I was to get an extra change of school during my primary education. To me changing schools would not have really mattered. That year at school had however been a lot better than the previous year; even receiving the cane several times during this school year did not cause any problems for me.

There was some ill feeling between my family and the landlord, over the way he treated my grandmother after my grandfather had died. My grandfather had worked for the engineering firm for many years. It was not that he was in some low-paid employment; he had been their accountant and company secretary. Having worked well past retirement, he had certainly given his life to the firm. They now regarded my grandfather as more of a nuisance in occupying a flat that had rising commercial value. With his death, they felt no more compulsion to offer his widow rented accommodation. Having lived in the property for many years there was the simple logistics of finding a suitable flat for my grandmother while needing full time nursing care from my mother.

53. 22.07.67 Letter to Rev. Gordon. E. Barritt. NCH London from Governor of Harpenden NCH.
Philip went home to his mother last evening and will be staying until 6th August. He will also be staying with her from 18th August to 3rd September.

54. 07.08.67 Report of Child Care Officer.
I called to see Philip who is at home on holiday. He is finding plenty to do and has been swimming practically every day. He is still a rather excitable child, who does not concentrate for long.

I spoke to his mother on her own and she said she was rather concerned about him, as she had seen his school reports. She has at last realised our cause for concern over Philip's lack of progress and is glad he will be seeing the Tutor in Charge soon. The mother is unable to throw any light on Philip's inability to concentrate.

The mother said that Philip has been well behaved and easy to manage this holiday and had no temper tantrums, as he has done at other times. When told that he should learn to control his temper he said: 'My blood just boils'.

The mother does not yet know where she will live when she has to leave this address in November. Her sister and brother in law are still exploring the possibility of buying a shop, in which she could help.

MY ANSWER.
During time away from the Home, I could always find things to do. If I was excited, it was down to the freedom I was allowed in London, rather than the restrictive life at the Home. It could take very little to get me into a rage; a short amount of teasing or when simple tasks did not seem to work and I could easily fly into a rage.

The only disappointment with the summer holiday in London, was to return to the Home, half-way into my holidays so that I could be taken on the 'family' holiday with the others in the group from the Home. This was my worst ever holiday there; the main event I was in trouble for was wetting the bed, and the only time my bed was without a rubber sheet covering the mattress. Soaking a mattress was the worst misdeed that could ever be committed by a child; to the Houseparent it was unforgivable, and I was given the slipper for each occurrence.

I managed to get short periods away from them during the holiday; it was by spending all my holiday pocket money on pony rides, the others having little interest in such activities meant I could be on my own for a little while each day.

When the 'family holiday' was over, I was allowed to return to London for the rest of the summer holiday. When my mother collected me, The Houseparent told her in front of me about my bed-wetting and all the wrong things I had done during the family holiday, and also that she had found it necessary to give me the slipper for my actions. During the trip back to London, I felt a little ashamed in front of my mother.

55. 12.09.67 Note to Sister Louise from the Houseparent of Philip.
I agree it would be interesting and very helpful to know more of Philip's capabilities, and perhaps it would be a good idea to get him tested soon, before he is due to move to senior school.

MY ANSWER
I was now in the top year of the primary school. The new class teacher had abandoned the Praise and Punishment system that I had become used to with my previous teacher – that method was, I think, starting to work. My new class teacher simply sent me to the Headmaster for even the most minor wrongdoing; there was now no praise for any of my work.

56. 14.09.67. Letter to Governor of Harpenden NCH from London NCH.
Thank you for your letter of the 12th September, which shames me. I have in fact had these children on my mind and was speaking last night about them.
I am sorry that I still cannot give you an immediate date. I am as you will realise, extremely pressed at the moment and I think it will be necessary for me to ask for the two children to be brought here. I will hope to be able to offer you a date, probably a Tuesday or Thursday the last week in September. It would be helpful if, when the children come, I could have an up to date school report and · also a report from the housemother.
Please accept my apologies for not having written to you earlier concerning this.
Note: To Sister Louise for Kevin and the Houseparent for Philip Howard. Would you please let us have a report on Kevin and Philip. We have asked The Headmaster for the school reports.

57. 21.09.67 Copy Letter to Headmaster Manland School from Stephens, London.. Original to Education Department St. Albans.
Thank you for the medical photographs, we have studied them, please find enclosed their return.
There is a general agreement between us, that your suggestion that the matter was not taken any further, would be the best course of action. This we feel is in the best interests of Philip. We can see no real benefit for him of having past and possibly upsetting memories brought back to him, in view of the problems that he may be currently going through.
We understand that with the new school year, there will not be any chance of a recurrence of past events. It was a little surprising that the whole matter was

185

not brought to our attention at an earlier point in time. This we understand was down to the delay of the photographs reaching you, due to their original medical purpose not having any relation to the current matter.

We can conclude that without the photographs little attention would have been given to the problem, there having been no complaints from either The Children's Home or the boy concerned.

Your decision we feel over this matter is the best for all concerned. It is a favourable result that the boy does not appear to have suffered any ill effects, that your recommendation that the boy not be involved in this matter, will we think benefit his school work. Any lasting visible effects should disappear over the course of time. It is always remarkable how youngsters can be so resilient to such events; we hope he will take it as part of growing up.

Should the school require a later update, and if there is any further correspondence between The Children's Home and us, we will inform you in due course, but we feel that this will now be closed at our end and they will correspond with yourselves if there is any further need.

MY ANSWER.

My original thought on this letter was that it was in relation to the gun pellet that had lodged in my knee. When they talked about the delay with the photographs, I took this to mean the medical X-rays that were taken during the Growth Study Tests. It was a few months after I was shot, that the X-rays were taken and the pellet was noticed. It was a further six months from this point before the pellet was removed. During my time at school, I did complain of a pain in my knee when I was involved in sporting activity, but at the time, little notice was taken of my complaint.

One of the photographs was in a school file. It was not of my knee in the photograph, but my lower leg, taken at the medical tests. At the time, I had an identical photograph, but was embarrassed when it showed the bruise marks on my legs from the cane at school. Quite early on, I removed the leg section on my copy of the photograph, so that the Houseparent would not get to know I was punished. I did not know at the time that the same photograph was sent to the school over the marks on my leg.

None of the adults said anything to me over the matter, even the Houseparent did not ask me about the marks on my legs that she must have been told about.

One odd memory that I can remember, was that at the end of the summer holidays when I had returned from London, the Houseparent had taken a good look over my body. At the time I took this to be a simple check to see what scars and injuries I had managed to acquire whilst playing in London.

Any injuries that I did have always did take a long time to fade away simply down to the shade of my skin. The marks from an earlier caning were probably still visible; more recent injuries from my play during the holidays may have slightly covered these up. The Houseparent had not made any comment at the time to me, so I had taken it that I was quite fit.

With the new year of school, I can now understand why my next teacher did not physically punish me in any way, and that for every event I was sent to the

Headmaster, where the only punishment I received during the last few months at that school was to stand outside his office during my free time or do a few lines.

The reason I find that this photograph was saved by the education department was that a record was made showing how the local schools punished children over the years. The photo of my leg had been saved as an odd example of such events. In the normal way after about ten or so years, most records of the education department were discarded.

58. 06.10.67. Note to Sister Louise in charge of Kevin and the Houseparent of Philip.

The Education Psychologist rang yesterday. She would like to see Kevin and Philip on Tuesday 10th October at 10am. The boys will have to go up to London to see her. Transport has yet to be arranged.

Footnote: I don't mind taking them up by train. R.F.

MY ANSWER.

The Home had now decided that they want to find out what my intelligence was and why my school work was poor. Although I did not appear to be unique, there was only one other boy from the Home who was going to be tested. A day trip to London was not really a holiday as we would be made to do similar work to that of school, but it was a day out that in the normal way we would not get.

The Houseparent took us both up to London early in the morning; it was a route I knew well. Finding which Underground lines we needed to be on, once our destination was given to me, was quite easy. If either of us had wanted to get lost and out of captivity, going in opposite directions would have been enough to cause problems. However any chance of freedom and a happy life ever again would have been nil.

Very little was explained to us about the day's events; apparently we soon would be back, but there would not be enough time for us to return to school. We expected to be going to a school for our test. Eventually when we did arrive at the location, but although the building resembled a school, there were only adults inside.

Instead of simply being sat down and given a written test to do we were separated. I would have my test first and the other boy I had come up with would be seen in the afternoon. The Houseparent was not going to be with us. I was led away with one of the staff; it was not that I was afraid, but everything was different from how I imagined it. The tests were my ideal form of exam; there was no need to give long written answers, just a single-word answer or the like was required. I was allowed short breaks between each series of tests. Some items were easy; others seemed impossible.

Apart from the actual tests, there were questions about life at the Home, school and when I went home, plus other questions on how I felt about various things.

The questions of did I like my trips to stay with my mother, and what I did on my visits. I could only say that it was my favourite activity and that I went swimming, to the cinema and to the park. I was asked if my mother punished me if I was naughty. I said that my sweets and going outside were stopped for that day; but my mother did not give me the plimsoll or cane any more.

There were questions about if I liked school and was I bullied. My reply was that I did not find school much fun now I had a different teacher. Any bullying was down to the colour of my skin; I was unable to explain to the others at school why I had a tanned complexion.

Time was spent asking if I had any problems living at Highfield; my main reply was that I would like more things to do and to have others of my own age in the flat to play with.

I was asked was I afraid at night and was my bed-wetting down to fear of the dark or something that I had not told the Houseparent about, and did the other children tease me. All I could explain was that it happened in the Home and during the summer holiday with the Houseparent when I did not wake up in time. The only way the others teased me was by watching me receive the slipper after wetting the bed. I was asked what did my mother say if I wet my bed when I stayed with her. My answer was that there had not been any wet beds during any of my visits to London.

The final question was what things would make my life happier. The only real suggestion I could give was that I would like to return to my mother. The answers I gave, possibly painted a rosy view on life at the Home, rather than how I really felt. In my mind the staff from the Home would soon be told of what I had said.

The tests for me ended at lunchtime. I was told not to talk about the test I had taken, as the boy who was to be tested in the afternoon would need to come fresh to them and should not know the answers.

Lunch over I was now shown to a small room. This had toys for very young children and a few comics that were not really of any interest to me. Although there was a door leading out to the garden, the weather was not that nice, and as I was in my best clothes any sort of play was out of the question.

Eventually the tests on the other boy finished, and we were left alone before the Houseparent came to take us back to the Home. Neither of us could really work out what all the tests were about, and there was little real explanation from the adults.

During the journey back, I was told that if the others in the flat asked why we had been up to London, it was best to tell them we had been given various school tests. Once back at the Home, there were questions by the others. There was very little I could tell them, other than that for half the day, we each had been given school tests to do.

59. 10.10.67 Note to Sister Olive from the Houseparent of Philip.

Lenton did not return by Green Line Coaches as arranged, but with Philip's mother, who looked exhausted. She chatted very freely over a cup of tea about wishing her parent could go into a home or at least away for a holiday. She said she had told her sister that she had done two years which she felt was her share. We did not discuss Philip as he was near us all the time, but I do feel she is worried as indicated in the report and when I saw her. If there could be another visit, I think we might get the answers to some of the questions.

60. 16.10.67 Report of Child Care Officer.
Although the Mother has been given notice to leave by the end of October, she still is not certain of her plans for the future. Her sister and brother in law are negotiating to buy a shop and if they are successful, the mother and grandmother will go to live with them. Meanwhile the mother hopes she might be allowed to stay in her present flat a little longer until arrangements are complete. If she goes to live with them she hopes to have Philip with her but it would be best if he could stay at Harpenden until the end of the school term and join her then. If he did this, the mother would continue to visit every third weekend even though it would mean travelling from the Isle of Wight. She agreed to let me know as soon as possible what her plans would be.

I had seen Philip a few days previously when he had been at Highbury to be tested by the Tutor in Charge. He appeared to be a little anxious about the future. His mother said that she would do her best to explain the situation to him although it is difficult as plans are so vague at the moment. She is very much looking forward to having him home. If there are any special recommendations following the Tutor in Charge's report, I am sure she would be co-operative in carrying these out.

MY ANSWER.
With all the events and plans going on around me, and not really being told anything positively about their plans for me, perhaps I became a little more unsettled with life at the Home. In my mind if my mother was planning to leave London, would I be able to go with her and if not, would she still come to visit me?

61. 10.10.67 Report by Tutor in Charge on Philip Test Date 10.10.67 Age 10 years 9 months.
Request for interview: by Governor of Harpenden NCH due to the child's poor progress at school, and behaviour difficulties within the family group.
Philip was given the Stanford Binet Intelligence Scale Form L/M, Children's Raven Matrices and Full Raven Matrices scales.
On Stanford Binet Form L/M Philip passed all tests at year 9, five at year 10, four at year 11, four at year 12, two at year 13, four at year 14, one at average adult level and failed all the superior adult level.
This gives a mental age of 12.6 and an IQ of 113.
The boy co-operated throughout the interview.
On Raven Matrices Children's Scale he obtained a score which placed him in Grade I indicating that he is intellectually superior.
On Full Scale Adult Tests, a score placing him in Grade III Plus, indicating that he is of good average intellectual ability.

Discrepancies on set scores showed slightly abnormal deviation indicating the score not to be completely valid, due to the boy's tendency to give up in the face of difficulty was marked in this last testing situation.

Philip is an attractive young boy who suffers from a degree of hypertension. Fundamentally an unhappy child: socially very ill adjusted.

The general tenor of his school reports and the Houseparents very helpful and detailed report is hopeful as he does show a slow erratic progress, this particularly in relation to his conduct at school. Scholastic attainment should certainly improve as the boy's emotional problems decrease.

I think Philip does in fact require more than average help and if he is to remain in the care of the National Children's Home, I would recommend that he be considered either for a place at the Harrogate Special Unit or an approach be made to obtain for him play therapy sessions at the St. Albans clinic.

He will be dependent on more than average adult supervision, guidance and company. He should be given as many opportunities for legitimate outlet of aggression as possible.

He is undoubtedly concerned about his colour and I believe about his father. He would appear to have no knowledge whatsoever about his father and I would strongly urge that his mother be encouraged by the Child Care Officer to realise Philip's necessity in this matter and to talk to him and enable him to have some image of his father.

Some of his schooling difficulties would undoubtedly be caused by his visual difficulties though I understand he no longer suffers from double vision. Nevertheless there would be a backlog of difficulty and associated emotional difficulty with this.

I note that the Houseparent states that his movements are clumsy and erratic and that he does appear to be over-active and over-excitable: to be a restless sleeper and very easily disturbed. I wonder whether he is a child who would be helped by some form of mild sedation. This is of course is a matter for a doctor to consider.

I feel very concerned for this child as I feel it would be very doubtful, without a great deal of support, that the mother would be able adequately to care for this boy and see him through his difficulties if he does return to her in the near future.

MY ANSWER.

The Houseparent told me that she had the results back from the test that I had been to. All I was told that I had done quite well and that all I needed to do at school was to try to concentrate. If more could have been explained over the results, I might have been able to understand that instead of my below-average results for my age at school, it might be possible for me to give above-average results for my age; it was that there were always so many other matters going on around me that prevented me from good work at school. I would have loved to see what the Houseparent said in the report about me.

62. 24.10.67 Letter to Houseparent of Philip from Tutor in Charge.

It was nice to see you again and I hope you and the boys weren't too weary with your long day.

I am sorry my reports are so long in coming but I have today given them to the secretary who will be getting off the copies to the Governor of Harpenden NCH. The delay has been due to pressure of work and ill health. I seem to be falling easy prey to anything that's going just lately, life like's that at times isn't it.

I feel very much concerned for Philip and you. Fundamentally he's a very nice child. You'll see my report and I can only hope that a little help can come from this. Do hope that Mr. Norman is able to start some of the woodwork, plays etc. There's such a lot in the youngster's mind.

MY ANSWER

The idea that an adult was going to let me do woodwork or the like, came to nothing. I was never asked once I had returned to the Home, if I would like to do any such hobby; if I had, then perhaps things might have been easier at this period for me.

It was an interesting comment that she was 'very concerned' for both the Houseparent and me. I wonder if she had the idea that we were not too happy in each other's company at times.

Since the start of the new school year, things had been a little unsettled for me. During the periods I was at school I was not very happy with the way I was treated, although I was never hit now at school, I was in constant trouble.

63. 01.11.67 Report of Child Care Officer.

Although the mother was due to leave her flat the following week, she still did not know where she would be going as her brother in law had not bought the business on the Isle of Wight. She promised to let me know as soon as any plans are fixed.

The mother was interested to hear about the Tutor in Charge's report on Philip, which confirmed our previous impression that Philip is intelligent but his performance up to now has been well below his ability.

Once more, we discussed the difficulties that the mother had when Philip was a baby. As she always lived in someone else's house, she had to keep him very quiet. We discussed the need for him to have more freedom in the future, and the ways in which he could most helpfully be occupied.

Apparently his uncle that they might go to live with is keen on carpentry and might encourage him in something like this.

We also talked about Philip's father and the need for Philip to know more about him. The mother assured me that she has always been open about this: has shown Philip photographs and explained to him why his father is not with him now.

The mother is concerned that Philip should have every opportunity to make the most of his abilities and said that if it was recommended she would willingly take him to a Child Guidance Clinic once he is at home with her. I think this might be very helpful to her as well as to him.

Report of visit to Harpenden Branch.
As it was the half term holiday, I saw Philip and took him out with Pamela and Susan. He seemed to thoroughly enjoy a race across the Heath rushing from one activity to another. This is probably the sort of activity that Philip needs but which is not possible when he goes to his mother for weekends and holidays.

MY ANSWER.
It was decided that I needed to let off more steam; taking me out and allowed to rush about was more interesting than being at the Home. Although we had plenty of open space, after a time it could get a little bit boring. When I was in London, there was plenty of time to run about if I was in a park, but as I was on my own, this was never noticed.

The matter of my mother explaining more about my father to me had been very little. It was true that I had been shown a selection of photographs of her friends, taken in the 1940s and 1950s but at no point was one picked out and informed that 'he was your father'. The only real information I had ever managed to get from my mother was that he had been born in Ceylon and had several older brothers. The actual reason for my mother and father parting had never been explained.

64. 03.11.67. Note to Child Care Officer.
I am not sure from the report of your last visit to the mother whether she is really planning to have Philip home at the end of the present term, or must this wait until the move to the Isle of Wight?

The point of this is, if Philip is to stay on at Harpenden whether we should do something about putting him in touch with the St. Albans Clinic. Would a change of school help him to make more progress with his work?

MY ANSWER
Some of the adults do not seem to have caught up with the latest position of my mother moving. Plans were already starting to be made for a change of school for me if I was going to stay at Harpenden for any length of time.

65. 15.11.67 Note from NCH.
Your comments have been noted, thank you. The mother lives in London at present but is likely to be moving to the Isle of Wight so the Harrogate Unit would be most unsuitable. When the move to the Isle of Wight is made, Philip is likely to join his mother.

Depending on the timing of this move a decision has to be made whether he attends the St. Albans Clinic, or returns to his mother when she is prepared to take him to the Child Guidance Clinic for help.

66. 17.11.67 Report of Child Care Officer.

It was felt that it would be wise for Philip to commence the Child Guidance Clinic whilst still at Harpenden if possible.

This would mean that if he does return to live with his mother it would be easier to arrange for him to be transferred than to have to recommend attendance again through the school or doctor.

Apparently Philip needs a good deal of attention but is not sufficiently confident to demand it in normal ways and makes himself noticeable by being aggressive towards the younger children.

The Houseparent does not feel that his mother is able to be sufficiently relaxed and warm towards him. It also appears that his other relatives give him practically no attention, although they live in Harpenden. It seems rather as if they are ashamed of him and it is quite possible that the find it very difficult to accept him in the family.

MY ANSWER

If my three sets of aunts and uncles that lived in Harpenden had been directly contacted by the Home, it might have been possible to get a different result over their visits. The other simple reason for little contact with my relatives who lived in the town was due to the limit of visits to every three weeks. As my mother wanted to see me as often as possible, it gave any other relatives little chance if they had wanted to have me for a day. If there had been a suggestion put to the two local sets of aunts and uncles that perhaps once a month after school I could go to tea with them, a different result would have been obtained.

67. 20.11.67 Letter to Mother from Governor of Harpenden NCH.

We have been advised by the Tutor in Charge to get in touch with the Child Guidance Clinic, and our medical officer Dr. Akeroyd confirms that it would be helpful to do so. I am writing to the clinic today asking for an appointment, and I think it would be very helpful if you could attend with the Houseparent and Philip for the first interview.

Any advice they can give us will of course be very useful not only for us at Harpenden, but it will also be very helpful to you later on when Philip is able to return to your care.

68. 20.11.67 Letter to St. Albans Clinic from Governor of Harpenden NCH.

I should be grateful if you could see Philip sometime in the near future. It is felt that as he needs more than average help, and our medical officer, Dr. Akeroyd supports a recommendation made by our educational psychologist that if possible he should attend play therapy sessions.

I think it would be helpful for you to see Philip's mother as well as his Housemother. I have mentioned this to his mother and I think she will be co-operative.

69. 22.11.67. Letter to Governor of Harpenden NCH from the Mother.
Thank you very much for your letter received this morning. I will of course be pleased to attend the Child Guidance Clinic with the Houseparent and Philip. I could see by his school reports something must be wrong somewhere. I am so disappointed, he seemed so much more sensible & co-operative since he has been at Highfield. I do hope the Clinic will be able to help.

Will Philip be able to come home for the week-end? If so I will come to meet him at 5.30pm on Friday 24th and we will return about 7pm on Sunday. My most grateful thanks for all the kind attention Philip is receiving.

69a. 23.11.67. Half-Yearly Branch Report By Houseparent.
Age 10 years and 10 months.
General condition: Good
Height 4ft 9in.
Weight 5st 10lbs.
Philip appears more settled and less aggressive at the moment.
There are some night-time disturbances.
Changes in child's own family: Grandfather Died.
Interests: Cubs, drawing.
Action: Philip has been referred to St. Albans Child and Family Psychiatric Clinic 20.11.67.
Action Required Plans for Philip to attend Child Guidance Clinic and his mother to go with him.

MY ANSWER.
The Houseparent now seemed to feel that I was less aggressive. Possibly as I was almost eleven, I was classed as one of the older ones with the odd extra privilege; life did seem a little better. The note says that I was interested in cubs. This was only because I was made to attend; refusal would have meant sitting on a hard chair facing the corner or doing extra chores.

The reference to the comment that I was suffering from night-time disturbances was not due to nightmares or bed-wetting, but simply due to a growing-up stage that I was going through.

Little had originally been explained to me over the changes I might find my body was going through with puberty. The Houseparent complained over the slight dampness I caused to my pyjamas and lower sheets on some mornings and then gave me the slipper. To all the others I was treated as if I had wet the bed. It was only later that the helper was able to explain what was happening to me. To save the embarrassment of having to regularly change my pyjamas and lower sheet each morning, I was provided with a pair of rubber pants to wear under my pyjamas. It was difficult to know if it was a punishment or to help me.

Since the start of the school year in September, life at school had not gone that well. The school decided that it might be best if an alternative school could be found for me. I was not told directly that they did not want me; it was hinted to me that as I did not seem to be happy there, there might be another school where I could improve my school work.

If it was a matter of getting into trouble at school, since I started the school year in September, I had not really been in any major trouble. If I did anything wrong, I was sent to the Headmaster and found myself standing outside his room. When he saw me, there was not any punishment other than having to do a few extra lines at odd times; even this work was not checked to see if I actually completed it.

They realised that I might be bright; they simply did not know how they could help me. The IQ test to them would normally mean I would be in the 'A' stream, but as they could only put my actual position in the lower half of the 'B' stream, something was wrong somewhere. Getting me ready for senior school appeared to be the solution, even although it was a little odd. I was looking forward to a change of school.

70. 12.12.67 Report of Child Care Officer.

I visited the mother in London, she is hopeful that, in February, she will move to Wiltshire, where her sister and brother in law are negotiating to buy a business. This has not yet been confirmed. She feels that it will be best if she goes first and settles in and then has Philip home, probably at the end of the Spring term in July.

I told the mother that we had been in touch with the Child Guidance Clinic and that it is possible that the clinic will contact her. She was pleased about this and would be willing, if necessary, to go to St. Albans.

The mother is hoping to have Philip home for part of the Christmas holiday, but not for Christmas Day as he would be the only child at home and would have a better time at Harpenden.

The St. Albans Clinic telephoned me to say that there was some doubt as to whether they would be able to work with the mother, as she was out of their area, although the mother might be invited to the diagnostic interview.

71. 20.12.67 Letter to Child Care Officer from Family Clinic.

I have discussed this case and we have come to the conclusion that the best plan would be if perhaps you could come along to the diagnostic interview when we can arrange it. We will not start any work with the mother as there is such a short time between now and February when she moves to Wiltshire, but we will pass the papers on to them so that they can make a fresh start there.

72. 27.12.67 Letter to Clinic from Child Care Officer.

Thank you for your letter and help with Philip. I shall be glad if possible to come to the diagnostic interview.

73. 27.12.67 Letter to Child Care Officer from Philip.

Thank you for your lovely gift of the scrapbook. I enjoyed Christmas, we had dinner in the evening so we could play with our toys after Chapel. I hope you had a very nice Christmas also. Love from Philip.

MY ANSWER.

This is the only surviving item of my handwriting from an early age. Although it is rather poor, this letter would have been one of many that I would have written after Christmas to the many people who sent me presents. One disadvantage of having many relatives, it was that there were a large number of letters to write. Possibly this was one of a number I had to write on the day, and by the time I reached this one perhaps it was a little hurried as I still had plenty of presents to play with.

74. 03.01.68 Letter to Mother from Child Care Officer.

We have just been given some theatre tickets for 'Give a Dog a Bone', for Friday, 5th January. I enclose four, and wonder if you would like to take Philip. Maybe Lenton and his mother would like the other two: if not, you could give them to another friend who might like them. I enclose the directions for reaching Westminster Theatre. The show is at 6.15 pm. I hope that Philip will enjoy the rest of his holiday.

75. 06.01.68 Letter to Child Care Office from the Mother.

Thank you very much for the tickets to see 'Give a Dog a Bone'. We took Lenton and his sister, and we all enjoyed it very much indeed. I think it's the most charming pantomime I have ever seen. After the show, the three children had their programmes autographed by nearly all the cast. Philip was thrilled to bits, the programme has been shown to everyone we know, thank you for the most helpful directions, I did not know where the Westminster Theatre was.

Philip went to the hospital to see my mother this afternoon, they allowed him into the ward, but she did not seem at all well and spoke very little. I don't think hospital life suits her.

Tomorrow afternoon we will be going back to Highfield. I expect Philip will find school a bit tame after his eventful Christmas holiday. Thank you again for the tickets and for all the kind interest you have taken in Philip.

MY ANSWER.
Taken to a major London theatre, was a real treat. This was perhaps one happy event that lodged in my mind; what the play was actually about was completely forgotten after a few months.
The song:
I Dream of Ice Cream, Sausages and Cake,
Things that you fry,
Things that you bake.
It's such a nice dream, I'm afraid to wake,
When I Dream of Ice Cream, Sausages and Cake.

76. 10.01.68 Report on Visit by Child Care Officer.
Philip was at home, on holiday and had Lenton, who is in his family group at Harpenden, playing with him.
Philip seemed to be enjoying his holiday. He was quite excitable and still spoke very fast, not really forming his sentences well and sometimes almost speaking nonsense.
The grandmother is still in hospital, having broken her leg again. This means the mother has been free to take Philip out this holiday.
Plans for moving to Wiltshire are still progressing, although no definite date had been fixed. It was difficult to talk in front of the children and I agree to call again towards the end of the month.
MY ANSWER.
A holiday in London and a visit on my birthday by the Child Care Officer and there was a very good reason for me to be excited. If she was unable to understand what I was saying, it was that I was teaching Lenton 'back-slang', a way of reversing the order of letters in certain words, so others could not understand what was said.
During the periods that my grandmother was in hospital, I often went with my mother on her visits. Other than on one occasion when I was allowed in to see her, I was not able to visit; there was a firm rule that children under fourteen were not admitted during visiting hours. My mother's visits were often for an hour or so. I was left outside the hospital entrance to wait until her visit was over.

77. 12.01.68 Letter to Governor at NCH Harpenden from Clinic.
Philip is still on our waiting list to be seen by a psychiatrist, but I am afraid we have not been able to fit him in yet. Our Social Worker has been in touch with the Child Care Officer. I think that it is unlikely that we shall be able to offer treatment for Philip.

78. 17.01.68 Letter to Rev. Gordon. E. Barritt. NCH London from Governor NCH Harpenden.
You will have received the copy of the letter from the clinic to me on 12th January, in which it says that it is unlikely that the Child and Family Psychiatric Clinic will be able to offer treatment for Philip.

In view of this I feel it is important for Philip to return to live with his mother as soon as it can be arranged.

MY ANSWER

The letter to the Home suggested that the Child and Family Psychiatric Clinic would not be able to offer me any treatment. The Home had the idea that I would have been with them for another six months or so; that would have allowed any problems that I might have to be sorted out before I was returned to my mother. This letter from the clinic changes all the plans the Home had over my future.

Their minds were made up; they wanted me to leave the Home. Did they have the idea that I could cause them a major problem? This was just at the point having changed schools that life at the Home was starting to get better.

If the Child Guidance Clinic had told the NCH that they could help me whilst at Harpenden, it might have been the idea of the NCH that I started a session as soon as possible. That my mother would be able to move to Wiltshire and settle down first would have easily come about. My leaving the NCH would then have been near to the summer; it might have even been suggested that I stay on longer at the Home to complete a Play Therapy course; this could have delayed my leaving by up to a year.

A course of Play Therapy sessions might have helped my emotional development; it could however have caused additional problems if I had decided that I could not stand living at the Home any longer. It was down to luck that the Child Guidance Clinic decided that they could not help me.

79. 23.01.68 Telephone conversation from St. Albans Clinic to Child Care Officer.

It was explained that as the mother was expected to move to Wiltshire in the near future, and take Philip with her, it was difficult to see the value of commencing treatment for Philip. This is partly because Philip would have to learn to relate to the people at St. Albans Clinic, and then would have to commence again in Wiltshire.

After some discussion, it was suggested that, if the mother does soon move, her address should be sent to the St. Albans Clinic and then The Clinic could write to the nearest Clinic in Wiltshire, explaining why he had not been seen, and asking that he should be seen in Wiltshire with his mother.

80. 23.01.68 Visit by Child Care Officer to Mother on 22.01.68.

The mother's plans for moving are still rather vague as she is waiting for her sister to sell her present house. As soon as this is done, the move to Wiltshire can be made.

The mother has become tired of waiting and wondered whether to act independently of her sister, but has done nothing really about this. Her own mother is still in hospital on account of her fractured leg, but has also been on the danger list, apparently having had heart trouble.

The mother said that after the Christmas holidays Philip had resisted going back to Harpenden. This is the first time it had happened. He also admitted to be worried about many things, but felt better after visiting his grandmother in hospital.

The mother had wondered whether she should keep him at home, as she is free to care for him, but did not do so.

1. Because she did not wish him to have another school. 2. Because she does not know if her landlord would give permission to have Philip home, especially as she should herself, really have left the flat by now.

The mother said that she does not find Philip too difficult to manage apart from his inability to concentrate, and his tempers. She is worried about his school progress, and would be willing to take him to the Clinic once she is settled in Wiltshire.

I had previously seen Philip at Harpenden on the 16th January 1968. The Houseparent had reported that his behaviour was very difficult and he seemed very resentful of authority.

I had spoken to Philip briefly, mentioning the fact that his mother was making plans to move and would have him as soon as possible. It is difficult to know how many of his problems may be associated with a wish to return to his mother, and how many are much more long-standing difficulties.

MY ANSWER.

There were reports from the Houseparent that my behaviour was very difficult in December but during November, there had been the mention that I was more settled and less aggressive.

I was told before Christmas that there might be a chance I would be moving to a different school and the possibility I would be moved to a different Home; this had apparently been suggested from the results of the tests. Knowing my mother would soon have to leave the London flat, I think a few things seemed to be going wrong around me. Little was actually explained to me about the various possibilities of my future; all that was ever said was that I should wait and see, which had me feeling even more unsettled and apt to cause problems.

81. 24.01.68 Letter to Governor of NCH Harpenden from the Mother.

When we returned on Sunday evening last, I mentioned to the Houseparent that my sister and her husband would be coming from Harpenden to London on Saturday to visit my mother in hospital, and would, if convenient collect Philip and bring him to London and I would return with him on Sunday evening letting you know as soon as I had arranged the time etc., it would be Saturday 3rd February at 12.15pm, they will give him lunch at their home.

I had a visit from The Child Care Officer on Monday and was very distressed to hear Philip was causing so much trouble to his Houseparent and everyone else. I will of course remove him at half term or before if you think it necessary.

As this situation has arisen, I have decided to abandon my family's problems and strike out alone. At the moment I am negotiating a position as housekeeper in Tenby, in South Wales on the sea front, it sounds most suitable.

I am so very sorry Philip's stay at Highfield has had to end like this, until two months or so ago he seemed so happy and much more reasonable.

82. 24.01.68 Letter to Governor of NCH Harpenden from NCH London.
Thank you for your letter. We enclose a report on discussion with our clinic and the mother, which took place prior to the receipt of your letter.

We note your comments about the advisability of Philip's return to his mother and agree that she should be visited again, with the suggestion that she might have Philip home soon, possibly at half term. As you will see from the report, this may depend on her landlord's agreement to Philip being in the house. The mother is in a state of indecision and a definite step on our part might help her.

MY ANSWER.
The NCH have the idea that asking my mother to take me back, will help her decide over the matter of my staying in the Home or returning to her.

83. 01.02.68 Letter to Clinic at St. Albans from Child Care Officer.
Further to our recent telephone conversation, I have visited the mother twice. She is still uncertain of her plans for moving, but as soon as we know her next address we will inform you.

It will be a great help if Philip's name can be transferred to a clinic in the area in which he will be living.

We are encouraging the mother to have Philip with her as soon as possible.

84. 01.02.68 Report of Child Officer.
I called to see the mother to discuss the Governor of Harpenden suggestion that Philip should return to his mother as soon as possible.

This was not difficult, as the mother had said on my previous visit that she had wondered if she ought to keep him at home. However, she still does not feel that it will be possible to ask her landlord for permission to have Philip, as they are living from week to week now, wondering when they will be told to leave.

The mother wondered why Philip should be anxious to come home now, as he has always seemed so happy at Harpenden. She also wondered what his behaviour difficulties were, as he is no more troublesome than usual at home, except that when he was told off by his uncle at the weekend he shrieked in a very unusual way. We discussed all these things.

The mother said that she has already replied to an advertisement offering a job and accommodation in South Wales. Her only fear is, that if she does anything to upset her family, there is no one who would stand by her if she were ill.

It appears the mother's brothers and sisters (she is one of a family of five) all rely on her to take the responsibility for her mother. I suggested that it may help her to be able to tell them that we are now asking for Philip's return home.

The grandmother is still very unwell and I suggested that it might also help the mother to see the Medical Social Worker to find out what kind of plans need to be made, in the event of her mother's discharge from hospital.

When the mother does leave the present flat there will be a great deal of clearing up to do. However at the moment there does not seem to be any definite steps she can take.

She assured me that she wants Philip with her as soon as possible, but at present she is still unable to give a definite date.

MY ANSWER.

The Home decided to encourage my mother to make the decision to take me back; it was by the request that I should leave Highfield. If my mother had decided to keep me in London after my last holiday when I told her that I did not want to go back to the Home, the NCH could have demanded a penalty payment of £150 from her – almost a years wages. Their request that my mother took me back, allowed my quick departure. No questions were asked by her to the NCH as to the actual reasons over their request for me to leave.

I always allowed my mother to think I was happy in the Home. I knew that it would have been impossible for me to live in London for any length of time whilst she was looking after my grandparents. I did not want her to think I was unhappy.

Life before Christmas in the Home had just not been easy; during my Christmas holidays while I was in London, I think I let my mother know that I was unhappy in the Home. If I behaved in an odd manner when my uncle told me off, it was that he took hold of me. With the memory of the Houseparent grabbing me, and an earlier memory of being touched, I reacted in a totally different way to normal.

85. 13.02.68 Report of Child Care Officer.

I called on the mother to find out exactly what the situation was as she had written to the Governor of Harpenden to say she would be having Philip permanently at the weekend (17/2/68).

The mother was obviously very worried, and the whole situation seemed very conflicting and uncertain.

The grandmother had come home from hospital the previous day, although she was not fully recovered and was obviously in mild heart failure, so the mother was back nursing her again. However her G.P. and the hospital have both said that she must return to hospital straight away if her condition worsens.

The mother did not get the job in South Wales, and although she is anxious to find a post like that where she can have Philip with her, she has no time to apply or attend interviews now her mother is on her hands again.

It seems that the house/shop in Wiltshire being negotiated by the sister and her brother in law will now not be available until 30th March, and the mother is very worried that the landlord will not continue to allow them to remain for another six weeks, as they were meant to be out by last October. She was awaiting confirmation of the moving date from her sister on Friday.

Despite all these problems, the mother was very cheerful, and quite determined to have Philip home at the weekend.

I assured her that he could of course remain at Harpenden until she moved to Wiltshire, and that this was probably the most practicable idea, but the mother was adamant that if he was unhappy at Harpenden he should come home, and that she would manage. She said that after all six weeks was only a bit longer than the summer holidays, and she had coped with him and her mother then, and as Philip had now been told he was coming home she would not go back on her word.

She was making arrangements for him to attend the local school where he went before going to Harpenden, but felt she would have to postpone the Child Guidance plans until they were settled.

Apparently she was not even certain that she would remain with her sister and brother in law in Wiltshire, but thought she might find another residential job where she could be alone with Philip, which of course would be possible if she managed to leave her mother in her sister's care for a change. I gather that the sister took very little interest in Philip, and she was worried that he might not settle with them.

The mother had obviously made up her mind to have Philip home, and said several times he was the most important person as far as she was concerned, and the sooner they were on their own together, the better. She did promise to contact us if things became too difficult during the next few weeks.

She hoped that the other sister and brother in law that lived in Harpenden would be able to bring Philip home by car at the weekend, and I promised to call soon to see how they were managing.

MY ANSWER.

At the visit to London at the beginning of February, it was hinted by my mother that I would soon be leaving the Home. If I had only been allowed to stay in London, life would have been great, but due to my grandmother needing a lot of extra care from my mother, I could not stay in the flat at that moment: it was the return to the Home to get ready for leaving that was the worst part of it all.

The final weeks were however odd. School had now become much better and even at the Home things seemed easier. As I was now regarded as an older one, having reached eleven, extra pocket money and the permission to go and visit a new school friend who was not at the Home was allowed once tea was over; this meant that the confines of the Home became less.

As to my forced activities, cubs was no longer obligatory, having fallen out with this activity a short while earlier, when a couple of us who by age were each due to be made Sixers, were told we were to remain Seconders whilst others were promoted in front of us. There were endless requests for me to remain in the Cubs, but I had stuck to my guns and said to the Houseparent that I no longer wanted to go; even talks with the Sister who ran the pack did little good to change my mind.

Eventually the Houseparent confirmed my leaving the Home. The others in the flat were not told until a couple of days before I left, over the plans for me to leave the Home. At school during the last week, only the teachers knew. On the last day, I told a couple of my friends that I would not be returning to school.

There was always the thought in my mind that, at the last moment, I would be informed that I would be remaining at the Home. I knew that until I actually left the grounds it would not have actually happened and even then, there was the possibility that I could always be sent back.

At the time I left the Home my mother questioned me as to why they had asked me to leave, but there was nothing I thought I had done wrong any more than usual to get this request made by the Home. In later years if I had been able to show her the documents of the time, it might have put her mind at rest over the final month or so of my life at Highfield.

FREEDOM 17.02.68
London is now mine. I can once again explore as much as I like in my free time by bus, underground and on foot without restriction.

86. 22.02.68 Report of Child Care Officer.
The mother and Philip were out at the library when I called the first time, and the mother's brother was looking after their mother.

When I called back later on, Philip met me at the door looking very cheerful and happy. He was obviously very pleased to be at home, and his mother assured me that everything was going well, at least where Philip was concerned.

He talked excitedly about what he had been doing since Saturday, but said he was missing Lenton from Harpenden, and was anxious about who was looking after the guinea pigs etc.

The mother is intending to write to the Houseparent that looked after Philip very shortly.

Philip's grandmother is much the same, and needs constant attention still. It was obvious that the mother is getting little sleep at night, and is on the go most of the time, but she was cheerful and uncomplaining, and obviously pleased to have Philip home.

So far they had still no news of the proposed move to Wiltshire, nor had the landlord commented on their still being in the flat, but the mother promised to let me know as soon as there were any definite dates.

The mother and Philip had an interview with the Headmaster of the local school the following day.

MY ANSWER.
In London I was happy, simply being on my own was all I wanted. It was easy to keep me quiet and not in the way, as I now had my own bedroom. Books and toys that I had brought from the Home could now be around me. My clothes were all in one place. With the short visits home, often there was a limited assortment of clothes but now everything I owned was here.

If I showed interest in the Home, it was down to the possibility that I might return. Knowing that during the day I would be sent off to school, even though the time I would spend at the school would only be for a short while, I was quite happy, although rather bored with junior school lessons.

87. 04.04.68 Report of Child Care Officer.
I called to see how the mother's plans were progressing.

Philip was busily cooking his tea, with his mother's guidance and talked cheerfully about his activities during the last few weeks.

He is obviously happily occupied at home, and I thought his speech and general behaviour were less excitable and disjointed.

However, he is not enjoying school as much as he did at Harpenden, and was looking forward to the Easter Holidays.

His mother was hopeful that there would be a good comprehensive school in or near Swindon that Philip will be able to attend when they move.

The mother at last has a more or less definite date for moving April 29th. She has been to a small village outside Swindon, to see the house and shop, and was quite pleased with all the arrangements.

The mother is hoping to get her mother into hospital for a fortnight while they pack up and sort out their furniture etc.

She promised to keep me informed as to their movements and any further developments.

MY ANSWER.
I was more settled in London. I could do what I wanted, when I wanted, and I was willing to fit in with what everyone else wanted to do. Here there were no petty rules that had been set for the sake of it.

The school I had been sent to was the same one I attended before going to the Home. I had soon made friends again with one of the boys who remembered me. The school had changed; there was now a new Headmaster and the buildings had been brought more up to date with bright colours and several new activities that were part of the daily routine.

One slight problem was that lessons were boring. Originally, I think I was in the 'B' stream when I first went there. As it was known that my stay was only for a short while, so that I did not disrupt the flow of lessons for others with the need to settle me into a new environment, I was now placed in the equivalent of a 'D' stream. Lessons were equal to those I had been given when I was first here. As long as you were quiet, you could do what you wanted – read, draw or do any activity as long as it was quiet. The books here had already been conquered, so much of my time was spent colouring pictures. It was fun for a few days, but not for several weeks. I was quite happy that soon we would move; although I liked London, to be free in the country seemed a good move to me.

88. 14.05.68 Letter to Clinic at St. Albans from Child Care Officer.
Thank you for this letter regarding the boy, Philip returned to his mother in February, and I have been visiting the family in London. The mother and Philip have just moved to a small village near Swindon.

Philip returned home as he was becoming increasingly unhappy at the Harpenden Children's Home, but he seemed to settle happily with his mother again. When I last saw the mother she suggested that Philip be given time to settle in the new home before Child Guidance was reconsidered.

As soon as we have the new address in Wiltshire, the Child Care Officer will call to see what the position is.

89. 14.05.68 Report of Child Care Officer.

I called at the London address, but there was no reply, and it was obvious that they had moved, as there were no curtains at the windows.

The mother said she would inform us of her new address, and discuss the possibility of Philip attending the Child Guidance Clinic in Wiltshire if necessary.

90. 20.05.68 Letter to Rev. Gordon. E. Barritt. NCH London from the Governor NCH Harpenden.

Thank you for the copy of the Child Care Officer's report on Philip and the mother has now given us their new address.

91. 18.06.68 Letter to NCH Bristol from NCH London.

Enclosed is a case history on Philip, who was at Harpenden, but recently returned to his mother and is now living near Swindon, Wilts. The family have been visited under Family Aid, and I should be glad if you could visit them at their new address.

92. 18.06.68 Case History of Philip.

D.O.B. 1957. Admitted 06.05.65

Harpenden Branch 06.05.65 to 17.02.68

Returned to his mother 17.02.68

Philip is the illegitimate son of Dorothy and Mr. Linton Jansen, a Singhalese, who was a trainee in hotel management at the time of their brief acquaintance. The mother lost all contact with him and his present whereabouts are not known.

The mother lived on the Isle of Wight where she was employed as a housekeeper. In February 1965 she had to give up her job to come to London in order to look after her ageing and invalided parents. One of the mother's brothers also lived with them, and there was neither room for Philip nor time to look after him adequately. His admission into care was therefore applied for. The mother had from the beginning intended this as a temporary measure, until she would no longer be needed by her parents.

The mother is an extremely conscientious person and has always been keenly aware of her responsibility towards her old parents, as well as her role in Philip's life. But although her three other married brothers and sisters all live in close proximity to London at Harpenden, none of them were helpful in sharing with her in the care for their parents, nor did any of them take an interest in Philip. It appeared that they were a little ashamed of him and were not willing to accept him.

After the death of the mother's father in May 1967, the threat of being evicted by the landlord continuously hung over her. Plans for the setting up a joint household with her sister and brother-in-law were slow to take shape and were not finalised until April 1968. In May her Sister and brother-in-law bought a house and shop near Swindon and the mother together with Philip and her mother, who is seriously ill with heart trouble, have now joined them.

Progress while in our care: -

Philip was admitted to Harpenden, as this was the most convenient Branch to enable his mother to visit him.

He was a highly-strung child, inclined to talk in a disjointed manner, but he was not lacking in confidence. He showed aggressiveness towards other children. There were some bed-wetting incidents until he became settled in the routine of Highfield.

Prior to coming into care he had attended a Primary school on the Isle of Wight, and the head teacher's report when he left this school observed that he was obviously in need of a stable background and missed the interest and concern of a father. Although his school work was below standard, it was felt that, given stability, he was capable of making good progress, academically as well as emotionally.

Philip settled well at Harpenden. His mother being very tied down at home by her parents' needs was able to visit him only once every three weeks. She had Philip home for all the holidays, but she had to leave him to fend for himself. Although Philip always enjoyed these holidays, he never resented having to return to Harpenden. His other relatives, in spite of living near to the Branch visited him only occasionally, nor did they offer to have him for a holiday.

Philip's progress at school remained unsatisfactory. He showed no improvement in his powers of concentration and his writing ability was particularly poor. In part this lack of progress was thought to be the result of double vision from which he had been suffering, and which was being corrected. In other respects, however Philip showed equal lack of improvement.

He remained excitable, had temper tantrums, was inclined to be jealous and aggressive, bullied other children, and was desperate for adult attention.

After the death of his grandfather, Philip seemed affected by the uncertainty of the family's future plans.

In October 1967 Philip was given a test in London. The report indicated that Philip was of good average intellectual ability (IQ 113), but that he suffered from a degree of hyper-tension, was fundamentally an unhappy child and socially ill-adjusted. He was undoubtedly concerned both about his colour and about his father, about whom he should be given some information. Concern was expressed about the mother's ability to see Philip through his difficulties, if he were to return to her. Philip would need more than average help and more than average adult supervision, and therapy sessions at the Child Guidance Clinic were recommended.

The mother was most willing to co-operate, but it was not thought advisable to commence treatment at the St. Albans clinic at this stage, in view of the family's plans to move to Wiltshire in the near future. Treatment was therefore postponed until the move to Wiltshire had taken place.

After the Christmas holidays it became apparent that Philip had not felt happy at Harpenden and was unwilling to go back. The mother was now determined to have Philip home as soon as possible, and Philip left Harpenden on 17.02.68.

Supervision under Family Aid was now carried on. Philip settled very happily at home, but did not like his new temporary school. The mother although working extremely hard, was obviously pleased to have Philip home.

93. 01.08.68 Report of Child Care Officer.

Both Philip and his mother seemed pleased to see me and they gave me a warm welcome. They are slowly settling down to country life, the mother is trying to make the best of things and Philip longs for London.

We talked about Philip's school and he is looking forward to going to the Senior School next term. This is three miles away but children are taken by coach.

Philip's bedroom is up in the attic and he was most anxious that I should go up the narrow staircase and also see the low beams. It is a pleasant room and he has all his own things about.

The living rooms are shared with the rest of the family, whom I did not meet, except for the grandmother who has her bedroom downstairs. I had a chat with her, she seemed really quite well and her speech was very good; the country life seems to agree with her.

I was able to have a talk with the mother on her own; she said that Philip is still very aggressive at times and she thinks that this is probably why he does not seem to keep the same friends for very long.

She has not yet sought advice from a psychiatrist for Philip and this I urged her to do as soon as Philip gets to the Secondary School; I suggested she sees the Headmaster and makes a request for Philip to see either the educational psychologist or a psychiatrist, and that she should do this as soon as possible. I will call again towards the end of the holiday to ensure that Philip has all he needs for school.

MY ANSWER.

The move to the country had certainly been different. I was now in an isolated village, although quite near to a town, and only a few buses ran at reasonable times. Most of the boys of my age had lived in the area all of their lives; it was a bit like at the Home, no one really knew of life outside the village. Unlike London I did not really have as much freedom indoors as I would have liked, as the shop and the location of excess stock came first; however my attic bedroom was my escape.

94. 02.10.68 Report by Child Care Officer.

The mother seemed to have settled into her new village although she said that life sometimes became rather boring as she only got out on Saturday afternoons.

207

She seemed quite relaxed and was prepared to settle as Philip was happy in his new Senior School and he seemed much better.

Philip is in the 'A' stream at school and he appears to be coping quite adequately: he gets a little homework, which does not worry him. He is now learning French and he was pleased to be doing some pottery: he also enjoys P.E.

I thought Philip's movements still seemed rather jerky but his mother said that she had not noticed this. She is delighted that he is so happy at school and there is no trouble going off in the mornings.

There is a good library in the school and Philip also has a ticket for the Swindon Library so he is able to get plenty of interesting books. He appears now to be a great reader. Philip told me that he had 'economised' in the buying of his comics and that he was saving his pocket money to buy a film projector.

The mother has not yet been to see the Headmaster: I said that I would be going to see him within the next few weeks.

It was encouraging to see that Philip and his mother both seemed settled and happy in their new surroundings.

MY ANSWER.

The first year of senior school was in a way a welcome change from the small village school. Life at the start of the new school year was a bit frightening as all new boys had to go through an initiation ceremony given by the older boys, and for most of the time there was continual teasing over the colour of my skin. It seems odd but none of them have actually met a dark skinned child; my light tanned complexion is the darkest they have ever seen.

The way the school runs with the need to change rooms for each lesson is something that I was already used to: for those from the village, that you do not spend your day in the same room seemed strange. Having spent only a short while at the village school, on arrival at the secondary modern there were no records of any previous schoolwork. After a short oral test, I was placed in the 'A' stream.

95. 22.10.68 Letter to Child Care Officer from NCH Bristol.

Thank you for the report on this lad. I think an early visit to his school should be made in order to acquaint the Headmaster with his early difficulties and to seek the Headmaster's advice on Child Guidance Referral.

I think it is unlikely that the mother will raise this with the school until Philip once again shows signs of disturbance and she is unable to cope with him herself. Early referral could minimise possible difficulties later.

MY ANSWER.

With my mother working during the week, there was no time for her to arrange an appointment for me with a Psychiatrist or Educational Psychologist. So nothing more was done over the matter of seeking help for me.

96. 21.10.68 Report of Child Care Officer on Visit to Philip's Headmaster.
I called to see the Headmaster to enquire about Philip's progress and to give him a little of Philip's background.

Philip is in Form 1A1 an un-streamed class parallel with 1A2, the lower streams in the first year are 1B and 1C.

He has settled down and as far as the Headmaster could say, he was making satisfactory progress; he had not heard anything to the contrary.

Philip had not shown any unusual behaviour, although he is the only coloured boy in the school. He was going through the normal teasing and trials of new boys and he has stood up to them very well.

Philip is not likely to be medically examined until well on in 1969. The Headmaster feels that Philip should be given 12 months to settle in the school and to establish himself but if there are any problems of behaviour or on the academic side then he will seek further advice.

Philip was absent from school on the day I called; he had a slight accident the previous day having been hit near the eye with another boy's ruler. It was thought that probably Philip had provoked the other boy, but no one had seen the incident. The Headmaster had made careful investigations.

I was able to meet Philip's class teacher, the Headmaster's wife. She reported that Philip was making satisfactory progress but that his writing was appalling. I told her about his jerky movements and his previous difficulty in coordination. She was concerned that Philip had not yet made any real friends apart from one boy in a more senior form.

I left them to go on to visit Philip and his mother and said I would let them know if Philip's accident was in any way serious.

The mother seemed very pleased and surprised that I had called.

Philip was at home with a cold but would be returning to school the next day. The bruise near his eye was only a minor one; he had not complained about it and it had given him no trouble. The mother told me that Philip seemed very happy at school. He had mentioned the teasing, but he had made light of it and seemed to have approached it in a very sensible manner.

MY ANSWER.
The Headmaster might have thought it odd to get a visit from a Child Care Officer rather than a parent. The Headmaster was a very traditional style of master; finding that one of his new pupils was in need of special treatment might have seemed a little strange.

The school was several miles away from the village and had the problem of no public transport between the two. We were taken by coach in the morning, and brought back in the afternoon. It was very difficult for any parent from the local villages to visit the school if they did not have a car of their own. Like most of my friends, their parents had never even seen the school, let alone spoken to any of the teachers.

Having been at the school for just over a month, perhaps my ability to get in any serious trouble had not really surfaced. The Headmaster noticed that due to my looks, I might have slight problems settling down; his view was that I should be given a year to see if any problems surfaced. If the Headmaster wanted regular reports on my activities, as I was placed in the form where his wife was the teacher, it could not have worked out better. The first report that could be given by my form teacher was that my handwriting was appalling, but I was making satisfactory progress.

I did have several friends. Although I was not really the studious type, running about games or playing with model cars during break time did not really appeal to me; in my mind, such things were not really part of senior school. Had there been the freedom to enter the library or some other practical way of passing the time, I would have been happier. Finding a boy from an upper form that seemed to have the same ideas as myself, it was easy to see why, during school time, I might not appear to be with my own age group. Once back in the village, our own age group tended to reform into one group except when a game of football was organised.

The Child Care Officer did not find that my eye injury was serious; that I seemed to be coping with the others teasing me, meant that little further notice was taken of that matter.

97. 20.01.69 Report of Child Care Officer.
I called to see the mother and Philip and first had a talk with the mother on her own. She is not really happy living with the family in the village: she never seems to get any time to herself and she is very tied to the house, she longs to get back to the Isle of Wight where she and Philip could have a flat on their own. But, she added, this certainly could not happen yet; these were just her thoughts and hopes.

After a time Philip joined us; he is still jerky in his movements and this affects his writing. His main trouble is that he will try to do everything far too quickly and therefore is not thorough.

He has periods of being teased at school but he seems to be coping with this. I had the impression that, although Philip says he is quite happy at school, this is not really so; he is just making the best of a bad job. He still talks of his previous school at Harpenden and the things he would be doing if he were still there.

The day I called, Philip said he might be moved into the 'B' stream. He said that he should never have been put into the 'A' stream and he thought he would find the work easier and be happier. He explained the work would be the same but the pace slower.

The mother said she wondered about going to see the Headmaster and what did I think. I urged her to do this especially as she has not yet been to the school.

MY ANSWER.
It was quite true that we found the village life rather stifling. For my mother, looking after my grandmother meant she was almost as confined to the house as she had been when in London. The only real time off was on a Saturday afternoon, when she took a half-day off. The pair of us would go into the local town or possibly a little further for a change.

Life in the village was rather limited in activities. Although I was quite happy living in the country and was happy to explore on my own, the surrounding area meant that even walking a short distance there were several hills to climb up and down. For both of us the idea of a seaside town or village was an appealing idea, and one that was a firm possibility in my mothers mind for some future date. If I had been asked if I would mind changing schools again, I would have been quite happy with the idea. Although I was reasonably happy at school, for many of the written lessons I was always near the bottom of the form; friends in the 'B' stream seemed to have a much more enjoyable day at school.

98. 15.04.69 Report of Child Care Officer.

I called to see the mother and Philip.

Philip seemed very well and was enjoying his holiday. He had just been in hospital for three days for the extraction of two of his adult front teeth in his lower jaw; he had apparently injured these during his time at Harpenden. He has now made a number of friends amongst the boys in the village with whom he goes out to play. He has also been to the Swindon Baths as he is a keen swimmer.

He is a little more settled at school; although he had been placed 28th out of 29 in his class, the remarks on his report had been encouraging, 'he worked hard and was interested'. However, Philip was rather worried lest he would be moved into the lower 'B' form next term. His deduction being that as five were to be moved up, then five would be moved down and he would probably be one of them.

Philip had been doing some oil painting and he had one of his little pictures already wrapped up to give me; it was quite a good effort. The mother said that his writing was still jerky but she thought it was improving gradually. Both the mother and Philip seemed happier and more settled.

99. 23.06.69 Report of Child Care Officer.

I called to see the Mother and Philip.

The mother seemed more relaxed than usual, possibly because her sister and brother-in-law were out and she and Philip were alone with her mother.

Philip had been at home all this week; he had cut his foot on some metal that had required some stitches, a pair of thick leather boots had prevented it from been very serious. It seemed to be healing satisfactorily and he expected to return to school the next week. He had missed the examinations but thought he would have to do them when he returned. Next term Philip thought he would be going into the 'B' stream of the second year and he was happy about this, as the pace would be slower.

The mother and Philip spent a day at Weston during the Whitsuntide holiday, which they had both thoroughly enjoyed. The mother was not expecting to get any holiday during the summer although she might get an odd day or two when they would be able to go out. Philip seems happy both at home and school but his movements continue to be rather jerky.

100. 12.09.69 Report of Child Care Officer.

I called to enquire how Philip had settled down at school. He is now in the 'B' stream and is doing more practical work, which seems to be suiting him better. He is particularly enjoying doing woodwork.

The mother said that he can write quite well when he tries but usually he is in such a hurry that the result is a scrawl.

During the holidays Philip had a number of friends at the house and they played mainly in the attic out of the way. Few of his friends are from the village, as they are mainly in the town where the school is situated.

Philip is very fond of an elderly widow who lives in the cottage opposite; she takes great interest in Philip and enjoys his frequent visits. They also go walking together with her dog. The mother is quite happy about this interest.

The mother is never very enthusiastic about her life in the village but as long as her mother is alive, I think she will be content to settle there to look after her and also her sister and brother-in-law.

101. 22.12.69 Report of Child Care Officer.

I called to take a special Christmas present for Philip on the 18th. The mother seemed very cheerful and quite happy about Philip; she appeared to have no worries and there were no complaints.

Philip came in whilst I was there; he had a half-day holiday from school which he was enjoying. He said school was all right but he had nothing special to tell me about it. He was much more anxious to show me his stamp collection. This is a new hobby; he spends nearly all his pocket money on buying stamps and he has a number of books in which he has them all classified. He was very enthusiastic. He seemed happy and well, and full of occupations.

102. 11.03.70 Report of Child Care Officer

I called to see the mother and Philip, primarily to ask them about a holiday in the summer.

The mother thinks it most unlikely that she could get away, even for a week, as apart from the house she must look after her mother.

I mentioned that it was possible that Philip could go on a short holiday. He would stay in a Children's Home at Dinas Powis in South Wales for two weeks. It was soon decided by Philip that he would like to go to Dinas Powis. I said that we hoped to arrange this holiday and I would let them know details nearer the time.

Philip has become very interested in woodwork; he showed me a bedside lamp he had made at school and a bagatelle board that his uncle had helped him make at home. He is still keen on his stamp collection and he never seems to be at a loss for something to do.

When I ask him about school he was not over enthusiastic: he is now in the 'B' stream and his mother said that he had some good examination results and had come 10th in a class of 36.

The mother seemed more settled than on some of my previous visits and there were no complaints.

103. 29.05.70 Report of Child Care Officer.

I called to see the mother and Philip chiefly to ask if she could contribute something towards Philip's holiday in the Children's Home in August.

The mother readily agreed to do this and will try and let us have something between Three and Five Pounds. She will be responsible for getting to Bristol by train where he will join the Mini-bus. Philip is looking forward very much to the holiday and thrilled to know it will be for two weeks.

He is reasonably settled at school but he is never very enthusiastic about it; he just says that it is all right. I will make a school visit before the end of this term to ask about his progress.

104. 05.06.70 Note to Child Care Officer from Holiday Organiser.

I have just realised that to pick up from Bristol will mean a detour for the group who will be travelling to Wales from Reading on the M4 route. Would you care to telephone the Swansea Branch to see whether he prefers Chippenham as being more convenient to both. He will be picking up at Reading at 1pm.

105. 20.07.70 Report of Child Care Officer.

I called to see the mother to make final arrangements for Philip's holiday at Dinas Powis.

Philip is to join the group at 2.30pm at Chippenham railway station on Saturday 8th August.

The trains and buses to Chippenham are not very frequent but the mother will take Philip on the train, which arrives Chippenham at 1.35pm. I said that I would be there about 2.15pm and I would look out for them.

Philip was not home from school when I arrived, but his mother was so pleased to tell me that he had done very well at school and had come 4th in his class: but Philip hoped that he would not be put up into the A class next term.

The mother said that Philip was looking forward very much to the holiday at Dinas.

106. 12.08.70 Receipt from NCH Bristol to Financial Secretary.

I enclose herewith Five Pounds received from Philip's mother as her contribution towards her son's holiday in the Children's Home at Dinas Powis. I shall be grateful if you would forward this receipt to the mother.

107. 13.08.70 Report of Child Care Officer.

The mother had taken Philip to Chippenham by train and I met them at the Railway Station.

Philip was most enthusiastic about his holiday and the mother said how lucky he was to be going.

We had about an hour and a half to wait for the Mini-bus.

Philip and Russell made a good relationship with each other; it looked as though they were going to be good friends.

The mother was just able to see Philip into the Mini-van before her train back to Swindon came in. She handed me an envelope containing a contribution towards the cost of the holiday; there was Five Pounds, which I later handed over to the Bristol Office. I said I would let the mother know about the arrangements for Philip's return journey.

108. 13.08.70 Letter to Child Care Officer from Mother.

Thank you for your letter, I have had three cards and a long letter from Philip, he sounded delighted with everything at Dinas Powis, and pleased to find he was the oldest boy. I will be at Chippenham Station on Saturday 22nd about 10.30am to meet Philip. Thank you very much indeed for arranging this holiday.

109. 27.08.70 Report of Child Care Officer.

I met Philip at Chippenham Railway station on the 22nd; he had come in the mini-van from Dinas Powis.

Philip looked very well and said he had thoroughly enjoyed the holiday.

The mother told me that she would meet Philip at the station at 10.30am but she had told Philip that if she was not there when the coach arrived to wait for her. Philip assured me that he would be quite all right waiting on his own. I therefore left him at the station in order to take Russell to Salisbury to catch a train to Weymouth.

As I was visiting Swindon on the 24th, I went to the village where Philip lives to enquire if he had to wait very long for his mother, on Saturday.

I met Philip in the street: he was on his bicycle on his way to the Post office. He said that his mother had arrived at the station as we were leaving so he had no time to wait on his own. I did not go to the house to see the mother, as the purpose of my visit was to make sure that Philip had arrived home safely.

110. 12.10.70 Report of Child Care Officer.

There is always a good welcome here; the mother is grateful for the interest we are continuing to keep in Philip.

As the mother was busy in the shop, first I had a good talk with Philip on his own. He had thoroughly enjoyed the holiday at Dinas Powis again, but with two reservations; they had all felt that rather too much of their time had been organised, although he had appreciated all the visits they had made; Philip would have preferred it if there had been more young people of his own age as when the little ones had gone to bed there was not much that just three or four could do.

Philip is still keen on stamp collecting and he showed me his British stamps; he has a wide collection and spends most of his pocket money on these. He earns a little extra delivering leaflets once a fortnight and this money is being saved for a bicycle tyre for Christmas.

He is not very enthusiastic about school, it is tolerable! But he seems to be keeping up with the work. He has a number of friends in the village and also in the town where the school is situated.

His mother joined us and she said how very much Philip had enjoyed his holiday and how wonderful it had been for him. She was most grateful to the

NCH for arranging everything: she would like to write to the staff concerned to thank them for all they did. As I did not have the correct address of the Swansea Branch with me, the mother will send her letter c/o the Regional Office.

111. 21.12.70 Report of Child Care Officer.

I called briefly to take a Christmas gift for Philip on 17th December. He was looking forward to breaking up from school on the following day, a day earlier than expected because of a conference. The mother said that he had made a very nice salad bowl in woodwork, Philip prefers the practical subjects at school and hopes to make a table skittle set next term.

Philip had done all his Christmas shopping and wrapped all the presents. He seems to organise his time very well and is rarely at a loose end. Both Philip and his mother were delighted to have heard from Harpenden and the mother was gradually getting a letter written in her reply as she has been busy helping in the shop and checking the stock etc.

112. 06.01.71 Letter to Mother from Bristol NCH.

Owing to reorganisation of regional boundaries, in order to line them up with Home Office and Local Authority regional boundaries, it has been necessary for us to transfer supervision of all administrative matters concerning Philip to the South-East region. All matters concerning his welfare and about which you normally wrote to this office should now be addressed to Highbury.

The Child Care Officer has also been transferred to the South-East Region and will continue supervision of Philip. These changes came into effect on 1st Jan 1971.

113. 01.03.71 Report of Child Care Officer.

I went to visit Philip and his mother on 26th February, she seemed pleased to see me: she and Philip always give me a welcome. The mother said that he was reasonably happy in the village but she found life rather monotonous and village life was very quiet.

Philip does not enjoy school very much but he evidently worked well as he had come 3rd in his class; his report had been very satisfactory but the general remark had indicated the comment that he must learn to stand on his own two feet.

This apparently referred to the fact that he gets very down when some of the boys call him 'wog' or 'chocolate boy' and he does not retaliate.

We talked about this together and he seemed to cheer up, as he had been particularly upset on that day. On the other hand he has many friends from both school and in the village.

Philip asked about Russell and if I had seen him lately: he and Russell had become good friends when they were on holiday together at Dinas Powis last summer. There is no doubt that Philip very much appreciated this holiday and I hope that it will be possible to arrange something for him this year.

114. 17.03.71 Family Aid Review.

The health of both Philip and his mother is very good.

The mother and Philip have a good relationship with each other and the family appear to be happy.

The mother looks after her mother and does all the housekeeping.

No financial assistance is required apart from help with a summer holiday for Philip. Material help is not required but emotionally, the mother does appreciate visits and discussions about Philip from time to time.

115. 31.03.71 Letter from Harpenden NCH to London NCH.

I enclose herewith a letter I have received from the mother of Philip, which is self-explanatory. We haven't the Birth Certificate on our file, and I can only conclude that it will be at Chief Office. I would be grateful if you could reply to the mother direct.

MY ANSWER.

The reason for the request for my birth certificate is so that I can show it to some of the boys at school, and finally prove to them that I was born in London and I'm not a foreigner. This might be the only way I can put an end to the constant teasing over the colour of my skin.

116. 24.03.71 Letter from Mother to Harpenden NCH.

May I please have the Birth Certificate of Philip, if it is still at the office, he was at Highfield 1965-68. I left it at the office on his arrival.

117. 01.04.71 Letter to Mother from NCH London.

Thank you for your letter of 24th March, please find enclosed the birth certificate of Philip, would you please be kind enough to sign the attached receipt and return it to me at your convenience.

118. Report of Child Care Officer.

As always I was given a very friendly welcome by both Philip and his mother.

Philip was looking very well; he talked more happily about school and seemed to be doing well. He had been given a patch of the garden at home to cultivate and he was keen to show me the variety of plants he was growing.

The mother also seemed more cheerful and she showed me, with pride, the improvements, which her brother-in-law had made in the garden.

Philip would very much like to go on holiday again. This year he will go to the Swansea Children's Home. This would be for two weeks 14th to 28th August. The mother expressed her gratitude that we were again giving Philip this opportunity; he would not otherwise get a holiday away from home. I agreed to let them know details about travelling nearer the time.

119. 19.07.71 Report of Child Care Officer.

I called to see the mother and Philip with details of the travelling arrangements for the Holiday in Swansea.

I had previously discussed the train times as to which trains the London party will be travelling on, this train does not stop at Swindon.

Philip will travel to Swansea on the train that leaves Swindon at 11.15 am. and arrives at Swansea at 1.40pm. He will be met at Swansea station; further details have yet to be arranged. The details for Philip's return journey have also yet to be finalised; he will probably travel on the train that leaves Swansea at 9.20 a.m. and arrives in Swindon at 11.41 am.

I agreed to let his mother know as soon as this was settled.

Philip had 'broken up' from school on the day I called: his mother had seen his report which had been returned to school; it had been a good report, Philip had come 4th in his class and had made good progress. I asked if Philip had any idea what he wanted to do when he left school. At present his chief interest is in postage stamps and he would like to get a job with one of the big firms in London.

His mother is quite agreeable for him to think along these lines; she would be happy to obtain work as a housekeeper. However, this will not be for another two years.

Philip is looking forward to his holiday in Swansea and his mother again expressed her appreciation that we were giving Philip this opportunity.

120. 10.08.71 Report of Child Care Officer.

I called to let Philip know what he is to do when he arrives at Swansea station on Saturday 14th August.

As arranged in consultation with the London party, Philip is to wait just outside the station by the ticket collector where he will be met.

The mother said how much Philip is looking forward to the holiday and counting the days. She is most grateful to us for giving Philip the opportunity of a holiday and she gave me seven pounds, which she had saved up as a contribution towards the cost.

Philip came in with his grandmother just as I was leaving and so I was able to have a brief word with him.

I will send the seven pounds to the office.

121. 23.08.71 Letter to Secretary from Office.

Swansea Holiday Project. I enclose the cheque for seven pounds in respect of contribution received from Philip's mother in respect of his holiday in Swansea. Will you please send a receipt to The Child Care Officer who will pass it on to the mother.

THE NCH REPORT ON THE HOLIDAY. August 1971.

Twenty children whose ages ranged from 10 to 15 years, spent two weeks holiday at Killay House, Children's Home, Swansea, from August 14th to 28th. The children were all either in NCH or Local Authority care under the Family Aid scheme.

Sister Stephanie Hall was in charge of the party at Swansea. The physical structure of Killay House in its beautiful grounds was ideal for the holiday plan.

Sister June was in charge of the branch at the time of arrival, and the welcome she and the staff gave the early holiday staff arrivals, and the hard work they put in making up beds and explaining the working order of the House, before turning out of the house into the pouring rain to a wet camp field, went a long way to make a successful start to the holiday. Those who normally lived at Killay House were sent away to live in a field for the two weeks that Killay House would be occupied.

The children came from a variety of backgrounds but their real need appeared to lie in the fact, that they required a holiday where they could relax away from family tensions, and, if possible, be given an opportunity to express some of the feelings brought about by such tensions.

All the staff were introduced to the children by name, explaining who they were, what they were doing prior to the holiday, and their ages. It was agreed that the staff could be called by their first names rather than their normal titles.

We explained that there were no fixed bed times, but the children could please themselves what time they went to bed, as long as it was before the staff. They would be told the night before what time breakfast would be, and if they did not wish to have breakfast they could remain in bed until the day's activities started. At first the children were very quiet about the house, but as they began to relax the house always seemed full of noisy chatter, and it must have been good for some of them to escape to their various rooms and places in the house and garden, where they could be on their own.

Towards the end of the holiday, settling down in bed became almost a ritual, when the children would ask that all the staff went to their rooms to tuck them up, kiss them good-night, and have a bedtime chat. These 'chats' were the times when the children shared with us their fears at night, such as the dark and bed-wetting; also their feelings about the tensions in their family lives. The staff were sensitive to these times, and it was felt that a large part of the benefit of this holiday was achieved at these times.

At first, the staff who had had little experience of this kind of structure were themselves wary, looking for leadership and watching out for incidents or unruly behaviour. They were able to discuss these things in the evening gathering of staff, and the way they co-operated at every possible level was outstanding. The children formed holiday relationships with the staff and each other, and there was a great deal of emotion shown at parting from each other on August 28th.

122. 07.09.71 Report of Child Care Officer.

I called on 6th September to see Philip and his mother, to hear about Philip's holiday in Swansea.

Unfortunately Philip had started school that day and as I called early in the afternoon I was unable to see him.

The mother said that Philip had thoroughly enjoyed his holiday; he had been pleased that there were several boys of his own age there including one whom he had met at Dinas Powis the previous year. Philip had thought it was grand to be allowed to call Sister Stephanie, Steve and the other members of the staff by their Christian names. This arrangement had obviously made the atmosphere less formal. Philip had been delighted to be able to spend a good deal of time on the beach and swimming; altogether he thought the holiday had been a great success.

The mother again expressed her gratitude to us for giving Philip the holiday.

123. 29.12.71 Report of Child Care Officer.
When I called to see Philip and his mother on 20th December, I was greeted with the news that they had moved to the South Coast.

The mother's sister said that their mother had died in October after having another stroke. The mother had then felt that she was free to apply for a job, which would enable her to be more independent and to live on her own with Philip.

The mother had subsequently accepted a post as a housekeeper in a family house. I was given her new address. She had been asked to start before Christmas and therefore moved two days ago on Saturday 18th December.

The sister said that the job sounded very pleasant, but it would remain to be seen how the mother and Philip settled.

The sister is prepared to have her sister and Philip back again should this prove to be necessary, she said that her sister had written to us to inform us of her move

On 21st December the letter from the mother was received informing of her new address.

On 22nd December I called to see the mother and Philip in their self-contained flat attached to the main house. They are very comfortably housed but as they had only moved on 18th December it was early days to say that they were settled. The mother does all the cooking and some of the housework in the large house with a permanent family of three, but there are frequent and numerous guests.

The mother has an agreement with her employer that the situation is reviewed after two weeks.

This is a start to a new life for Philip and his mother; if the mother can cope with the work it should prove very satisfactory. The house is situated in an affluent residential part of the town about one mile from the centre. Philip will have some distance to travel to school and the mother was going to make enquiries at two schools after Christmas. The Headmaster of Philip's school had given her two schools to which she should apply.

I asked the mother to let us know if after two weeks it was necessary to return to her sister. If we did not hear from her, I would call early in the New Year to see if Philip was settled in a school.

124. 21.12.71 Letter to Child Care Officer from the Mother.
Things are happening so fast here; I think I'd better let you know what's afoot.

The sad news first, my mother died suddenly in October, she was quite well in the evening & I went in her room about 10.30 p.m., then about mid-night I heard her shouting, she was having another stroke which lasted until 4 a.m. when she died.

Now for happier things, Phil & I are off to the South Coast on the 18th. After waiting weeks & writing dozens of letters, the right job seems to have come along; I am to be housekeeper in a large beautiful house. We have our own flat, two bedrooms, bathroom, sitting room (with TV), it's rather a pity Phil will have to change schools just in his last year, but I think this position is too good to miss.

I was invited to the prize giving at the school as Phil won his form's Progress Prize, a nice book; he was twice rewarded as his aunt & uncle bought him a very smart radio for 'good effort'. I do hope we will see you either before we depart or when we are at our new address.

125. 04.01.72. Report of Child Care Officer.

I called on 3rd January to see if Philip and his mother had settled in, and to hear how she managed all the Christmas arrangements.

As far as the mother is concerned, everything went satisfactorily and she is prepared to continue; the final decision naturally rests with her employer.

Philip will attend one of two schools; both are about one and a half miles away from where he is living. The mother said she had been advised to wait until Wednesday 5th January before making enquiries.

Philip hopes to leave school at the end of term, when he is anxious to work in one of the town's stamp shops. Stamp collecting had been Philip's one real hobby and he would like to make enquires fairly soon regarding a possible vacancy for an assistant. Philip already knows of four or five stamp shops.

I recommend that visiting continue for a few more months, possibly until Philip is settled in some work, when this case could then be closed.

126. 10.02.72. Report of Child Care Officer.

I met the mother by chance in town; she was out shopping and had just recovered from an attack of influenza.

She seems settled in her new job and as far as she knows everything is going satisfactorily. Her sister and brother-in-law visited and they were impressed with the present situation.

Philip is attending a boys' school; he has been persuaded to stay on at school until he is 16 and to take examinations.

The mother said that there is strict discipline at the school and Philip has a good deal of homework. Philip has settled happily, and gets down to his homework without any trouble and appears to be working well.

I would recommend that consideration could be given to the possibility of closing this case at the end of March, after I have made one more visit.

127. 08.05.72 Report of Child Care Officer.

Visit of 04.05.72 The Mother is now very well settled in her job as housekeeper in the large private house.

Philip is doing well at school and had recently had a good report. He will be staying on until July 1973 in order to take several subjects in examinations. He maintains his great interest in 'stamps' and definitely wants a career in this line. He thinks that the school will give him good help in finding a suitable job and will seek further advice from the Careers Adviser if necessary. Philip has already made some enquiries in the town about opportunities in the work he wants to do and is very hopeful of being able to find what he wants.

As both the mother and Philip are so well settled financially and materially, I suggested that they were no longer in need of our help and support. The mother thanked us for all that we had done for Philip as well as for her and for the interest we had taken in both of them.

In view of this satisfactory situation, I recommend that we close this case.

128. 22.05.72 Letter to Bristol NCH from London NCH.
We note your comments. This is receiving our attention. I should be glad if you would kindly let us have the main file in due course.

129 10.05.77 Letter to NCH London from Philip.
Asking if any records were held and would it is possible to have a copy of them.

130 17.05.77 Letter to Philip from NCH.
Replying to request to see file.
We do, of course, have records of your three-year stay at Harpenden, which are not possible to be copied.

You did come up to Highbury in October 1967 when you were rather unsettled at Harpenden and when it was felt that tests might indicate some other means of helping you. Of course, it was shortly after this that you returned to live with your mother, and as far as we could tell, this was what was required.

I do not know if you would wish to take this any further either by correspondence or by coming up to Highbury for a talk, but perhaps you will let me know how you feel.

MY ANSWER.
The reply that they do have a file is interesting, but I was now twenty, I just did not feel like either writing to them or even going up to see them. How could I ask them about things that I did not know if they knew about? My three years in their care were a bit mixed up in my mind. I wanted to forget about the matter but I couldn't. There are so many things that I would like answers to, but I would find it difficult to ask the questions.

It was twenty years later when I saw my file.

THE CHILDREN IN CARE

It might be unkind to name the other children who were also in care at the same time, and who have now started new and productive lives. I have changed the names of some children unless they have allowed me to use their real names. I am sorry if those persons with the names I have used were in care, but they do not feature in this work. The adult names have also been reduced to related employment titles. However Lenton and Kevin are real names, and are ex-members of Harpenden who wish it to be known they were in care and would very much like to find others who were in care at the same time.

Those who knew me at the Home will have the knowledge that their past is quite safe. I will leave it to them to open up their own Pandora's box.

If you were in the NCH and would like to see your file, please contact the NCH at 85 Highbury Park, London, N5 1UD or your local regional NCH office.

MY FINAL THOUGHTS

The National Children's Home did its best to give children a good start in life. Without their intervention, my life would never have been so varied and interesting as things have turned out. If I had lived in the London flat from the age of eight, with little opportunity for my mother to supervise me, there would have been a very good chance that with my ability to get into mischief, many serious events may have soon occurred.

The staff in the Home were devoted to looking after children. The Sisters did not simply look after us for set hours of the day; other than allowing them days or part of the day off each week, they provided all our needs for every moment of our lives, just like true parents. There was a build up of trust between the Sister and the child. With the arrival of Houseparents, providing they took on the role that the Sisters had evolved, they too could be completely trusted by the children in their care.

My views on life in the Home might seem to some who were there during the same time as far more restrictive than they experienced. This might be down to the Sisters who looked after us. They may have experienced far more freedom and affection. To me, this highly organised upbringing I experienced in the Home, did give me a much better advantage in later life.

The NCH has given me an outlook on life that the ordinary child would not have experienced. Life outside the Home was not comfortable for every child. For most of the friends we met at school, they would have had a happy family life; however there would have been a few that suffered far worse experiences through ill treatment and neglect than we ever imagined – they needed to keep silent, allowing their family to stay together. During my stay at the Home, it was the most miserable chapter in my life, however, without their help, my life could have easily been far worse. Their simple acts of kindness, kept me from far worse experiences.

PUNISHMENTS

During my childhood, I was always worried and uneasy over the punishments I might receive. The physical punishments I received from both my grandmother and mother, were given more with kindness than anger; if I could understand what I had done wrong, it was thought I would not do the same thing again. The only exception with punishments from my mother would be the plimsoll for my bed-wetting at the age of seven. This did little to stop the problem; if anything, it made me more fearful and caused even more problems.

My first encounter with the cane at school was soon after my seventh birthday. It was a punishment that I did not really deserve, but did me little physical harm and might have even been an ideal point to show me how I should act at school. The physical action and pain of the cane was soon over and more or less forgotten by the end of the lesson. The psychological effects remained in my mind the longest. From then, I knew what the cane was like, and although frightened of it, once it had been given, that was the end of the punishment.

The majority of my physical punishments during my later childhood were unjust, but taken with the matters I was not punished for, made the score about even. At the time, I experienced several feelings: there was the fear of the punishment combined with anger, as often what I was about to be punished for had not been my fault; then followed the pain from the actual hits and an equal amount of pain when others witnessed my tears.

If the Sister or Houseparent had not been able to use the slipper, I might have become a problem, and any form of easy family life could not have been possible. Giving me extra chores might have been a solution; but without any worse punishment being available, I might have ignored chores set as punishments and caused more problems. However, if there were no physical punishments that could be given, I might have turned out to be a calm well-behaved boy. Without the fear of punishments, many of the problems that seemed to cause conflict might not have occurred.

If I could not be given the cane or the slipper, I would have been strong enough to stand up to Sister and other adults and request a few changes: I do not want to drink tea – it makes me sick. At night if I want to go to the lavatory – please don't stop me. I would like to go for walks on my own outside the grounds. I don't want to go to Cubs. I don't want to go to Sunday school. I don't like parsnips. Will you keep my sweets safe so I may have some each day? I don't want to escort a girl to school. Please may I visit my friends after school? Please may I visit my local relatives? Ten simple matters, which, if I had the courage to put the requests to the adults, might have made three years of my life far easier for the staff. A child in care today might get most of these simple wishes granted without any problem.

ON LEAVING THE HOME

My mother knew that I had not been very happy during my stay in care. She suggested that I should start afresh, and forget about the past few years. If I put my mind on schoolwork and made new friends, there would be plenty to occupy my mind. The matter of starting afresh, to my mother seemed a simple thing to do, for me it was a different matter; trying to forget the previous three years was impossible.

On leaving the Home, there was always the worry that for whatever reason things did not work out, a return to the Home might occur. Over the next few years, I was still a little worried about my future. There was always the thought that living with my aunt and uncle might not completely work out. If on leaving the Home, I had been able to go and live with my mother as I had previously done, life might have been easier.

With my new friends, there was a gap of three years. When they told me what they had done over the past few years, I had the problem of trying to explain my life, and at the same time not admitting to having been in care and away from my mother.

There was never any resentment against my mother for sending me to the Home. Circumstances at the time made it appear to the adults that this would be the most favourable option.

MY FILE

At the time I left the Home, my mother questioned me as to why they had asked me to leave. There was nothing I thought I had done wrong any more than usual to get this request made by the Home.

Until I received my file, I had little idea why the NCH had asked my mother to take me back. When I did get my file, I found that, by asking my mother to remove me, it would be the easiest way for my mother to make the decision if I should stay in the Home or return to her. This simple piece of information shown to my mother might have made things more easily understood. Obtaining my file however came a few months after her death.

KEEPING IN TOUCH WITH THE HOME

I remained in touch with Sister after I left the Home. Originally, she had moved into a retirement flat on leaving us. Life might have seemed a little dull, as within a short space of time she took on the position of a housekeeper and companion. In later years, I visited her in Harpenden on a couple occasions. When she decided to move down to the West Country, we still kept in contact and I visited her occasionally. Sister managed to keep fit and enjoyed an active life for many more years.

Sister however was not the only member of staff that I was in contact with. There was still news from the Home and the Houseparent. After leaving the Home, each Christmas we received a newsletter listing all the events that had happened to the family during the year and how everyone was getting on. The newsletters were written at the end of each year, typed up and duplicated at the main office. They were sent out to relatives of the children, past residents of the family group and any friends known to the Houseparent.

The first Christmas after I left, there was a brief mention in the newsletter that year of how I had left the Home and was living with my mother. The next letter mentioned that the older children had now left school and gave the jobs they were doing. The newsletter that came three years after I left was the last I received of news of the Home; its content was much like the previous ones, listing all the events of the year. It must have been compiled around the start of November. At the very end of the newsletter, an extra paragraph had been personally written by hand in the distinctive writing of the Houseparent. The death of the younger member of the group whom I had shared a bedroom with was now reported. His death occurred while the newsletter was being produced. An earlier paragraph had been left in of his events during the year. The illness that he had always suffered had finally caught up with him. To the adults it was known in advance that his life was going to be short. Yet as children, although we had been required to take extra care over him by way of diet and medication, we had never been informed that his life would end so soon; he had lived almost the same life as the rest of us.

A few years after I left, the Houseparent left the Home and returned to London. She sent a Christmas newsletter informing us of the new events in her life. A few years later, there was a party for her mother. Several friends of the Houseparent were going; it was mentioned that a couple of the girls that I had been at the Home with were going to attend so it would be nice if I could come. On the day, only one of the older girls that had been in our flat was able to attend, but it was an interesting meeting to reminisce on the events of our lives. I remained in contact with the Houseparent for several more years, until a swift illness cut short her life at a far younger age than most of us would have expected.

After I left the Home, I've returned on several occasions to see if it was still as I remembered it. The National Children's Home at Harpenden closed down in 1985, but took on a new lease of life for a Christian Group – Youth With A Mission. The Houses and grounds are still as I left them all those years ago.

Philip J. Howard

Some additional items on the history of The National Children's Home and the various branches of the NCH, together with other related matters of life in care are to be found at

www.theirhistory.co.uk

If you have any further information on life in care please email theirhistory@ntlworld.com or write to:

Their History,
Dalkeith Publishing,
P.O. Box 4,
Bournemouth,
BH1 1YL, England.